I am always inspired and challenged by Jamie Buckingham's writings. He has made me laugh, brought tears to my eyes and challenged me in more ways than one. In his recent encounter in the battle against cancer, Jamie challenges us to greater heights of faith while at the same time helping us guard against presumption. Through the continuing manifest miracles, healing and personal comfort, we will draw even more life and inspiration. This may very well be his greatest contribution in all of his writings.

— James Robison, international evangelist

In spirit I lived through each day of this experience with Jamie. His refusal to capitulate to the enemy is an inspiration. Jackie's role as a prayer-partner-wife is unforgettable. The combination of distinctive word pictures, penetrating insights and invaluable teaching on being an overcomer make this book a five-star production.

— Leonard LeSourd, author, former editor-in-chief of *Guideposts*

Following Jamie and Jackie through their wrenching personal experience, you learn with them God's greatest lesson: how to wrestle with the devil until we win; how to wrestle with God until He wins.

— John Sherrill, contributing editor for *Guideposts*

Some people are survivors. Others are more than conquerors. This book is a powerful story of the latter.

— Bernie May, U.S. Division Director, Wycliffe Bible Translators

John and I are so thrilled that Jamie has written a book that will bless multitudes of people all over the world. Only a person who has gone through something like this can offer the same comfort that the Lord Jesus has given them. Jackie and Jamie are tremendous people of faith and power, and we are so glad that "through God they will do valiantly because He has tread down their enemies."

— Dodie Osteen, co-pastor, Lakewood Church, Houston, Texas

If you are suffering physically, this book will be a tremendous encouragement. If your body is strong, let this book point you toward spiritual health as well.

— Pat Robertson, president, Christian Broadcasting Network

AFTER HEARING THOSE DREADED WORDS
— INOPERABLE CANCER —
GOD TURNED TRAGEDY INTO A

SUMMER of MIRACLES

JAMIE BUCKINGHAM

Creation House
Lake Mary, Florida

Creation House
Strang Communications Company
600 Rinehart Road
Lake Mary, FL 32746
(407) 333-0600

Unless otherwise noted, all Scripture quotations are taken from the Holy Bible, New International Version. Copyright © 1973, 1978, 1984, International Bible Society. Used by permission.

Scripture quotations marked KJV are from the King James Version of the Bible.

CONTENTS

FOREWORD

JAMIE BUCKINGHAM AND I FIRST MET IN THE early 1970s when he was writing my biography, *Shout It From the Housetops*. We have been friends ever since, and I have often invited him to be my guest on "The 700 Club."

Last July I was shocked when the phone call came: "Jamie Buckingham has been diagnosed with terminal cancer."

In *Summer of Miracles*, a master at telling other people's stories describes his own struggles during the weeks and months after his diagnosis — how it felt to have an enemy in his body, rushing him toward death.

His story is a beautiful example of the body of Christ rallying around a wounded member. The church Jamie pastored stopped business-as-usual and fell on its knees before God. Pastors and leaders around the country called their congregations to prayer. Neighbors and friends were there to help.

His story shows the tenacity and tenderness of a marriage of thirty-six years and the joy of being surrounded by children and grandchildren who are serving the Lord.

Jamie reproves us "busy" Christians whose lives too often become centered on God-activities instead of on God. "I've spent more time with my calendar than I've spent with You, Lord," he said after the diagnosis. God is teaching us that ministry must not — cannot — substitute for a daily relationship with our Creator.

I am reminded of the words of Paul to the Corinthians during his third missionary journey. Paul had been beaten, stoned and shipwrecked three times. He had been hungry, cold and naked (2 Cor. 11:24-27, KJV). He did not pretend that he did not have any problems. Instead he rejoiced in the victory that he received through suffering.

> We are troubled on every side, yet not distressed; we are perplexed, but not in despair; persecuted, but not forsaken; cast down, but not destroyed; always bearing about in the body the dying of the Lord Jesus, that the life also of Jesus might be made manifest in our body (2 Cor. 4:8-10, KJV).

If you are suffering physically, this book will be a tremendous encouragement. Let God use it to help you turn tragedy into triumph. Immerse yourself in the healing Scriptures.

If your body is strong, let this book point you toward spiritual health as well. Make your priorities God-centered. Learn to support and pray for those around you who are battling physical pain.

When you are open to the Spirit of God, any season can be a *Summer of Miracles*.

Pat Robertson
Christian Broadcasting Network

PREFACE

This is a book about miracles. Not ancient occurrences in faraway places. It is about real, tangible, measurable miracles. It is a true account of the miracles that took place in my life in the summer of 1990 after my doctors had diagnosed me with inoperable and untreatable cancer.

This is not the first book I've written about miracles. In the early 1970s I wrote two books for the late Kathryn Kuhlman, who had one of the most significant healing ministries in history. I approached that writing assignment — and the miracles people said they had experienced in her meetings — with skepticism. For years I had lived in a theological climate which affirmed biblical miracles but found no place for miracles today. Advanced medical science had replaced divine healing, and psychology had replaced deliverance from demons. Death and suffering from diseases too big for medical science to cure — such as cancer, multiple sclerosis, Lou Gehrig's disease or Alzheimer's disease — were looked upon as the "will of God."

I believed in answered prayer. I just had trouble believing in miracles, because I had never seen one. The concept of accepting a thing simply because it was in the Bible ran cross-grained to both logic and my academics. Until I saw, I was unable to believe.

So I approached my writing assignment for Miss Kuhlman with a skepticism that bordered on cynicism. My job was to interview people who said they had been healed of incurable diseases. She asked me to talk to these folks, talk to their families, talk to their doctors and talk to other medical people who had treated or examined them before and after the so-called miracles took place. Then I was to write their stories.

I had heard stories about healing miracles since I was a child. Frankly, I didn't believe them. They were like the wild stories of creatures from outer space that appeared on the front pages of tabloid papers in supermarket checkout lines. They just didn't ring true. I thought the people exaggerated, engaged in wishful thinking, had not really been as sick as they said or wanted to convince others so badly they made things up.

In writing, that is called fictionalizing.

The other hindrance to my belief was the lack of credibility on the part of the storytellers. I heard stories of miracles from people whose lives did not reflect God's integrity. I heard stories of miracles from men and women I didn't trust in other areas. I listened as television preachers told stories of miracles then used them to raise money for themselves. I had real problems believing that was the way Jesus performed miracles. Despite my desire to believe in miracles, the miracle-workers got in the way. Then there was the problem of what I perceived to be a lack of journalistic integrity in the way the stories were told or written. So I entered the writing projects for Kathryn Kuhlman much as a Missouri farmer would listen to a Texan brag about the size of his watermelons: "If you want me to believe, show me."

The two books, *God Can Do It Again* and *Nothing Is Impossible With God*, contained the stories of twenty people. All had been miraculously healed. Some had been healed of multiple sclerosis. Some of cancer. Some of horrible skin diseases. Some of congenital defects. Some had suffered bone injuries and reported instant healings. All these people had attended a Kathryn Kuhlman miracle service.

As I traveled across the country from Texas to California, from Oregon to Canada, from New England to the Deep South, I gradually became convinced that healing miracles were still taking place. My mind-set shifted from that of a cynic to an objective reporter to an open believer in miracles.

Later, before she died, I wrote eight other books for Kathryn Kuhlman — each one centering around some outstanding miracle healing. After she died I wrote her biography. I had become a firm believer in miracles.

But all these were books about divine healings experienced by others. They were secondhand stories. I believed in the miracles. I rejoiced over them. I wrote about them. After each research trip I returned to Florida and reported them to the church I pastored. But they were all stories of miracles that happened to other people.

Last year, just a few months before I was diagnosed with cancer, I wrote another book about miracles. I called it *Miracle Power*. In the book I analyzed ten of the miracles of Jesus and related them to miracles happening today. I quoted C.S. Lewis's definition of a miracle as "an interference with nature by supernatural power." This is done when God superimposes His high, invisible law over the visible laws of nature.

"The supernaturalist," I wrote, "while not denying the laws of nature, believes also in a higher set of laws which govern the 'heavenlies.' These laws are invisible and are activated by various factors — none of which seems consistent with our Western logic.

"Prayer is one of these factors which activate miracles.

"So is faith.

"Sometimes miracles occur when no one asked for them or even believed they were possible. Such miracles seem to take place simply because God willed them into being. All are, however, merely the imposition of God's higher law over His lower law."[1]

But I've since discovered there's a vast difference between writing books about miracles and experiencing one.

I had, on occasion, thought I would like to receive a personal miracle. There had been some. But they were all "little miracles." I had been healed of minor cuts and bruises. There were times when planes were delayed just for my benefit. Once I almost stepped on a rattlesnake, but someone warned me not to put my foot down. Then there was the time — in fact, it happened on two occasions — when I prayed during an outdoor service, and the rain, which had started, stopped instantly.

What, I wondered, would it be like to receive a really big miracle? What I did not take into account were the suffering, pain, anxiety and total helplessness people experience before they are in a position to receive such a miracle.

Others in my family had gone through such experiences.

In February 1983 my wife, Jackie, made an appointment with her gynecologist to check some lumps in her breasts. He sent her to a surgeon. The surgeon examined her and said immediate surgery was necessary. The first step was a surgical biopsy of lumps in both breasts. He wanted us to sign a surgical release giving him permission to extend the biopsy surgery — and remove more tissue from the breasts — if the initial tests showed the lumps were cancerous. The tests, using sample tissue removed during the biopsy, would be conducted quickly while she was still under anesthesia.

Jackie and I were part of a small group in our church, the Tabernacle Church in Melbourne, Florida. We had been in relationship with these four families for five years. Before making a decision, we looked to the group — and to the Lord — for direction. The meeting that week was in our home. Following dinner, we gathered in our living room. The two of us knelt on the floor. The others laid their hands on us and anointed us with oil in the name of Jesus Christ. The group prayed for healing for Jackie and wisdom for the two of us as we made the critical decisions that lay ahead. Despite the threatening circumstances, we felt peace. We also felt we should not sign the surgical release.

Two days later I sat with Jackie in the surgeon's office as she told him our decision.

The doctor agreed reluctantly. "It's your body."

Jackie entered the hospital, and the surgeon removed the lumps. The tissue was rushed downstairs from the operating room to pathology. Within thirty minutes the report came back. The tissue showed signs of malignancy. However, because we had not signed the surgical release, the surgeon sewed her up and sent her to the recovery room — then back to her own room to spend the night before going home. At the same time he requested a full pathology report. That report, he said, could take several days.

I talked with the surgeon as Jackie was coming out of the anesthesia. He outlined the possibilities as we stood in the hall outside her room. It all depended on the final pathology report. Based on the preliminary report from the frozen section, however, he said one of three things would happen:

• I could take her home, let the incisions heal for a few months, then bring her back for a radical mastectomy followed by radiation treatment.

• I could take her home the next day but bring her back the next week for the radical surgery. If this was done, we might escape treatment.

• If the cancer was already in her system, the prognosis was chemical treatment followed, perhaps, by death.

The final pathology report came four days later. The doctor called. The earlier diagnosis on the tissue was "misleading." The tissue, treated with various chemicals and examined under the microscope, was nonmalignant. The radical surgery he had projected was not necessary.

It was a week before we realized what had actually happened. Aside from the miracle — for which we praised God — came the realization that had we signed the standard release, the surgeon would have gone ahead and removed both breasts. Later, when he did remove the stitches from the biopsy incisions, he told Jackie she was a very "lucky lady."

She smiled and corrected him. "Not lucky. Blessed!"

Miracles were coming closer to home.

On January 1, 1990, six months before I was diagnosed with cancer, another miracle took place in our family. My daughter-in-law Michele, the wife of my oldest son, had been helping me in my job as editor-in-chief of *Ministries Today*, a magazine for pastors and leaders. She was an outstanding writer and editor, and I had convinced publisher Stephen Strang to name her as my full-time associate editor. Michele and my son Bruce live on our family compound, and she would be working out of her home, just as I did. Her job officially began on New Year's Day.

That morning she woke with partial paralysis on the left side of her body. Her arm, hand and fingers were useless. Her left leg was dragging. She felt dizzy and nauseated. The symptoms persisted, and the next day she went to a neurologist. He immediately ordered a computerized tomography scan of her brain and did other exams. His initial diagnosis was multiple sclerosis. Michele's home group joined our family — especially her husband — in concerted prayer. We called the church into prayer. The symptoms got worse.

Then a woman in the church, Mary Derrington, called Michele with a vision she had received while praying for her. In the vision she saw a black dot on Michele's brain. Then she saw the "finger of God" reach in and touch the dot, and it disappeared.

The next day the doctor called Michele and Bruce and asked them to come by his office. The CT scan, he said, showed a "black dot" on the side of her brain. On the basis of that and the symptoms, he confirmed the multiple sclerosis diagnosis. The disease was "incurable." He gave them a book on MS and suggested they learn to live with the disease — until it finally killed her.

Their home group went on the attack with spiritual warfare. Bruce, who was a former congressional assistant and now public information officer for NASA at Kennedy Space Center, began fasting. My wife, Jackie, insisted Michele "throw the book [about MS] away."

"Read the promises of the Bible, not the curses of man," she said. Michele agreed. Round-the-clock prayer on the part of many in the church went into effect. Less than a week later the symptoms disappeared. Totally. Randy Wisdom, an Air Force medical doctor in their home group, examined her. There was no trace of the previous symptoms. She was able to return to work with no additional problems. She was healed.

But the biggest test for me was yet to come. Six months later I sat in a doctor's office following a routine physical exam and was told I was going to die of cancer. What followed is what this book is all about.

Jamie Buckingham
Palm Bay, Florida

NAGGING SYMPTOMS

IT BEGAN THE LAST FRIDAY OF JUNE, THE SUMMER of 1990. I sat in the office of a young internal medicine specialist. I had gone for a routine physical. Now he was telling me I had cancer — and that I was not going to live very long. From that moment until now everything about me has changed radically. The diagnosis catapulted me into a new dimension of life. Suddenly I was helpless, face-to-face with a reality bigger than I. Some sinister force was trying to direct — to take — my life. I seemed caught in its inescapable power, no longer able to plan my future, no longer master of my body nor captain of my soul. I was being wrenched by an evil force greater than anything I had ever experienced.

I had been feeling punk for almost three months. No energy. Tired Although I was fifty-eight years old, I was in excellent health, proud of my athletic ability. Besides regular games of racquet ball, I played basketball on the half-court behind our house several evenings each week — plus a game on Sunday afternoons. Most of those in our games were twenty-five years younger than I. While not as strong or as fast as my two sons nor my three sons-in-law, I was proud that I could not only keep up, but I could also outlast them.

Pride, I now realize, was one of the controlling forces of my life.

My heart was strong, my muscle tone good. During the last eight months I had led two fourteen-day hiking and mountain-climbing trips to Israel. Two years before I had hiked down and back up the Grand Canyon. The next year, along with my home group, Jackie and I had climbed down the canyon and rafted the Colorado River for five days. I had never been sick, never been a patient in a hospital.

Therefore this strange lack of energy was a mystery. I had noticed it off and on over the last several months, but it wasn't anything serious enough to cause alarm. In March Jackie and I had flown to Panama, where I preached in a small church in Gamboa on the Panama Canal. At that time I blamed my listlessness on the Central American heat and humidity — plus the oppressive political situation. Yet I had been in similar situations many times before and was always full of energy.

In early June we spent the weekend with Jack and Barbara Taylor in Fort Worth, Texas. Jack, a former Southern Baptist pastor and now a traveling teacher, was a dear friend as well as one of my columnists for *Ministries Today* magazine. I had no idea the major role Jack would play in what was about to unfold.

The Taylors' family had gathered for a Father's Day dinner on Sunday. Sitting at the table, I suddenly felt weary. I lasted through the meal, but then, joking about Sunday traditions, I headed for my bedroom and an afternoon nap. I was to preach that night in Dallas. Jack and Barbara drove us over. In the car we talked about the dangers of physical and spiritual burnout. The year before Jack had almost died following complications with open-heart surgery. He had learned to recognize the signs of overwork. He urged me to do what he was struggling to do — slow down.

I agreed. I always agreed when I got into these kinds of conversations with my friends. In fact, it had become something of a joke. "Jamie is always saying he's going to slow down. If that's the case, what's he doing in Indonesia? Or Seattle? Or Arizona?"

Or one of any forty places I might visit in a year. This time, however, I didn't have much choice. I was really pooped.

The following week I was scheduled to attend the annual meeting of the Charismatic Bible Ministries on the campus of Oral Roberts University in Tulsa, Oklahoma. Monday morning as we flew home from Dallas I told Jackie I didn't want to go.

"I feel like I'm close to the edge," I told her. "I know you enjoy the conferences, but I just don't have the energy to keep going."

"Everyone's been telling you to slow down," she said understandingly. "All you have to do is call Oral Roberts and tell him you'll not be there. If anyone understands overwork, he does."

But Jackie was not convinced it was merely overwork. She knew there were spiritual battles raging in my life. I was working three full-time jobs. I was the senior pastor of the Tabernacle Church in Melbourne, a church I had founded almost a quarter of a century before which had now grown to several thousand people. I was editor-in-chief of *Ministries Today*. I was writing on deadline every month for *Charisma & Christian Life*. I was producing videotapes and Bible curriculum workbooks. Besides that I was traveling constantly — at home and overseas — speaking, doing research and leading conferences.

Jackie knew, after thirty-six years of marriage, when I was drawing from God's spring and when I was dipping runoff water from my own cistern. Now, looking back, I remember the words of a friend who once told me he had discovered that even if his lamp had run dry he could keep on burning. But he was burning wick — not fuel.

I had, I believed, dropped into the wick-burning stage.

Jackie's primary concern was not the burnout. It was the cause. She knew I thrived on work. I loved getting up early and working on manuscripts, loved the staff meetings with my pastors at the church, loved preaching in my church, loved traveling around the world, even loved the constant writing deadlines. She knew, however, that I was no longer plugged into God. She knew I was no longer depending on the One who had called me; I was drawing on my own strength, leaning on my own understanding.

She also suspected there were unknown areas of spiritual rebellion in my life. She was not sure of the details but easily recognized the symptoms. I seldom read my Bible unless I was preparing a sermon. I seldom prayed with her — despite her constant yearning for me to do so. I seldom, if ever, talked of my activities with her, much less sought her advice. She knew of the double life I had once lived in the past. The sexual indiscretions. My noncommunication made her fearful it might have returned. Unable to talk to me about her fears and unwilling to talk to anyone else, she pulled back. She talked to God — asking Him to intervene in my life.

Back home from Texas, I attended an early-morning breakfast with Gene Berrey and Don Lees, elders in the church and close personal friends. Gene and Don also belonged to our home group — a small group which met weekly for prayer and fellowship. After breakfast at a local restaurant we stood chatting on the sidewalk before they headed to their jobs. I was scheduled to drive on to the church office for a meeting with some of my pastors. But, standing there talking, I felt suddenly sleepy. Instead of heading to the church office I drove home.

17

Jackie was surprised to see me. "I thought you had an appointment at the church office."

"They can handle it without me," I said and headed upstairs to my bedroom to do something I had never done in my life — take a morning nap. As I climbed the steps I felt a strange exhaustion, accompanied by a slight breathlessness. Something was wrong with my body, and I didn't know what it was.

That afternoon Jackie insisted I make an appointment with a doctor. It had been almost twenty years since I'd had a thorough physical examination. She was adamant that I call a doctor.

I balked. I was too busy to spend two hours in the office of a strange doctor getting poked, mashed, whacked and stuck. Besides, except for these little indicators, I was in excellent shape.

One year earlier our church had purchased a long-term disability insurance policy for all the pastors. Those of us over fifty-five were required to have a basic physical exam. The insurance company had sent a nurse out to the house. She checked my blood pressure, took blood for a blood count and ran a urinalysis. I had just come off a lengthy fast preparing for a trip to Israel and felt great. My blood pressure was 110/70, my resting pulse 55 and my cholesterol 170.

That same week my son-in-law Jon Moore, who at that time worked as a cardiac rehabilitation specialist at our local hospital, had suggested I come in for a treadmill exam. "Anyone your age who is as competitive at basketball as you are needs a heart check," he insisted. The cardiologist who monitored me on the treadmill confirmed my heart was in excellent health.

Now, however, just a year later, something was wrong in my body. Maybe I needed to increase my vitamins. Maybe I needed zinc or iron. Reluctantly I agreed to the physical exam. As I now look back on that time period, I find it hard to believe I never related my physical condition to my relationship with God. When you're healthy, you don't need God — that was what my actions said. I had made some recent decisions about reestablishing my relationship, blaming the fracture on my busy schedule. Just the day before I had spent an hour in prayer in a feeble attempt at repentance. But, as with most of my repentances in the past, it seemed shallow, although it was the best I could do without external pressure.

Agreeing to the exam raised another problem. Even though I knew a number of physicians around the nation — some being personal friends — I did not have a hometown doctor. During the past twenty-five years I had only gone to doctors for short-term treatment.

"Why don't I just let Randy check me over?" I asked Jackie. Randy Wisdom was a military physician, stationed at nearby Patrick Air Force Base. He played a mean trumpet in our church orchestra and belonged to my son Bruce's home group. He was also a regular among those who showed up at our house several times a week to play basketball.

"Randy won't examine civilians," Jackie said. "You need a thorough checkup."

Although Randy's family practice was limited to military personnel, Jackie found him to be a supporter of her cause. After one of our evening games, she cornered him on the edge of the court, still hot and sweaty.

"Will you please tell my husband he should get a physical exam."

"Do you think he'll listen if a civilian doctor tells him to stop slapping my head on defense?" he joked.

"Don't you guys ever get serious," Jackie complained, shaking her head. "He complains of these symptoms but won't do anything about it."

Randy agreed. Given my age, the nagging symptoms and the fact I had not had a thorough physical in more than twenty years, he felt Jackie should make an appointment for me — whether I wanted it or not.

Earlier in the year Jackie had taken her mother, Daisy, who lived with us, to an internal medicine specialist. She decided to contact him. The next day, when I came home from our Tuesday morning church staff meeting, she was just hanging up the phone.

"I called the doctor. You have an appointment next Thursday. Mark it on your calendar."

"Honey, not that week. I'm supposed to go to the dentist on Tuesday. I don't want to see two doctors in the same week. See if you can put it off until next week."

She sighed and rescheduled my appointment for the following Thursday, June 21. Neither of us realized at the time how important that postponement was. God was already directing the schedules. From that point on I would be out of control as He, from the hidden side of the loom, wove the threads of my life into a tapestry which would not only save, but change, my life.

Jamie Buckingham

Jackie Buckingham

Two

DEATH SENTENCE

It WAS EARLY WEDNESDAY MORNING BEFORE MY doctor's appointment on Thursday. Jackie was still asleep when I slipped out of bed, pulled on my shorts and sweatshirt and went downstairs. Brooks Watson and I had a 6:30 A.M. appointment to play racquetball at his condominium development. The den was dark. Outside the sky was turning gray, heralding the approach of the dawn. I sat on the floor in front of the sofa and laced up my racquetball shoes. I remembered back eight years when I started getting serious about my physical condition.

It began the morning of my fiftieth birthday. I had been standing in the shower, praying about my future. I dreaded hitting fifty. Fifty was old. Old was not something I wanted to be. My prayer was more of a lament than praise for being alive.

Then, with the water streaming over my head, I heard an inaudible voice. It was one of the few times I had known for certain that God was speaking to me. I knew it was He because it cut across my fears and apprehensions and injected a totally new line of thinking.

"I want to give you another fifty years of life."

"Lord, one-hundred-year-old people are useless. They sit in wheelchairs in nursing homes, staring at the walls, vegetating."

"If you cooperate with me I'll give you another fifty years of productive and creative life."

"What do you mean, 'cooperate'?"

But He was gone. The only sound was the running of the water in the shower. I looked down and saw the size of my stomach. My body was being crushed to death by fat. Cooperate, I realized, meant getting my body in shape — something I had neglected for years. It meant losing 60 pounds off my then 230-pound frame, starting an exercise program and changing my diet, which up until then had consisted of eating almost everything in sight.

That had been eight years ago. I had not only lost the weight, but kept it off. I was proud — there's that word again — of my physical condition. But over the last several months I had stopped doing my sit-ups. As a result a slight stomach bulge — complete with sidehandles — had reappeared. Maybe that's the reason I was feeling punk, I concluded. I resolved that morning, sitting on the floor of the den, to start my sit-up program again.

I lay back on the carpet in front of the fireplace. The light of early dawn was just easing through the windows. After stretching for a few moments I bent my knees, put my hands behind my head and pulled my body forward from the waist in the familiar sit-up maneuver. Something was wrong. I could barely pull up. I tried another. There was a strange tightness — almost a cramping — across my upper abdomen. I berated myself for letting my body get out of shape. A year before I had been able to snap off one hundred sit-ups without even breathing hard. I tried one more and realized I simply could not pull up. No problem. I'd start back gradually. Soon I'd be back to where I used to be.

Brooks Watson was an old friend. Like Gene and Don, he was a member of our home group. He was also a next-door neighbor. I met him at the racquetball court. He had brought along a business acquaintance and suggested we play "cut-throat" — two playing against one and rotating after every serve. After a brief warm-up on the court — stretching our legs then banging the ball for a few minutes — we started the game. A fierce competitor, I was determined to win.

Less than five minutes into play I began to feel winded. That was not unusual, for I was running well and swinging hard. I knew if I kept going I'd push through and the second wind would follow. It always happened — both with racquetball and basketball.

But this time the second wind didn't come. Instead I grew increasingly exhausted. It was an eerie feeling. I slowed my playing, hitting some ceiling shots rather than my usual slammers against the front wall. It didn't help. Standing against the back wall, waiting for the serve, I was forced to lean against the wall for support. I could barely catch my breath.

It was my time to serve. I stepped to the line and realized I had lost the strength to swing the racquet. There was an awesome tightness across my torso, just below my rib cage. There was no pain, but I couldn't draw a deep breath.

Pride kept me from admitting my problem.

"I need a drink of water," I gasped, trying to keep the other men from knowing anything was wrong. "I'll be right back."

Stopping for water was permissible. Other men I played with did it all the time. But if my partner headed for the water fountain, I'd remain on the court, banging the ball against the wall until he got back. This time I used thirst as an excuse to try to catch my breath.

Outside the door of the court I paced back and forth along the little hallway, gasping for air. I could hear the other two men hitting the ball back and forth, waiting for me to return. I could breathe, but the oxygen didn't seem to be getting into my lungs. I felt faint.

It was the same sensation I had once, several years before, when I was researching a book on jungle pilots in the Amazon jungle. I had been sitting in the co-pilot's seat of an ancient DC-3, flying over the Andes. Because we were going to have to climb to eighteen thousand feet to cross the mountains, the pilot had given me a little plastic tube to stick in my mouth. The tube was connected to an oxygen bottle under the seat. But the tube was kinked, and as we climbed over the snowcapped peaks my body reacted from oxygen starvation. I almost passed out before I discovered the problem. Now this morning I felt the same sensation. There was some kind of blockage just below my rib cage which prevented me from drawing a deep breath.

I thought about lying down but was afraid I wouldn't be able to breathe at all if I did. I kept pacing, gasping, lifting my arms trying to pump air into my lungs. It was as though there was no oxygen getting to my blood cells. My entire body was suffocating. I felt ridiculous.

My strength gradually returned, but I was wrung out — as if I had just finished running a marathon. I staggered back on the court, smiling grimly as though nothing were wrong.

"Let's play."

This time I paced myself. I didn't go after the tough shots. I didn't swing hard. On several occasions I could feel the exhaustion racing back. When that happened, I slowed to a walk, playing like an old man. I didn't care who won, just as long as the game was soon over. When Brooks's companion said he had to go, I welcomed the chance to quit.

"Don't you want to play one more game?" Brooks asked, knowing I was always eager to stay as long as anyone was willing to compete.

"Not today," I replied, anxious to get home and lie down. I was mystified by what had happened to me.

Driving home, my sweaty back sticking to the seat of my pickup, I again tried to identify the feeling I'd had. It was vaguely familiar. I didn't think it was my heart, for my pulse seemed normal, and there had been no pain. Then I remembered an instance, about a month earlier, in the Atlanta airport. I was changing planes. The evening flight from Los Angeles had been late arriving in Atlanta. I was carrying my twelve-pound portable word processor, plus my briefcase. I had to run up the escalator and down the long concourse to catch my connecting flight to Florida. I had made similar sprints many times in the past with no problems. This time, however, when I reached the counter, I was totally winded. It only lasted a few seconds, then I was OK. But I remembered how I had been mystified. How could this happen since I was in such good shape?

Now, driving home from the racquetball court, I had just experienced the same feeling — only this time it was much, much worse.

The rest of the day went OK, but the memory of what had happened on the racquetball court nagged me. That night, sitting at the supper table, Jackie looked up from her plate.

"Do you feel bad?" she asked.

"I've felt better," I admitted. Then I told her what had happened that morning on the court.

She reached over, put her cool hand on my arm, then felt my forehead.

"You have a fever," she said, her own forehead wrinkled in concern. "Why don't you go on to bed early? I'll clean up the kitchen."

That was all the urging I needed.

Upstairs I rummaged through the drawer of Jackie's night stand and finally found the thermometer. It had been years since I'd had a fever. I lay on the bed, thermometer sticking out of my mouth, feeling silly. It registered 100.5 degrees. Low grade, but an indicator — something was wrong in my body.

"It's a good thing you're going to the doctor tomorrow," Jackie said. "It's time to find out what's wrong."

I didn't know it at the time, but postponing the doctor's appointment for a week, the experience on the racquetball court and the fever were all divinely instigated. Had that strange series of events not taken place — in that order — things might have been much different. The Master Weaver was deftly pulling the threads to form a pattern only He could see.

The next morning the fever was gone. By 9:30 I was sitting in a small examining room as a young nurse drew three vials of blood out of my arm.

"You're Bonnie's dad, aren't you?" she asked, referring to our second daughter. "I went to high school with her." Somehow the little identification made me feel I wasn't completely among strangers.

Moments later the bearded young doctor came in. He introduced himself and immediately started asking questions. He was cool, precise, matter-of-fact. A classic product of computer-age medicine. I told him about my energy loss, about the strange instance on the racquetball court and the fever the night before. He scribbled notes on a clipboard then asked me to disrobe and lie back on the narrow examining table. He poked and probed my abdomen; felt my neck, shoulders and groin for lumps; listened to my heart and lungs with a stethoscope; then donned gloves and made a rectal exam.

"Everything seems OK," he said. "Your prostate is a little enlarged, but that's normal for a man your age. I don't feel anything wrong in your abdomen, but we'll know more when we get the results back from the blood test." He made an appointment for a chest X ray the next day and told me to come back the following week — the last Thursday in June.

Saturday night Jackie and I drove to Vero Beach, the little town where both of us had been born and raised. I had agreed to officiate at a marriage vow renewal ceremony for friends on their twenty-fifth wedding anniversary. That night I didn't feel good. The low-grade evening fevers had continued. Jackie tried to talk me out of going. But friendships count, and I had agreed to read their vows before a packed crowd in the church auditorium. We skipped the reception, however, and headed home early.

Driving back home on the interstate, I was aware of Jackie, sitting in the dark beside me, praying softly.

"You're concerned," I said gently.

"Something's not right," she said. "But don't forget — God is in control." It was a theme from which she never wavered — even during the darkest days ahead.

The next morning, Sunday, I felt better. The fever was gone. I preached at both morning services in our church. Oddly, the preaching exhilarated me. However, the energy seemed only for the moment, and by the time I got home I was exhausted. A long afternoon nap helped, and that evening I joined my young friends on the basketball court behind the house.

"You're pushing yourself," Jackie complained. But I felt I needed the exercise — and enjoyed the game. That night, right on schedule, the fever returned. The low-grade fever continued the rest of the week, arriving at sundown and disappearing at dawn. It was just enough to keep me feeling bad.

Thursday morning I was back in the doctor's office for my second visit. Jackie had offered to go with me, but I explained it was merely routine. I sat on the examining table with my shirt off, waiting for him to come in. I was pleased that a week of dieting had reduced my little tummy bulge. I couldn't help but think I looked pretty good for a man my age.

The doctor began talking as he came through the door. "All your tests look good," he said, his eyes on the notes in his hand as he talked. "The only thing I notice is a slight drop in your red blood count. I understand you told my nurse you've continued to run a slight fever at night."

He paused for a moment, scratching at his beard. "Ordinarily I wouldn't do this. However, because of your fever — and that little spell on the racquetball court — I've ordered a CT scan of your abdomen. You need to stop by the hospital this afternoon and pick up your barium drink. They'll do the scan first thing in the morning."

He must have noticed the puzzled look on my face. "It's merely a precaution," he said. "It will show up a lot more than a regular X ray. I'll call you when we get the results."

That night the fever disappeared — and never returned.

The next morning Jackie and I braved our way through the unfamiliar ground floor corridors of Holmes Regional Medical Center in Melbourne. Much of the new, sophisticated diagnostic equipment was located in this area. We spotted the little sign that read "Radiology." Earlier that morning I had force-swallowed the contents of two-and-a-half containers of the chalky, orange-flavored barium drink. The nurse had told me to save the last half-quart to drink just before the exam.

Jackie waited in a side room while I followed the attendant down a narrow hall and into a room which contained a sparkling white, seven-foot-tall, donut-shaped machine. In front of it was a narrow table on rails which would slide back and forth through the donut. Behind the glass was a sophisticated control panel. On the other side of the small room I recognized the familiar lead shield where the technician would stand while taking the X-ray pictures.

"Get as comfortable as you can, because you're not to move until we finish," the technician said. "Put your hands over your head, away from your sides. The table will slide slowly through the scanner. It will stop momentarily, and I'll ask you to hold your breath as I take the pictures. Then it will move back slightly until we've taken a number of 'slices' — of your abdomen."

I chatted with the technician as we got ready for the exam. It never occurred to me the X rays might reveal something ominous in my body. Something deadly.

That afternoon I was home alone. Jackie had gone to the grocery store. I was working at my word processor when the phone rang. It was the nurse — my daughter Bonnie's friend — in the doctor's office.

"The doctor asked me to call. Would it be possible for you to stop by the office before closing time? He wants to discuss the results of your exam." It sounded so innocent, so innocuous. Yet I sensed a dark foreboding.

"I'll be there in twenty minutes," I said.

This time I didn't disrobe. I simply sat on the edge of the examining table listening as the doctor, in an impersonal monotone, talked about the results of the test.

Holding his notes in his hand, he said matter-of-factly, "The tests show a number of enlarged lymph nodes in your abdomen. They are definitely cancerous. There is some possibility it may have spread into one or both kidneys. We'll have to wait until Monday, when I'll get a urologist and another radiologist to read the scans."

I just stared at him. Here was a doctor who had no idea who I was. He had to glance at the sheet in his hand to know my name was "Mr. Buckingham." He had not asked if I was married, had children or had ever done anything worthwhile in life. I was, to him, a case study. A human creature sitting on the edge of his examining table in a body he believed was about to die.

"My preliminary diagnosis is non-Hodgkins lymphoma," he continued, still reading from his notes. "It is treatable but not curable. It seems to have spread into one of your kidneys and perhaps into other organs as well. We'll want to run more tests next week to be sure."

I was too stunned even to ask questions. I simply sat, staring at him as his voice droned on. What was it like, I wondered, to tell a man he was about to die?

"Unfortunately, your prognosis is not good. Less than 2 percent of the cases with this type of disease live beyond five years, but you can't bank on that. If this is growing as fast as I think...." He shrugged and didn't continue.

"What action do you recommend?" I asked, realizing my mouth had gone dry. My voice sounded as if it were coming from the next room

"I want to schedule exploratory surgery early next week. After that we'll know more."

"Surgery?" I had never been a patient in a hospital, had never spent the night in a hospital room. Now this doctor, whom I had met only once before in my life, was saying I was going to have to be cut open so others could peer into my abdomen.

"The surgeon will make a vertical incision," he said. "It's major surgery, so you'll be in the hospital at least a week, depending on how well you do. Fortunately you're in good health."

I wanted to know who would assist during the surgery. "The only surgeon I know is Dr. Jackson, who did the breast biopsy on my wife several years ago."

"I've never worked with him," the doctor said, jotting notes on his pad. "I prefer another surgeon who is just as good. I'll call you Monday and let you know the schedule. Wait here a minute. I want my nurse to draw some more blood. Then you can leave."

Nothing else. He had just passed a death sentence on a man he'd met only once before. Now he was walking out of the room without even a "God bless you" or "I'm sorry for having to report you no longer have a future."

I waited as the nurse came in, smiling. Did she know? She must. But she gave no indication. She chatted amiably as she strapped the rubber tube around my upper arm and felt with her finger for the vein.

"Do you think it's going to rain?"

I grunted. Inside my mind was screaming, Do you think I'm going to die?

"See you next week," she said. And she too was gone. I walked through the door and caught the elevator down.

I was too stunned to think. "God, what's happening?"

The elevator doors opened on the ground floor. I looked up. There was Lewis Likens holding his little daughter, Rachael. Lewis was the age of my oldest son, Bruce. They had been good friends in high school. Later, Lewis had served a stint on our church staff before going into secular work. His parents were our personal friends, longtime church members and down-the-street neighbors.

"Hi, Jamie," he said cheerily. "We're just riding the elevators while Denise is in the pediatrician's office with Jeremy. How're you doing?"

What should I say? How was I to answer? He seemed so full of life and joy. His little girl was giggling, eager to make another ride on the elevator.

I desperately wanted to say, "Lewis, I've just been told I'm going to die from cancer."

Instead I lied. "I'm OK." I put on a crooked smile.

"Great to see you!" he said as he stepped into the elevator. "Wave at Pastor Buckingham," he said to Rachael. She grinned and waved, eyes sparkling with life, as the doors closed. I turned and walked out the main door to the parking lot. It had just started to rain.

THREE

PARADISE LOST

I DROVE HOME WITH TINY RAINDROPS SPATTERING against the windshield. The skies were dark. Thunder rumbled and wind whipped the tops of the palm trees along the road. One moment I had been living as though I had another forty-two years. Now I had no promise beyond today.

Life, which I had so taken for granted, now stood out in stark relief. It was all around me. I rolled down the window of my pickup so I could see life. Smell it. I noticed the little tufts of green grass growing up through the asphalt — fighting to stay alive against all odds. As I turned off Palm Bay Road toward my house, two dogs came running out of a yard, tails wagging, barking happily. I felt tears coming to my eyes. On the electric wires running parallel to the road, two mockingbirds sat, singing in the rain. Water dripped from the green fronds of a cabbage palm.

My mind raced back to my childhood, walking through the "hammock" — five acres of a thick, tropical jungle of oaks and palms behind our house in Vero Beach, just a few miles down the Florida east coast. Suddenly I was there, barefooted, slingshot in hand, following that twisting trail that led back to the tiny stream. A summer shower had cooled the air; my shirt was sticking to my back. I opened my mouth and stood under the drooping fronds of a cabbage palm and let the rainwater run into my mouth.

I choked back the tears of homesickness the thoughts generated. I pulled into our long, winding driveway through the tall pines. Ahead a tiny caterpillar, a fuzzy-wuzzy out of my childhood, was inching across the narrow drive. I slowed and swerved to miss him. How precious life was.

The house was empty when I arrived. Jackie was still at the grocery store. On the breakfast table was an earlier message from Steve Strang, my magazine publisher and friend. It had come in over the fax machine, and my daughter Sandy, who worked as my secretary, had left it there so I'd be sure to see it.

"We're shifting your September column to October. [I wrote a monthly column in *Charisma* magazine titled Last Word.] Write something for our anniversary issue. Talk about the future. You're at deadline."

Suddenly I heard a voice whispering in my spiritual ear. It was a voice I would hear many times during the next three weeks — the voice of Satan. He began, as is so often the case, by quoting a scripture, one I remembered from my youth: "Strike the shepherd and the sheep will be scattered, and I will turn my hand against the little ones" (Zech. 13:7).

"God has finally given up on you," the voice continued. "You have strutted like a peacock, doing your own thing. Now He has struck you with cancer, and your family and your church will be scattered. God has turned His hand against the little people — your grandchildren and the children of the church. All will be scattered, and many will perish. You are doomed."

There followed, in quick order, many other accusations — flashing through my mind like summer lightning across the night sky.

- You have no future.
- You are filled with sin.
- You go in your own strength and rely on your own understanding.
- You judge God's people, sneering at them with your writing and preaching.
- You don't pray.
- You spend more time with your calendar than with your Bible.
- You're unfaithful to your wife's unconditional love.
- You don't take time with your children or grandchildren.
- You're too busy with God's work to spend time with God.
- You're proud!
- Now it's time to pay the price. You will die.

I could feel a cold, clammy hand wrapping around my mind. Hope, that one necessary ingredient to all life, was gone. I was already dead.

Outside I heard a car door slam, then Jackie's familiar footsteps on the tile floor of the screened back porch. I waited until she set the groceries on the kitchen table. A bunch of bright yellow bananas topped off the brown paper bag.

"We need to talk," I said. "Come in the den."

She listened as we sat side by side on the love seat. I spoke only a couple of sentences, and her face became a mask of anguish.

"You're not going to leave me," she sobbed, bright tears bursting from her eyes. She reached over and grasped my arm with both hands.

"I may not have a choice," I choked out.

Then something happened. I have thought back on that moment many times, recalling the instant change I saw take place. Although her face was wet with tears, I saw a small light flickering in her eyes. Then it became a dazzling brilliance. Her entire face radiated with a supernatural glow. In the midst of her tears, she smiled.

"God has just spoken." Her voice was a whispered shout. "He said, 'This is not unto death.' "

Then, just as suddenly, she balled up her fists and shook them. "I rebuke you, Satan!" she said with the anger and sternness of a she-bear protecting her cub. "In the name of Jesus, you cannot take my husband."

"But he's right," I said, shaking my head. "I have been on a path of self-destruction. I have gone in my own strength. I've lived as if God would not hold me accountable. My life is filled with sin — "

She broke in. "Then we shall repent together until we are assured that the sin is gone — from both of us. We cannot bribe God or buy your healing. Jesus bought it with His blood at Calvary. But we can come into God's presence with clean hands and a pure heart — and we'll do it together."

She grabbed my hand and held it tightly. "You may walk through the fire, but it will not kindle upon you. You will emerge on the other side."

Hope was restored.

FOUR

THE FAMILY

FRIDAY EVENING THE FAMILY GATHERED.

Fifteen years ago Jackie and I had bought a new two-story, brick house that sat on twenty acres of rural land in an undeveloped section of Palm Bay — Melbourne's next-door neighbor. The front part of the property was heavily wooded with tall, stately pine trees mixed with cabbage palms and thick clumps of palmettos. The rear half of the land was in fenced pasture, complete with a small lake. Across the years we had raised horses, cows, even a few pigs. Then our five children, who had gone off to college, married and returned home. We gave each of them an acre of land. Four of the five had built their homes next to us — meaning we finally had to pull down the pasture fence and get rid of the animals. Only our daughter Bonnie, her husband, Marion, and their two children lived off the compound. But they were only ten minutes away. When the family gathered — including Jackie's eighty-three-year-old mother — there was a total of twenty-five.

We piled in the den. The two infants were put to bed upstairs. The rest of the grandchildren sat on the floor. Jackie's mother, who lived with us, was not there.

She was, mercifully, in an assisted-living facility recovering from a broken hip. The others were seated on the couches or in the big bean bags on the floor. I outlined, as accurately as possible, what I had been told.

Sickness was a stranger to our family. Death was unimaginable. With the exception of some complications with pregnancies, normal childhood diseases and Jackie's bout with breast biopsies, no one in the family had ever been sick. None of the boys had ever been in a hospital. Nor had I. I wasn't even born in a hospital. I had been birthed in the second floor of a garage apartment in Vero Beach. The town's one physician, along with my dad, who "caught" me, had been there to welcome me into the world. Now that journey seemed almost over.

For me to sit in our den on that June night, in the middle of what seemed to be a perfect family setting, and talk of death was like announcing the intrusion of a dragon into Camelot. The reaction on the part of my grown children and their spouses was instant — and uniform. My oldest son, Bruce, took the lead.

"Dad, there's no way we're going to let Satan do this to you. Cancer is evil. We will fight it with the weapons of spiritual warfare until it is gone and Satan is driven from your body and from this property."

Our youngest son, Tim, the cowboy in our family, approached it at another level. "You're not going to give in to this, are you? Or don't you believe all that stuff you've been preaching all these years?"

"What do you mean?"

"Well, does God heal or not? You've been saying He does. You've written all those books on miracles and healing. Do you really believe it, or should we all just stop going to church?"

"Hey, that's not fair." It was Sandy, the youngest daughter. "The doctor's just told Dad he might die."

Bruce reacted. "No, it is fair. That's what it's all about. Either God is who He says He is, or we're all a bunch of fakes."

My three sons-in-law were equally adamant. All are mature Christians, active in our church. Two of them, along with four of my own children, are alumni of Oral Roberts University. They were stunned, but reacted with positive support and deep faith. The five young women — all of whom I loved equally — were fighting back the tears. But no one flinched.

"We need to pray," my oldest daughter, Robin, said. "We need to do it now. The children need to join us."

Involving the children in prayer, I was to discover later, was one of the powerful — perhaps the most powerful — secrets to healing. It was to happen time and time again, both in my presence and apart from me. It would involve not only my own grandchildren, but all the children of our church.

I sat cross-legged in the middle of the floor. Everyone hunkered around —

34

straining to lay their hands on me in the middle of the prayer pile.

Everyone prayed out loud. Some in tongues. Some with weeping. Some with strong, authoritative voices. I stopped trying to listen as the tears began to flow. It had been years since I'd cried. Now the tears flowed freely, tears which, even as I write this almost a year later, are still flowing.

We slept little that night. Jackie and I had much to talk about. It seemed imperative, if she were to walk with me "through the fire," that we be in absolute unity. That meant I needed to confess all the hidden things of my life. Most of them were unnecessary. She knew about them anyway and stopped me before I got started — even the old infidelities, doors long closed. But she needed to know of my willingness, for I did not see how I could get right with God, much less approach Him, if there were any hidden things between me and the one He had ordained I should live with and be faithful to all my life.

Lying in bed on my back, my hand in Jackie's, I listened as she prayed — her voice often choking. I felt the tears spilling out the sides of my eyes, running down my cheek and soaking the pillow. My relationship with God was a simile of my relationship with Jackie. We slept in the same bed, had the same name and enjoyed occasional times of brief and exciting intimacy. But at heart I was an adulterer. I did not share my deepest thoughts with Him. I came to God only on my terms, not His. I had a mistress — my "ministry." Although innocent to the eye, my ministerial mistress received far more affection than the One to whom I was vowed.

As with God, so with Jackie. I had boxed her out of my life. I resented the fact that she had but one purpose in life — to be my wife. I knew if I honored that purpose, it would mean I would have to restrict myself and allow that purpose to call forth a corresponding reaction on my part. I was afraid of that, afraid it would hobble me, afraid it might take some of the excitement out of my life. And I thrived on adventure and excitement. I loved seeing how far I could venture into danger without getting harmed. To give all my devotion to God — or to my wife — might mean losing the thing I cherished most, my self-will, the power to sit in the captain's chair of my ship and call all the shots in my life.

Now that most cherished factor of life had been snatched from me. The cancer in my body was in control. In my unwillingness to turn my life totally over to God, another force had sneaked in and taken the helm — assigning me to the ship's dungeon, where I would die a miserable death. Yet, despite this shift of control, my wife was still there, squeezing my hand in the middle of the night, pouring out her intercession to God on my behalf.

What a fool I had been to neglect her.

What a fool I had been to neglect Him.

35

Four Eagle Scouts - The Buckingham brothers
Walter Jr.   Clay   Jamie   Laddie

Vero Beach Florida

Christmas 1948

age   24   21   16   15

(Top) The Buckingham brothers: Walter Jr., Clay, Jamie and John (Laddie), 1948

(Right and above) Jamie Buckingham and Jackie Law: sweethearts since high school

FIVE

A BASE OF PRAYER

THERE'S NOTHING THAT WILL ORDER A MAN'S priorities," Samuel Johnson once wrote, "like being sentenced to hang in a fortnight."

I identified with Johnson's felon and spent Saturday morning ordering my priorities.

It had been a sleepless night. Before dawn I was in my study writing a note to Sandy, my daughter and part-time secretary. "Cancel everything on my calendar through September except my duties at the church."

I looked around my study at all the familiar things, the pictures which swept memories into my mind like wind blowing leaves at autumn. Each picture represented an important event in my life — places of great significance. Standing at the Western Wall in Jerusalem. Climbing through St. Stephen's gate on Mount Sinai. Paddling a dugout canoe in Irian Jaya. Standing beside a beached Catalina seaplane on the Amazon River. In front of that wonderful little church in Czechoslovakia — the one with the huge chalice on the steeple.

Then there were the pictures of people who had meant so much to me across

37

the years: my family; my brothers John and Clay; my brother Walter, who had died in 1966; my dad, standing in the middle of an orange tree surrounded by wonderful, golden fruit. There were John and Elizabeth Sherrill, Catherine Marshall, Len LeSourd — the gang that made up the first *Guideposts* writers' workshop where I had gotten my start as a professional writer. I gazed at pictures of Kathryn Kuhlman, Corrie ten Boom, Pat Robertson — all those with whom I had written. And, of course, the many reminders of Jackie, centering around a brown sepia photograph of the blonde-haired fifteen-year-old I fell in love with when she was in the tenth grade in high school — and I was a year older. How long had I loved her? Through two years of high school, four years of college, thirty-six years of marriage. "For her sake, Father, don't let her become a widow. Let us die together, living out the years You promised."

My gaze shifted to the picture over my desk, the only picture of Jesus we had in our house. It was an artist's rendition of the good Shepherd, holding His staff, leaning far out over a deep, craggy ravine to rescue a lamb trapped in the rocks. In the background a giant predator bird circled. My eyes strayed from the pictures of family and friends and fixed on that one picture. Jesus! I felt tears again. Was I slipping off the deep end emotionally?

Jackie walked in, still in her nightgown and robe. I looked up, trying to say something sensible.

"I'm clearing my calendar," I said. "For years I've wished for some kind of excuse to stay home. I never dreamed it would happen like this."

She looked over my shoulder at my calendar.

"Why didn't you cancel the October hiking trip in Israel as well?"

"I can't cancel out the entire future. I've got to have something to hope for, something to look forward to besides dying."

"Good!" she smiled.

"We're supposed to fly to California next week," I said. "I hate canceling that."

"You don't have any choice. If they do surgery...." She paused, then continued. "Besides, Bernie will understand. Maybe you can work with him using the phone and fax."

Bernie May was president of Wycliffe Bible Translators, one of the world's largest missionary organizations. For a number of years I had helped with his writing — and been something of a personal consultant. Helping him meant helping get the Bible translated into all the languages of the world. It was my own little mission project.

Across the years Bernie and I had developed a deep personal relationship. He once described it like the one which existed between David and Jonathan, who "became one in spirit with David, and he loved him as himself" (1 Sam. 18:1).

Jackie and I had planned to take our ten-year-old granddaughter April Moore with us for her first trip to California. Now all that would have to wait. I had no choice but to cancel. I knew Bernie was out of town, but I typed out a brief fax message to his wife, Nancy, knowing she would not only contact him, but begin to pray.

There were three more people I needed to contact.

The first was my friend and sometimes business associate John French. John and his wife, Barry, lived in Phoenix. They had a summer cottage on Lake Michigan as well as a home on Cape Cod. Although they are Episcopalians, they also are nonresident members of a group of Christians called the Community of Jesus, who live on the cape. Several years ago John and I entered into a business partnership to create and market Christian video curriculum to be used in prisons. We had made a number of trips to Israel together, using the video crew from the Community of Jesus, and videotaped on-location material to be used in conjunction with Bible study notebooks I had written. I was the creative half of the company; John, the marketing half. We sold these tapes and workbooks to the Christian market, then used the profits to give the material to prison ministries. I knew John and Barry would not only pray but would involve the powerful prayer warriors at the Community of Jesus.

I typed out a short message, dialed John's fax number in Michigan and fed the paper into the machine. I wondered what it would be like if one of my dear friends sent such a message to me. How would I respond? I wished I had spent more time praying for John when he was in the hospital in Boston, recovering from open-heart surgery. Was everyone like me, too busy to pray for their friends — even when they might be dying? I hoped not.

The final two people I called lived in Florida. One was my friend and publisher Steve Strang. I called him at home. He was up early and listened as I told him the news. "We serve a God who is bigger than cancer," he said softly. Then he added, "Stop everything else you're doing and get well."

"I can't stop, Steve. Michele can pick up the editing slack, but life comes from spreading the gospel. I've got to keep on writing. For my sake. Besides, I need for my readers to be praying for me."

It was, I realized later, one of the better decisions I made. Before the ordeal was over, thousands of letters would come from magazine readers all over the world. They told of incredible prayer experiences of people I will never meet this side of glory.

My final phone call was to Len LeSourd. Len and his deceased wife, Catherine Marshall, had been dear friends to me for a long time. Before Catherine died, they had founded a small organization for intercessory prayer called Breakthrough Inc. Jackie and I served on the board, along with several others — most of whom had been associated with *Guideposts* magazine, which Len had edited for twenty-eight years and where I had once served as a roving editor. For more than a dozen years we had sponsored and encouraged intercessory prayer — encouraging people to call or write their prayer needs to our organization, which then directed these needs to hundreds of intercessors all over the nation. Now it was my time.

Len's wife, Sandy, answered the phone, bubbly as usual. She listened silently as I told her what I had told the others.

"Len's on the phone," she said, her voice choking.

"It's not your time to die, Jamie," he said matter-of-factly. "We're going to mobilize the Intercessors. It's time for spiritual warfare. Satan is not going to win this one."

I hung up and sat quietly, looking at the wall beside my word processor. Years ago I had pasted pictures of these four friends — Bernie May, John French, Steve Strang and Len LeSourd — on the wood paneling along with a number of other pictures of friends I knew I would contact sooner or later. I had put them there as prayer reminders. Every day when I sat down at my computer, waiting for it to boot up, I would glance at the wall and pray for my friends. Sometimes I sat there for a long time, even after the computer was ready. Now I desperately needed their prayers.

"Don't let me down," I whispered out loud. "I need you!"

I glanced down at my little pocket calendar — my constant companion — then at the airline schedule books scattered on my desk. I felt tears coming back to my eyes.

"I spend more time with my calendar than I do with Your Bible," I confessed out loud. "I spend more time making travel arrangements than I do praying. I spend more time writing memos, letters and fax messages than I do interceding for my friends. Forgive me, Father, and give me a second chance."

I picked up the phone and dialed the familiar number of my travel agent, Hanna Shepherd, remembering the agency was open on Saturday until noon.

"Cancel all my flight plans through September."

"You've finally decided to take a vacation," she joked.

"Not quite." Then I told her the news.

She was silent on the other end of the line. I remembered. Her husband had died of lingering cancer several years before.

"I'll pray for you," she said awkwardly but sincerely. She was wise enough not to say more.

I had one more fax to send. I sat looking at the little black box with the phone receiver on the side. Like my doctor, it was simply a messenger of good or bad news. Whatever I fed into it, it fed out on the other end of the line. What a marvelous instrument.

A little voice spoke to me, using a favorite computerese phrase: Garbage in, garbage out.

I sat looking at the keyboard of my computer where I was about to type one more message. "I've been putting garbage into my soul," I confessed to God. "Television, newspapers, magazines, the books I read, the movies I see. Even though I disapprove of the industry, I enjoy seeing and reading the results. Is it possible this has filtered into my system, lodged in my kidney and become cancerous?"

There was no answer, but I remained convicted. It was time, past time, for a mighty cleansing and purging that I might be clean and pure in every area.

I typed out a brief message to my friend Jim Jackson in Montreat, North Carolina. Jim's organization, Christian Believers United (CBU), sponsored many of the teaching conferences where I often spoke. I had worked with him for years. I was the president of the National Leadership Conference; he, the executive director. Jim also acted as my tour host on the several tours I had led to Israel, helped make the land arrangements when we took our video crews for filming and was currently planning the hiking tour we were to take in October. I knew he would enlist prayer support from the hundreds of people who support the CBU ministry.

I got up and walked back into the kitchen, where Jackie was sitting at the breakfast table.

"I've called Don Williams, and he's going to call the pastors and the church staff," she said. Don, a retired army colonel, was my loyal associate at the church, coordinating the work of the other staff pastors.

"Is he OK?" I asked.

"He was crying," Jackie said, tears coming to her own eyes. "I've also called all the members of our home group. They are all praying. You need to call your brothers and sister."

"Not yet," I resisted.

"You need their prayers," Jackie said. "We cannot make it without prayer."

I had always been reluctant to ask people to pray for me. I was healthy. I had enough material possessions, an almost perfect family and virtual self-sufficiency. So many were worse off than I.

Yet Jackie was right. This time I had no choice. Unless God intervened — and prayer was the key to His intervention — I was going to die.

I sat down at the breakfast table and called my brother John in Birmingham. A year younger than I, he was a doctor serving on the faculty of the medical school of the University of Alabama as well as holding down his own private family practice. A dedicated Christian, he had foregone the riches often found

41

in the practice of medicine to spend most of his time working with poor families who could not pay and building a Christian medical clinic in Central America. He listened as I told him what I knew. I knew that he knew the situation was grim. He asked a few questions, made me promise to call him daily as new facts appeared and committed himself to pray for me. He told me he would call our older brother, Clay, a retired U.S. Army major general now in full-time ministry with the Officers' Christian Fellowship, and our younger sister, Audrey, a housewife in Missouri. I felt better after talking with him.

An hour later Audrey called. I was five years old when my parents adopted a newborn girl to go with the older boys already in the family. I remember sitting in my older brother Clay's bedroom the night before they brought her home from the hospital. My parents, sensitive to the situation, brought us in on the decision. My mother suggested five names then allowed us boys to pick the name we wanted. We all agreed on Audrey. From that time on we never considered her adopted. She was our baby sister.

For a number of years she had lived in the town of Fredericktown, Missouri. Her entire family was active in a little charismatic church. I could hear the tears in her voice as she talked over the phone.

"As soon as John called, the Lord told me to read Isaiah 38," she said. "It's for you, Jamie. Read it now."

There was more to the conversation, but as soon as I hung up I told Jackie what had been said then picked up my Bible and walked out into the front yard. It was the last day of June. The towering pines that surrounded our house were a bright green against an azure sky. The thick carpet of St. Augustine grass felt good beneath my bare feet. I walked in a big circle around the yard, reading aloud Isaiah 38.

Somehow, in my study of the Bible, I had missed this fascinating story from the life of King Hezekiah, king of Judah seven hundred years before Christ. I remembered reading some of the stories of Hezekiah found in 2 Kings and 2 Chronicles. I had even led expeditions through Hezekiah's Tunnel in Jerusalem, a quarter-mile-long watercourse which runs underground through solid rock from the Gihon Spring to the Pool of Siloam — one of the world's most incredible engineering feats. But for reasons unknown I had never studied the little section of his life described in Isaiah 38.

Hezekiah, still a young man, had become ill and was dying. (He became king of Judah at age twenty-five and reigned for twenty-nine years.) Isaiah the prophet came to his palace with a message from God: "Put your house in order, because you are going to die; you will not recover" (v. 1b).

The prophet then turned and stalked out of the palace. As he was leaving, the Bible says, "Hezekiah turned his face to the wall and prayed to the Lord,

'Remember, O Lord, how I have walked before you faithfully and with whole-hearted devotion and have done what is good in your eyes.' And Hezekiah wept bitterly" (vv. 2-3).

I sat down on the front steps. Devastated. Is this what God told my sister to tell me to read? I was already at the breaking point emotionally. I did not think I could stand another prophecy of doom — even if it was given to a man twenty-seven hundred years ago. I turned back to the parallel passage in 2 Kings 20 and continued reading.

"Before Isaiah had left the middle court, the word of the Lord came to him: 'Go back and tell Hezekiah, the leader of my people, This is what the Lord, the God of your father David, says: I have heard your prayer and seen your tears; I will heal you. On the third day from now you will go up to the temple of the Lord. I will add fifteen years to your life. And I will deliver you and this city from the hand of the king of Assyria. I will defend this city for my sake and for the sake of my servant David' " (2 Kin. 20:5-6).

Fifteen years. The day before I would have shaken it off as nothing. After all, hadn't God promised me another fifty years that morning in the shower? And only eight of those years had passed. But the news of the previous afternoon had changed everything. Today I would gladly welcome such a promise.

I turned back to Isaiah 38. The rest of the chapter was a song, composed by Hezekiah after his healing. I got up from the steps, almost overcome by the potential of the promise I had read. Was God actually speaking to me out of the life of this man who had been dead nearly three thousand years? Were our paths parallel? Would He treat my repentance with the same mercy with which He had treated Hezekiah's? The Bible still in my hand, I got up and once again started my circular walk around the lawn, reading out loud from Hezekiah's song of remembrance. I began to weep. His words were my words.

> I said, "In the prime of my life
>   must I go through the gates of death
>   and be robbed of the rest of my years?"
> I said, "I will not again see the Lord,
>   the Lord, in the land of the living;
> no longer will I look on mankind,
>   or be with those who dwell in this world.
> Like a shepherd's tent my house
>   has been pulled down and taken from me.
> Like a weaver I have rolled up my life,
>   and he has cut me off from the loom...."
>   Isaiah 38:10-12

43

There was more, but by now the tears had blinded my eyes. I could no longer read but only walk through the yard realizing how common was death. All my life I had been healthy. I had never once considered the thought of dying — nor had I feared it. I had been frightened on a number of occasions. Once I almost stepped on a rattlesnake while rock climbing in the California desert. Another time I was caught in a rock slide on the side of a steep mountain in the Sinai Peninsula. Another time the engine on my single-engine Bellanca quit momentarily while I was flying over the mountains of north Georgia. But facing a life-threatening disease was like taking a blow in the solar plexus from a heavyweight boxer. It may not show up on the outside, but inside everything is messed up. All my prayers were focused keenly. To face death brazenly when you are young and healthy is one thing. To face it when you have been told by medical authorities that it is imminent is quite another.

I wiped my eyes and continued reading Hezekiah's song:

> I cried like a swift or thrush,
>   I moaned like a mourning dove.
> My eyes grew weak as I looked to the heavens.
>   I am troubled; O Lord, come to my aid!
>
> Isaiah 38:14

I read on. He talked of the "anguish of my soul" but promised God he would walk "humbly" all his years because God had had mercy on him.

Mercy. What a wonderful word! "O God, that is what I cry for. Have mercy on me." Tears dropped onto the pages of my open Bible. Was it fear of the cancer? No, it seemed more like grief. Deep grief. Something was dying *inside* me. I was grieving for it.

At the close of the song, after Hezekiah had received his assurance of continuing life, he shared a remarkable revelation of self-understanding:

> Surely it was for my benefit
>   that I suffered such anguish.
> In your love you kept me
>   from the pit of destruction;
> you have put all my sins
>   behind your back.
> For the grave cannot praise you,
>   death cannot sing your praise;
> those who go down to the pit
>   cannot hope for your faithfulness.

44

The living, the living — they praise you,
    as I am doing today....

                    Isaiah 38:17-19

I closed the book, too overcome to read more. A brilliant realization dawned in my mind, like the sun breaking through dark clouds following an afternoon thundershower. There was purpose in this. It was for my "benefit that I suffered such anguish." God was allowing this to happen to me. He may have permitted it, but He had not caused it. The cause was Satan, the murderer of the brethren, and God was still in control. Even though Satan was wrenching my body, lacerating my emotions, God was still in control. He was allowing Satan to buffet me to keep me "from the pit of destruction."

That's where I had been heading. No, I wasn't hell-bound. I believed too strongly in the sustaining power of Jesus Christ to think I could do anything that would cause Him to turn His back on me. But my self-centered life-style had for years been leading me downward toward destruction rather than upward toward His presence. That is why, when I received the news the day before, I had cried but one prayer: "Your face, Father, is all I long to see. Just to be in Your presence is enough."

God was allowing this thing to happen to me because He loved me. Because I was a sovereign vessel, chosen by Him for good works. Now all my sin was behind me. I could come into His presence holy. Purged. Cleansed by this powerful force which had swept through my body.

I went back in the house. It was noon, but Jackie had not prepared lunch. We were alone.

"Jane Berrey called," she said. Jane and her husband, Gene, were part of our home group of five families. They were close friends. "She said God told her to tell you to read Isaiah 38."

I stood there, my finger still in the pages of the Bible where I had been reading, and started to cry again. I could almost hear the sounds of battle over my body, as the angels of God clashed swords with the demons from hell. Things were happening in that invisible reality called "the heavenlies" — things far beyond my control.

45

SIX

SUNDAY I

THE TABERNACLE CHURCH WAS BIRTHED IN MARCH 1967. During the two years prior to that I had been evicted as pastor of two Southern Baptist churches — one in South Carolina and one in Melbourne, Florida. I was at the end of my spiritual tether (which was not very long back then). A small group had followed me out of the Melbourne church and formed another church. Disillusioned and frustrated by the system, we began a quest for spiritual truth. Within a year the entire church was ejected from the Baptist community. We became an interdenominational body comprised of people broken by the denominational systems and shattered by the world.

But it was a good thing that had happened. We doubled in size. Then doubled again. I began writing full-time — books and magazine articles — as well as preaching on Sundays. Leaders were raised up to take care of the pastoral duties. The church continued to grow until it became one of the largest churches in the area, with multiple staff and several thousand people who called the "Tab" their church home.

Even though my own ministry had expanded far beyond the influence of my local church, I remained their spiritual overseer and looked to them as my spiritual family. Relationships, I believed, meant everything — especially in times of crisis. Now it was my time to rely on the relationships I had established across the years. I had nowhere else to turn except to my church for help.

They responded instantly. Their shepherd had been struck with what seemed to be a mortal wound. But instead of scattering, the sheep rallied, holding him up so the Lord could heal him. The head of the church intercessory prayer chain mobilized her troops. The pastors and church staff stopped everything they were doing to intercede. Hundreds of others began to fast, even before there was any official word of my illness.

Sunday morning, following the dark news on Friday, I sat in my usual place on the front row in our simple, familiar auditorium. The worship time that morning had been subdued. Many of those present had already heard the news. I was aware of people glancing at me. I knew they were praying, even though they did not yet know the details. When I stood to face them, I could sense their concern.

I had always been frank with the church. Very little went on in my life, or the life of my family, which I did not share from the pulpit. It embarrassed some and threatened others, but I believed the best way to disciple others was to live an open life before them — sharing personal victories and defeats and letting them see God at work in their shepherd.

I began my sermon that morning with a frank report of the situation as I knew it. I then told them the medical diagnosis — and the prognosis. At that time I was classified as having lymphoma. The doctors were recommending more examinations that week followed by exploratory surgery. The disease was incurable. My life on earth was determined by the rate of the cancer's growth.

What follows is an edited version of the transcript of what I said to the congregation that morning.

My Sermon

I confess to you I have been running primarily in my own strength and leaning primarily on my own understanding — rather than trusting God. Yet I do not believe God is punishing me, rather I believe there is purpose in this cancer attack. God is simply reminding me that He wants me to return to His ways.

These last thirty-six hours have been days and nights of marvelous change in my life. I've renewed my relationship with God as Father, walking intimately in His presence. I've not heard Him speak, but I know He has been listening as I have spoken to Him — something I've not done a lot of recently. I am trusting Him to continue to change me until I am the kind of man He wants me to be.

I've also entered into a new relationship with my wife. We've spent thirty-six years together during the last two days. She has fearlessly let me talk to her about my sins — and about my fears. She has not winced as we've talked about how much longer I might have to live. However, she has been honest with me at the same time.

She's pointed out, for instance, the fallacy of my reliance on physical exercise as a life source. I have told her on a number of occasions, "If I don't exercise, my body will die."

She has now responded, "Exercise is not your source of life. Diet is not your source of life. God alone is your source of life. Man does not live by bread alone, or by exercise alone, but by the words that proceed out of the mouth of God. That's where life comes from."

She's reminded me that when God told me, eight years ago, that I would live another fifty years if I cooperated with Him, I translated that to mean weight loss, diet and exercise. I failed to understand that "cooperate with God" meant obedience in all areas of life.

I now see the wisdom of that.

I don't want to be operated on. I've never been a patient in a hospital, much less had surgery. But if that is the method God chooses to change me, to get me back into His will, then I will drink from that cup.

On the other hand, when the doctor asked me in his office how I felt about his diagnosis, I said, "I don't believe it." Jackie says that is good theology. I am not denying the presence of cancer in my body. The CT scans show the tumors. But I am not going to confess that I have cancer. The cancer is trying to have me — but I am going to resist it. The pictures may show it, but I don't have to accept that it is deadly or that my condition is terminal. It's there temporarily, as far as I am concerned. But my body is the temple of the Holy Spirit, and I serve a God who is much bigger than facts and circumstances.

As I prayed about this service, I felt God saying I should come to you this morning and ask you to pray for me. I don't do that very often. There are a number of reasons why I've been reluctant. For one, I know some of you are worse off than I am. You've been battered and bruised and cut on a lot more than I'll ever be. So I've been hesitant to ask you to focus your prayers on me. But as I prayed God said that this time it was very important for you to pray for me.

Even though God is using this to change me, I am convinced it is an attack of Satan. There is no way I can look at cancer and say, "God brought this on." God does not visit us with cancer. The essence of cancer comes from Lucifer. Lucifer was an angel who rebelled against God and was cast out of heaven, taking on the name Satan.

Lucifer's rebellion is a perfect description of the character of cancer cells in the body. Instead of being in submission to the system God has ordained, they have decided to grow at their own speed. They set themselves up over all the other cells — destroying anything that gets in their way. They are in rebellion to God's perfect system of life and health. As a result they are destructive rather than constructive. It is right to cast them out of the body.

Pray for Jackie. It is imperative she be strong in the midst of this. God has done a special work in our relationship over these last two days. Every time I woke up last night I could feel her hands on my body, making the sign of the cross on my back and shoulders. I would doze off, knowing she remained awake all night long, lying close beside me, praying softly in the Spirit. Please pray for her. Ask God to give her strength to walk through this fire with me and not be burned.

Pray also for my family — my sons, daughters and their spouses. Pray for the little people — the children — who live with us. This is my primary support system.

Pray for the leaders of this church. I don't know how long all this is going to take. I have no idea what is going to happen. I don't know if I will be separated from you for a time. This is a time for God to call forth new, young, emerging leaders. If it is necessary for me to get out of the way so this can happen, then I am willing.

There is a possibility I am reaping what I have sown. I have been prideful, rebellious and independent in many of my attitudes. Now I find that some of the cells in my body are reflecting those attitudes. Whether that is true or not, I ask you to believe with me that as I die to my pride and arrogance and willful disobedience, God will quickly put these cancer cells to death. I am praying that for myself — and I am praying that for this church as well.

Yesterday afternoon I spent a lot of quiet time with God. At one point, sitting in the den, I picked up the newspaper. I glanced at it and dropped it on the floor. "It's not very significant, is it?" Jackie said.

We've turned on the tape player, and our house is filled with the sound of praise and the music of Scripture choruses. We've cut off the TV, and I'm not sure we'll ever turn it back on. Television is not wrong. We simply have no interest in it. His presence has been all our hearts have yearned for. Pray that we will enter that presence and never depart.

I have shared all this not just to ask you to pray for me and to pray for this church, but because I see some spiritual principles emerging which affect us all.

Yesterday I read again the story of King Jehoshaphat's battle against the enemy forces coming to kill him and destroy the nation of Judah. It's found in 2 Chronicles 20.

The southern kingdom of Judah had been through a series of evil kings before

Jehoshaphat came to the throne. A godly man, he did two things in the beginning of his reign. First, he got rid of all the corrupt civil leaders and appointed righteous judges.

Second, he appointed holy spiritual leaders. He removed the corrupt priests from the temple and in their stead appointed Levites and priests and heads of families to administer the law of the Lord and to settle disputes. He told them to serve faithfully and wholeheartedly and in the fear of the Lord.

Then, interestingly, he and his nation were suddenly under satanic attack. The pagan forces from the other side of the Jordan River had banded together to march against Judah. His couriers, alarmed, brought word that their enemies had forded the Jordan and were encamped on the shore of the Dead Sea where the springs of En Gedi empty into the sea. They would soon be marching up through the pass and would surely overwhelm Jehoshaphat's small army. It was an impossible situation.

At that point Jehoshaphat did three things:

(1) Although frightened, "he resolved to inquire of the Lord" (2 Chron. 20:3). He said, "This thing is too big for me. I'm going to see what God wants to do."

(2) "He proclaimed a fast for all Judah" (2 Chron. 20:3). He asked the people to fast and join him in prayer seeking God's answer.

(3) "The people of Judah came together to seek help from the Lord" (2 Chron. 20:4).

At that gathering, Jehoshaphat made a profound speech, concluding with these words: "O our God...we have no power to face this vast army that is attacking us. We do not know what to do, but our eyes are upon you" (2 Chron. 20:12).

That's the word God has given me for this hour. I don't know what to do, but my eyes are upon God. I can stand in front of the mirror and look at my tummy and say, "Everything's OK in there." But saying it doesn't make it OK. Positive thinking does not make it OK. All the love and loyalty of friends and family will not heal. Too many of my friends who love God and have loving families around them have died of cancer. Love and loyalty and positive thinking do not heal. Only God heals!

He can do it with medicine. He can do it with treatment. He can do it with surgery. He can do it by simply touching the disease with His finger. But God alone heals.

So Jehoshaphat stood before the people and confessed he was helpless — but not hopeless. He put his trust in God. Suddenly a man in the crowd, Jahaziel, began to prophesy. Jahaziel came from a long line of musicians dating back to Asaph, David's chief musician. His words rang like thunder above the crowd.

"Listen, King Jehoshaphat and all who live in Judah and Jerusalem! This is what the Lord says to you: 'Do not be afraid or discouraged because of this vast army. For the battle is not yours, but God's.' "

I woke many times during my fitful sleep last night with those words ringing in my ears: The battle is not yours, but God's.

Jahaziel followed this encouraging word with specific instructions. God was saying, through this prophet, that Jehoshaphat should take the initiative and march down against them.

But "you will not have to fight this battle. Take up your positions; stand firm and see the deliverance the Lord will give you.... Do not be afraid; do not be discouraged. Go out to face them tomorrow, and the Lord will be with you" (2 Chron. 20:17).

Early the next morning they set out to march down through the Negev desert, across the steep mountains and into Wadi En Gedi to confront the massed armies of the enemy. This time it was Jehoshaphat who prophesied to his small army of soldiers and priests: "Have faith in the Lord your God and you will be upheld; have faith in his prophets and you will be successful" (2 Chron. 20:20).

So confident was he of the pending victory that he put the Levites, his choir of praise singers, at the front of the army. They marched into battle singing, "Give thanks to the Lord, for his love endures forever."

What a way to fight a war! What a way to win over cancer! Trusting God. Fasting. Hearing prophecy. Obeying the Word. Facing the enemy with praise.

The rest is history. When they arrived, they found the enemy had turned on themselves and slaughtered each other during the night. When they crested the last hill and looked down on the enemy encampment, they saw the result. It is described in detail in verse 24: "When the men of Judah came to the place that overlooks the desert and looked toward the vast army, they saw only dead bodies lying on the ground; no one had escaped."

I want to close my sermon by letting you know where I am standing. In that verse in my Bible I have scratched through the word "bodies" — and written in the words "cancer cells."

I had finished preaching. I then asked Don Williams, our pastoral coordinator; Don Lees, one of our elders; and my two sons, Bruce and Tim, and my wife to join me on the platform. I wanted the congregation simply to wait on God and see what the Father had to say in reply to all that had been said.

We stood, arms around each other's waists. Then a voice spoke out of the congregation. I glanced up. It was Don Hoenig, a messianic Jew who still wears his yarmulke to church.

"God has not raised up a wimpy army." He was speaking loudly and with authority. It was not prophecy, but exhortation. "We are not experiments. We are children of God. It is time for the body of Christ to point their Christ-centered finger in the face of the devil and say, 'Get off my back. We don't have to put up with you any longer.'

"I believe our pastor is a catalyst to show the church that we have not taken a stand, and it is time to begin to see ourselves as who we are — who God says we are. I do not accept the lie of the devil that he is to die. We are more than conquerors, and the devil has no place in our lives. We are created in the image of God. God does not have cancer, and the cancer will not have you."

There was a loud murmur of affirmation across the congregation. Then Don Lees, standing beside me on the platform, spoke. More exhortation.

"Be reminded that this is a battle. It is not just a sickness that is trying to afflict Jamie. It is a battle for the kingdom of God in this church. You are citizens of God with us. We are lively stones, built into a temple which God inhabits by His Spirit. God is building His temple in our lives.

"When Nehemiah was called to reestablish the temple in Jerusalem, he was threatened from many sides. Sanballat and Tobiah were there, challenging him, threatening him. They were the bearers of fear. The warfare was so fierce that Nehemiah told all the laborers to gird themselves with swords while they were working on the wall.

"Today, as we rebuild the wall, we are in a battle. The sword of the Lord, which is the Word of God, is our defense. As we pray, lift your expectation from Jamie to God. Ask God to heal your hearts. Heal your thoughts. Ask God to heal Jamie's hurt and Jackie's hurt so they can receive from God."

Don then prayed a powerful prayer, anointing Jackie and me with oil, rebuking Satan and the rebellious cells in my body.

The men left the platform, and I asked the people to stand for the benediction. Suddenly a young man came rushing down the aisle and onto the platform. He was Don and Linda Lees's son-in-law, Dale Velie. Dale owns a little lawn-care business, and I had always seen him as a quiet, submitted, humble young man. This time, however, he turned and looked at me with fire in his eyes.

"Stand before me!" he shouted.

Surprised, but by this time ready for anything God wanted to do, I turned and stood facing him.

"God told me to stand before His servant and tell him the words He would give me."

He paused, seemingly confused. Then he lifted his head and spoke in a voice that startled everyone present:

"I used you as a pioneer over twenty years ago that My people would follow you and receive the baptism of My Holy Spirit. I began to lead you. I moved on the hearts of those following you — not following you but following Me through you. They responded. Now there is a greater work, a greater glory, a stronger and more powerful thing which I have called you to pioneer. I must do it this way for there are those who will not receive it in any other way.

"I must have you, Jamie Buckingham, on the earth. I cannot use you in heaven to write. I cannot use you in heaven to minister to My people on earth. I cannot use you in heaven to preach. I need you here. There is a great and mighty thing I have planned for this church — this Tabernacle Church — to do. It will come about. I will put My revelation in your heart and spirit, and you will give it to My people. They will be free because they will see Me. As they see Me as Freedom, they will be free. As they see Me as Healer, they will be healed."

The service was over. But somehow all of us had a feeling the experience had just begun.

SEVEN

GETTING READY TO DIE

SUNDAY AFTERNOON BERNIE MAY CALLED. HE HAD just returned to Huntington Beach from Dallas. Nancy, his wife, had received my fax message and called him. He waited until he got back to California before calling. I was overwhelmed by what he said.

"I talked to God after Nancy called," he said. "I told Him, 'Lord, if you can take my life and spare Jamie's, please do it. I am happy to go to glory. My work is almost finished, but Jamie's work is not over.' "

"I can't handle that kind of love, Bernie," I said seriously. "Why not just ask God to keep me alive so I can help you?"

He laughed. "I can pray that kind of prayer too. But what I prayed first is how I really feel."

I hung up and sat looking at the huge pile of unanswered mail on my desk. I wondered if I would ever be able to answer it. Would Sandy, who handled most of my secretarial work, have to prepare some kind of black-edged form letter? "I'm sorry to inform you that my dad...." I tried to shake off the thoughts, but my mind was full of them.

Outside my study I could hear my sons and some of the men from the neighborhood bouncing the basketball, getting ready for the usual Sunday afternoon game of half-court. I went upstairs and told Jackie I was going outside to play. She was lying on the bed reading her Bible.

Her face showed deep concern. "Are you sure?"

"I'm tired of thinking death thoughts. I need to think life."

She reached up, squeezed my hand and smiled. "Try not to get hit in the stomach."

The game was invigorating. "Don't go easy on me," I insisted. They didn't. On two or three occasions I felt a return of that same suffocating feeling I had experienced on the racquetball court the week before. When it started, I slowed down — but kept going. Obviously there was something wrong in my body, but I was determined to keep on playing. Besides, as long as I was playing, my mind was not reminding me that I was about to die.

The reminders returned that night, however. We went to bed early, lying side by side, praying. Jackie read Psalm 30 and Psalm 91. They were to become great pillars in my life over the next thirty days, holding me up when I felt like falling.

We prayed, but not for ourselves. Something was happening, something I could not explain. Instead of praying for ourselves, both of us felt compelled to pray for others. Intercession. We began by praying for our five children, their spouses, their children — calling each name and asking God to intervene in their lives during this time of crisis. We knew that as the night wore on, each of those five houses would be houses of prayer. We knew the little ones, and their mothers and daddies, would be kneeling beside their beds praying for me. Then we shifted our prayers to all those who had called or made contact with us over the last two days. The list was long, for Jackie said the phone had rung continuously while I was outside playing basketball.

A siren sounded faraway in the night, its wail drifting through the trees and into our bedroom window. A police car...fire truck...ambulance? It was a signal someone was in trouble. We interrupted our prayers for our friends to pray for that unknown person in crisis. How sensitive we were to the trouble all around us. How great our need to pray for those known and unknown.

In my memory I went back thirty-seven years to my advanced English literature class at Mercer University. Professor W.T. Smalley was sitting behind his desk rocking back and forth, his one good eye closed. He was quoting melodiously from Tennyson's "Morte d' Arthur":

> The old order changeth, yielding place to new,
> And God fulfills himself in many ways,
> Lest one good custom should corrupt the world.

Comfort thyself: what comfort is in me?
I have lived my life, and that which I have done
May he within himself make pure! but thou,
If thou shouldst never see my face again,
Pray for my soul. More things are wrought by prayer
Than this world dreams of. Wherefore, let thy voice
Rise like a fountain for me night and day.
For what are men better than sheep or goats
That nourish a blind life within the brain,
If, knowing God, they lift not hands of prayer
Both for themselves and those who call them friend?
For so the whole round earth is every way
Bound by gold chains about the feet of God....[1]

This compulsion to pray for others was a new experience. I had taught on prayer in our church, even conducted prayer clinics for others. Jackie and I were actively involved with the Breakthrough organization. But this was different. I had read of intercessors, such as Rees Howells and Praying Hyde, who prayed for hours at a time — often through the night. I often wondered how that could be possible. Now it was not only possible; it was natural. It seemed to be a source of great power, of great comfort, as though I were pleasing God by praying for others in my time of deepest need. For the first time I could feel with those in pain, those in deep trouble. It was as if I had taken their burden on my own shoulders. I felt as if I could — perhaps should — spend the rest of my life praying for others.

I recalled being with Bill Bright, the founder of Campus Crusade. Bill and Jack Hayford had asked several of us to meet in Chicago during the Reagan-Carter presidential campaign. Bill shocked us when he said he was laying down most of his evangelistic activities to devote his life to intercessory prayer. He was convinced that situations — especially world situations — could only be changed permanently through prayer.

My mind flashed to a quiet dinner I had with George Cowan, former international president of Wycliffe Bible Translators, in his tiny little apartment in Southern California. Afterward he asked me to stay and watch the evening news on TV with him and his wife. I remember how impressed I was. The reason they watched the news each night was so they could pray for world situations. During the commercial breaks they muted out the sound and prayed out loud for the people and events seen in the last segment. Cowan, one of the world's great missionary statesmen, had laid aside his scholarly approach to ministry to devote his life to prayer. He was in charge of the Wycliffe prayer chain, sending out prayer requests to Wycliffe members all over the world. During the last few years he had organized thousands of people who agreed to pray daily for the Bibleless tribes of the world — by name. I even had the name of one of those tribal groups pasted on the wall of my study, reminding me to pray for the Tawusay tribe in Irian Jaya.

I lay in bed with these images swirling through my mind. I could feel the radical changes taking place in my spirit.

I drifted in and out of sleep, waking to find myself praying for various people the Lord seemed to bring to mind. Most of the time I was praying out loud. Softly. When I did, I would hear Jackie joining me, adding more names. We spent the night, as we would spend many nights in the future, sometimes sleeping, most of the time praying. When I would drift off to sleep, I was aware of Jackie's hands on my body, touching gently, moving across my chest and stomach, finger-tipping in prayer for me.

Early Monday morning I dressed and went downstairs. The thought of the pending surgery terrified me. I knew I needed, somehow, to work my way through the fear. Old memories of others who had gone through exploratory surgery haunted me. I recalled the sad comments. "The cancer had spread everywhere. They just closed him up and sent him home to die."

"Why, God, does my mind always race forward to the darkest scenario? Why doesn't my mind focus on life rather than death?"

I went back into my study. Years ago we had enclosed the two-car garage and made it into three rooms, two of which I used as offices. The other was a bedroom where Jackie's mother slept. This morning I was alone in the wing of the house, because Daisy was still in the rehab center recovering from her broken hip.

I stood in front of one of my bookcases. I knew what I was looking for. More than twenty-five years earlier, John Sherrill, then senior editor of *Guideposts*, had gone through cancer surgery. John and his wife, Tibby, had since become dear friends. We had served on various editorial boards together and remained on the board of Breakthrough. He had often talked of his earlier battle with cancer. I remembered he had written about his surgery in the first chapter of his best-seller *They Speak With Other Tongues*.

I found the original hardback he had given me. It was inscribed inside the cover and dated: October 1967. He had given it to me at the first *Guideposts* writers' workshop. He was teaching, and I was a participant. It was John who had recommended me to Dan Malachuk, a beginning publisher in New Jersey, to write my first book, *Run Baby Run*, the life of Nicky Cruz. It was an instant best-seller and had catapulted me into the wonderful world of writing.

I took the book back into the kitchen and sat down at the table. I started at the beginning, once again impressed with the beauty of the flow of words as they came from John's pen. I read deep into the first chapter as he told in detail the story of his cancer surgery — and the excruciating pain that followed. Is this what I should expect? I shuddered, closed the book and sat staring out the back door into our backyard. Beyond the clumps of palmettos I could see the two houses on the back side of the pasture where Bruce and Tim lived with their families. How blessed I was with family and friends. I grieved over having to leave them.

Jackie came down and stood behind me, her hands on my shoulders. "It's the beginning of a new week," she said.

I reached up and put my hand on one of hers. How familiar the touch of her fingers. I remembered what it was like holding her hand as we walked in the surf late at night, the warm Atlantic washing over our feet. I was sixteen — she, yellow-haired and full of life at fifteen. How we had loved each other back then. Surely God would not snatch me away from her now, just as we'd fallen back in love again. She bent over and kissed me on the cheek. "God is in control," she said. "He is a God of miracles."

I squeezed her hand, and she stepped around the counter into the kitchen. Ordinarily I would have been at the coffee maker, brewing up the morning's supply. But strange things had been happening. Friday, as I was driving home from the doctor's office, I had stopped at a familiar traffic light. As I waited for the left-turn arrow to turn green, I had heard a voice, deep in my mind: "You've drunk your last cup of coffee."

Over the last dozen years, since someone had given us the coffeemaker, I had drunk at least four mugs a morning — laced with artificial sweetener. I had never given much thought to the warnings. I never felt it was a moral or a health problem. Now, for some unknown reason, I had been told, No more coffee!

It wasn't a big deal. I never felt addicted. I just liked it. I had an electric warmer next to my word processor and liked to sip while I was writing. Now that little pleasure was gone. Oddly, I didn't care. Even the smell of the coffee Jackie was brewing for herself had no appeal to me. Was this change a prelude to even larger, more significant changes to come in my life?

The phone rang. I reached over and picked up the receiver.

"Jamie!" I instantly recognized the cheery voice. "This is John Sherrill. Len [LeSourd] called me yesterday and told me the news. I was up early this morning praying for you, and the Holy Spirit said I should call you now. Is this a bad time?"

"You'll never know just how *right* this time is," I said. Then, looking down at his book still open on the breakfast table, I knew God was in control. I laughed. It felt good.

We chatted for a while, then he said, "The real reason I called was to talk to you about surgery. Len said you might be having exploratory surgery this week. You may not remember, but I had cancer surgery a number of years ago. It was followed by excruciating pain. Since then I have learned some things about pain, and I wanted to share them with you."

"Just keep talking, John," I was still chuckling. "One day I'll tell you all that preceded this conversation. You are simply continuing a little talk I had just begun with God about you. You can't imagine what your call is doing to me. Please keep talking."

"I discovered a fascinating truth about the difference between mind and spirit," he said. "Before I went into the operating room, I did all my homework, wanting to submit to the surgeon. I was determined to cooperate fully with the medical authorities. Later I discovered one area I had not known about. I could submit my conscious mind to the knife but had failed to work on my subconscious. As a result, my subconscious mind — the spiritual part of me — was resisting the knife. That's where the pain came from. You see, my conscious mind was relaxed and submitted, but once I went under the anesthesia, my conscious mind was no longer a factor. From that point on my subconscious was in control — and that part of me violently resisted the knife's intrusion. That's the reason my lungs collapsed, my muscles went into spasms and I had all that pain."

Then he did what I've grown to expect of John. Without changing gears or even asking my permission, he began to pray over the phone. "Lord, I ask You to show Jamie how to instruct his subconscious mind to submit to Your will. Show him how to resist Satan in his conscious and subconscious so that he will come through surgery without pain."

Suddenly the fear — the terror — was gone. I hung up and turned to Jackie.

"That was a miracle!"

"What do you mean?"

I told her about John's book and what had been going on in my mind just before he called. "And I haven't talked to him in more than a year."

"I think we're going to see many miracles before this is over," she said. "I think it's going to be a summer of miracles. After yesterday's church service, too many people are praying against Satan. He can't win the war. Many are fasting this week. They told me so yesterday. Prayer support is building around the nation.

"Yesterday morning, while you were preaching, God gave me a verse for you. I wrote it down. This morning I pasted it on the mirror in our bathroom upstairs so you'll see it every morning and every evening. It is the flag you are to wave in Satan's face every time he tells you you're going to die. It's Psalm 118:17 (KJV): 'I shall not die, but live, and declare the works of the Lord.' "

As she fixed the toast, I opened my Bible and read it for myself, then underlined it and put the date beside it: July 1, 1990. God knew how much I was going to need that verse as the day — the week — wore on.

Mid-morning the phone rang again. It was the doctor.

"I've had two radiologists and a urologist look at your CT scans," he said in his matter-of-fact tone. "We've revised our diagnosis. You have renal cell carcinoma — cancer of the left kidney. It has metastasized into your lymph glands and possibly into other organs as well — pancreas, spleen, liver, maybe even the other kidney."

"What's that mean?" I could feel my mouth going dry again.

"It means the cancer in your kidney is spreading. It is inoperable and probably untreatable by ordinary means. The urologist said it would be impossible to remove the kidney because of its size and deterioration. It also means we'll not do the exploratory surgery."

I heard the phone click as Jackie picked up the extension. I was unable to swallow, unable to speak. I was glad she was on. My mind seemed drugged.

"I'm scheduling you for a kidney biopsy tomorrow at Holmes Hospital in Melbourne. You'll be an outpatient, but you will need bed rest in the hospital for eight hours following the biopsy. You'll need to check in at 9:00 A.M. I'd like to see you in my office at 2:00 P.M. this afternoon for some more blood work."

That afternoon I sat on the examining table in the doctor's office. Jackie was beside me in a chair. The nurse's needle had once again sucked blood from my arm. Smiling sweetly, she had departed. Jackie and I were alone. Holding hands. Moments later the doctor came in, holding my file in his hand.

"Unfortunately, your prognosis is not good," he began. "Renal cell carcinoma can also spread into the bone or into the brain."

My mind was playing tricks on me. I pictured myself playing a Humphrey Bogart part in a black-and-white movie. My next line should have been, "How long do I have, Doc? Tell it to me straight."

But nothing came out. I just sat on the edge of the table, my feet dangling stupidly above the floor. Jackie was gripping my hand.

"How long has he had it?" she asked.

He shrugged. "There's no way to tell. It may have been growing for years. It may have started just a few months ago. Interestingly, fast-growing cancer is easier to treat than the slower-growing varieties. But in his case there's just no way to tell. There is evidence it is now growing rapidly and we don't have much time. We need to run more tests."

Astute! The word came to my mind. Someone recently had described me, during one of those silly introductions people give before the guest speaker stands, as having an "astute mind." Now an image appeared. It was a flat plain — stretching as far as my mind's eye could see. The grass was dead. Brown. There was no vegetation.

Another image appeared. It was a television screen, the kind they use to monitor heartbeats with the little green line jumping up and down. Only this one had a solid green line. No bleeps or blips. It was a symbol of being mind-dead. Maybe that was the reason I couldn't think. Maybe the cancer had already crept into my brain.

Gradually I returned to reality. The doctor was describing the biopsy procedure for the next day.

"The CT scan shows your left kidney tumorous, three times its normal size. However, to be sure it's malignant we need the biopsy. It's done with a long needle monitored with the CT scanning equipment. They'll use a local anesthetic, and you'll suffer some discomfort but little pain. You should be able to leave the hospital about 5:00 P.M. after you've rested a while."

"Is there a chance the tumors are benign rather than malignant?" Jackie asked, her voice coming from a hundred miles away.

"There's always a chance," he said. "But we'll know more after tomorrow."

For the first time I spoke. My mind was clear again. I slipped off the exam table and looked the doctor in the face.

"My life is at stake here, and there's something I need to know."

"Of course."

"Are you a Christian?"

He didn't even blink. "No."

It was the first time I could remember that anyone ever answered me with a forthright no when I asked that question. Invariably people said, "I grew up in a Methodist church," or "I was confirmed as a Catholic." But he was as consistent with his spiritual answer as he was with his medical answers. Straight and to the point. I appreciated his honesty but knew I had to continue.

"Then you need to know where we're coming from," I told him. "My wife and I — by the way, her name is Jackie, and mine is Jamie, not Mr. Buckingham — are risking our lives and our eternities on the belief that God is real and that He has revealed Himself through Jesus Christ. I am the pastor of a local church. My entire life is based on one single fact: that God is who He says He is, that He loves us and that Jesus is His Son — the Messiah. I believe in prayer — in talking to God and having Him talk to me. I am surrounded by many people in this community who are, right this minute, praying for me. I believe He is in control of all that is happening in my body. I also believe that God alone heals and that it is His will that I be made whole. In short, I have put my trust in Him. I am grateful for all you've done and are doing, but you need to know that I do not look on you or the medical profession as my source of life. I look to God."

A faint glimmer of a smile crossed his face. "I understand. Prayer certainly won't hurt you any."

He reached out and shook my hand. "Good luck. I'll contact you as soon as we get the biopsy results."

Outside in the hall, waiting for the elevator, Jackie gripped my hand tightly. Looking up at me, she said softly, "I'm proud of you."

Somehow I felt she was speaking for God also. What had that verse said? "I shall not die, but live, and declare the works of the Lord."

As we got into the car to drive home, I realized I now had a reason to live — and I had just made a down payment on it in the doctor's office — to "declare the works of the Lord."

Slowly it was beginning to dawn on me. We might be helpless, but we were not hopeless.

That evening our home group was to meet at Al and Saundra Reed's house, just a mile down the road. Our group was comprised of five couples from the church, old friends we had known for many years. We met every Monday night. Each family brought a dish. We'd eat, then spend a couple of hours ministering to each other.

Jackie was in the kitchen, mixing up the big salad she was taking. I had just come in from my study, where I had been working on deadline material for the magazine. Our son Tim, who installed irrigation systems for a living, had just come from work. He was standing in the kitchen, his grimy shirt wet with sweat. He was talking to his mom. She had just told him about the conversation with the doctor and the biopsy scheduled for the next morning.

Tim had recently turned thirty. Although he was powerfully built, with large shoulders and a barrel chest, his blond curly hair gave him a boyish look.

He looked at me. "Mom just told me about today. Now I've got something to pray for. I'm going to believe the biopsy will show the cancer is gone."

I was impressed with the strength in his voice. While the rest of our children had taken active parts in the church, Tim and Kathy had always been "back-rowers." Deeply devoted to his three children — and to God — Tim had a natural affinity for down-and-out people. He felt uncomfortable among white-collar types. After high school, he had worked for two years as a cowboy on a large ranch west of town. Then he and Kathy left for agriculture school. Following graduation he managed a cattle ranch in Georgia. Later they returned home, hoping to find work in ranching or farming. Nothing opened. He had raised a few animals on our property but had to be satisfied working at a low salary with a friend in our church who had a small irrigation business. Now I sensed something was happening in his spirit.

He nodded and smiled. "Just wait. God's gonna take that cancer right out of your body."

Just as Tim left, the phone rang. It was Bernie May — his second call in two days.

"I didn't tell you yesterday, but I was scheduled to speak to all our office workers in the headquarters building during chapel time this morning. After I got your message I tried to back out. I didn't want to speak. I didn't have anything to say. I tried to call Joe France, who had scheduled the chapel services, and back out. All I got was his recording device.

"Sitting at my desk, phone in hand, I heard a little voice whispering: 'Use the chapel time to pray.'

"We had 110 present. I shared with them the concerns of my heart — especially my concern for you.

"Then I told them what God had told me as I prayed for you. One: Jesus loves me, this I know. I think it was Karl Barth who said that sentence contains the most profound thought known to man. Two: God is in control. He's never surprised by events. Three: I can trust Him. And four: I can't quit. I've got to keep going.

"Then we broke up into groups of three. I asked each one in the group to pray intensely for two minutes just for you. That's 220 minutes of prayer on the part of 110 righteous men and women. God says that kind of prayer 'availeth much' [James 5:16]."

That night after dinner the ten of us sat in the Reeds' living room. Gene Berrey, the group coordinator, voiced the feelings of the entire group. "We may have other things to talk about tonight," he said, "but let's put them aside. There's only one thing we need to do. We need to let Jamie and Jackie talk to us. Then we need to pray for them."

Gene had been a friend for many years. We had made several overseas trips together, including a missions trip to the Orient and two trips to Israel. Quiet, undemonstrative, he had a keen, almost sly, sense of humor — and a brilliant organizational mind. He was an ideal leader for our group.

"You've heard news any one of us could hear," Gene said tenderly. "Tonight we want to give you a chance to react. Tell us your feelings. Let us become part of those feelings with you. Jackie, you first. Then Jamie."

The next two hours were filled with tears. I didn't realize how desperately I needed, how desperately Jackie needed, to talk out the feelings. We were being bombarded with bad news. What had seemed horrible on Friday had become terrifying today. I found myself weeping as Jackie talked. When it was my turn, I broke down in front of the entire group. I didn't care that I was sitting there crying into my hands, gasping for breath, trying to choke out how I felt about death, leaving Jackie behind, leaving the children. Yet I knew God was in control, and despite the swirling waves of emotion, I felt solid Rock under my feet.

When it was over, Gene asked a penetrating question which even now, as I write this, echoes in my mind.

"If God were to say, 'Jamie, I'm going to give you a choice. You can come on home to Me now and enjoy all the wonderful blessings of heaven, or you can stay on earth, but you may suffer much pain and even heartbreak.' Which would you choose?"

The question startled me. I looked around the room at my friends. Brooks and Laura Watson had been part of the original group that started the church. Brooks was a building engineer and developer. Earlier, Laura had helped me editorially, working closely on many of my manuscripts. Al and Saundra Reed were also "charter members" of the church. Our kids had grown up together. Al was an electrical engineer, and Saundra was the financial administrator at the church. Both were like family to us. I glanced at Don and Linda Lees. Like Gene, Don was a corporate manager as well as an elder in the church. I depended on him so much for spiritual wisdom. Then I looked at Jackie, my childhood sweetheart, my wife of thirty-six years, with whom I had just fallen back in love.

"I can't make a choice," I told Gene. "I would have to tell God: 'Lord, whatever You want me to do — go or stay — I will do.' "

"Perhaps," Gene said, "that's all He's been waiting to hear you say."

Then he added, "For more than twenty years you've been teaching us how to live. Maybe now you're to teach us how to die."

It wasn't what I wanted to hear. But deep inside I knew it was what I needed to hear. Life and death are but two sides of the same coin — a coin that was now flipping through the air.

(Top) Jackie Buckingham

(Right) Tim Buckingham, Jamie and Jackie's youngest son

EIGHT

THE BATTLE
OF THE MIND

I WAS SURPRISED HOW UPBEAT I WAS FOR THE KIDNEY biopsy. Both my sons, Bruce and Tim, had stopped by on their way to work before we left the house. Each had prayed with us. On his way out Tim had said, "Dad, I've been praying constantly. For the first time in my life I have faith — faith to believe the biopsy is going to show no cancer."

Now I was back at the hospital. The biopsy took place in the same room and on the same table where I had my CT scan. Only this time I was on my side, and they had IVs running into my arm. A doctor deadened my left flank, then explained the procedure.

"I'm going to insert a long, skinny needle into your side. It has a small set of sharp pinchers on the end, enclosed in a shield. We will guide the needle by watching it through the scanner as it enters your body. Once it has touched your kidney, we open the pinchers, and it takes a 'bite.' Then we pull the tissue back into the shield and withdraw the needle. You'll need to wait on the table until the pathologist is confident we have a good sample. Then we'll wheel you up to your room. You'll need to lie still on your back for eight hours before going home.

You may get up to go to the bathroom, but be sure and check your urine for blood."

I did not know until the following week, when I overheard a conversation between Randy Wisdom, my military physician friend, and my brother John, who flew down and spent the night, that this is an extremely dangerous procedure. In fact, many doctors refuse to do it for fear the cancerous tissue will leave "tracks" when the needle is withdrawn — that is, spread the cancer to other parts of the body.

Blessed by ignorance, however, I lay on the table chatting with the doctor and the technicians throughout the procedure. Only once, when I felt the needle take its bite out of my kidney, did I feel any extreme discomfort. The entire procedure took less than two hours. After the doctor was satisfied they had a good sample, I was lifted to another gurney and rolled out to the elevator. Jackie was waiting and walked beside me as I was pushed to a quiet room on the north end of the hospital. This was the twenty-three-hour wing, for outpatients who were not admitted into the hospital but required bed rest before returning home.

Jane Berrey, Gene's wife, was in the room when I arrived. Although Jane's a nurse at the hospital, she had taken off that day so she could sit with me.

"Have you heard what's going on at the church office?" she asked.

Of course I hadn't heard anything.

"They cancelled the regular Tuesday morning staff meeting. They all arrived at 7:30 A.M., put the phone on the answering service and locked the doors to the office. The entire staff is inside praying for you. Saundra just called to get a report. She said it's wild. People are weeping and lying on the floor, crying out to God. There's a lot of deliverance taking place, and they're laying hands on each other for healing. She said it would probably go on all day."

I couldn't comment. Everything seemed out of control, and I was helpless to do anything about it.

I slept most of the afternoon, aware that Jackie and Jane were there, sometimes talking softly, sometimes praying. I felt calm. Peaceful. Others were fighting the battle I was too helpless to fight.

At 5:30 the nurse came and told me I could leave. Jackie went down to get the car and bring it to the door. She met us at the door with the car. I felt strong, but she refused to let me drive home.

"Don Williams called. The pastors and staff want to come out to the house to pray for you."

"What did you tell them?" She could sense my reluctance.

"I know it's been a long day for you. But they've spent the entire day in prayer. Something is going on in their lives. Don said he'd never experienced anything like it in his life. They've had some kind of visitation from the Holy Spirit, and they need to share it with you."

It was after six when Don, my pastoral coordinator, arrived with the pastors and staff. All of them could not come, but there were about a dozen present. I was sitting in the den in a recliner when they came in. It was awkward. Always before I had been in charge, in control. Now they were controlling me. Yet I loved them, not just as my co-workers in leadership, but as precious men and women of God. They came in and sat around the room, on the sofas and on the floor.

"We love you," Don said, his voice breaking.

Suddenly I began to weep. God had entered the room with them, and without warning my emotions turned loose. I tried to hold back the tears but could not. It was even more traumatic than the night before, when I had sat among the members of the home group and cried. This was a deep sobbing, wrenching things loose from far below the surface.

The room exploded in prayer. Whatever it was that had taken place in that all-day prayer meeting had been transferred to my den. Everyone was praying out loud. Some were shouting, binding Satan. Others were crying out to God on my behalf. The very house seemed to be shaking with the force of it.

I was vaguely aware that Jackie, sitting on an ottoman in the middle of the room, had fallen backward onto the carpet. Several had caught her, and now she was stretched out on her back in the middle of the room. At least three of the staff were kneeling around her, praying for her, laying hands on her. She was weeping convulsively.

Then Jimmy Smith, a traveling evangelist/teacher on our staff, stood over me. I could hear his voice through my tears as he commanded a "spirit of control" to leave me. The room echoed with the shouts and prayers of the others. I could feel myself resisting Jimmy's spiritual pressure.

Then, in the midst of this turmoil, I heard another voice — a quiet inner voice — speaking.

"Why do you struggle so hard to hold on? You are obsessed with control. You control your family, your children and grandchildren. You control the church. You control everyone who comes into your presence. You are proud of being a controller. That's why you are so full of grief. You are afraid if you die, your family will perish also, the church will fall into ruin, and all your projects will go for naught. You are a proud, haughty, controlling person. Proud you are in control of your body; proud you are in control of your life. Now it is time to turn loose."

I could hear myself screaming a long, savage "Noooooooo!"

"Give it up," Jimmy commanded, standing over my chair. "Turn loose."

"I can't," I wailed. "If I turn loose I'll die." I could feel my face contorting, straining to hold on to my control of life.

Then it was over. Something released in my deepest part. It was as if I had been swimming against a fierce current, knowing I was being swept toward a deadly waterfall, when suddenly I was swept into an eddy and tossed onto the shore. The room was still filled with a torrent of emotion, but my spirit was free.

Jimmy had left. I could hear him wandering through the other rooms of the house, praying loudly. Jackie was still on the floor, and two of the ladies and at least one pastor were kneeling over her, fending off the evil spirits of fear and death. I sat watching, no longer weeping. As I had feared dying, she had feared widowhood. She too was being set free.

Someone had gone into the kitchen, found a large basin and filled it with water. Another went into the utility room and came back with a towel. Don Williams took the basin and knelt before me.

"We've spent the day washing each other's feet. Now we've come to wash yours. It is our sign of servitude and submission — to God and to you as our spiritual leader."

"Please, Don," I begged. "I can't — "

"God told us to do it, Jamie. It is for you as well as for us. Just sit there and let us show our love."

I felt him removing my shoes, then my socks. I closed my eyes, knowing if I looked I would once again burst into tears.

"I should be washing your feet," I moaned. "All of yours...."

"We are doing this unto Jesus," Don said gently as he lowered my foot into the warm water, then removed it, rubbing it gently with a towel. As a newborn kitten is licked clean by the mother cat, I felt I was being bathed in liquid love.

I looked up and saw Inez Thompson kneeling before me. Inez was the only woman pastor on our staff. Seventy years of age, she had been with me from the formation of the church. She was in charge of our ministry to senior citizens, the poor, as well as all special projects. She was Saundra Reed's mother, and to some degree the mother of the church.

"No, Inez," I said. "Not from you. Please."

Gently she lowered my other foot into the water. "Ten years ago," she said as her hands lovingly massaged my feet, "I had cancer in my kidney. You came to the hospital and said if I needed a kidney transplant, you would donate one of yours. That's how much you loved me. Now I wash your feet as my spiritual leader."

I put my hands over my face as the tears once again streamed down my cheeks. I was aware, only vaguely, that they had moved the basin and were washing Jackie's feet the same way. I did not know how much my system could take before it went on spiritual overload and blew all circuits — forever.

Our youth pastor, Jim Bartholomew, was kneeling before my chair. He reminded me, in a soft voice, of my sermon the week before the cancer was diagnosed. I had preached from Mark 2, the story of the paralytic who had been brought to Jesus on a stretcher carried by his four friends. When they couldn't get into the house, they had gone up on the roof, removed the thatch and let the man down through the roof to Jesus' feet.

"Remember what you taught us," Jim said. "Jesus was impressed with the faith of the man's friends. You reminded us how important it is to have friends who will hold you up when you have no strength, folks who will bring you to Jesus. Then Jesus spoke forgiveness to the sick man. After that he was healed."

Jim looked up in my face. "The cells of your body are sick because they don't know Jesus has forgiven them. When they hear that message, they will be healed, for healing is found in the atonement of Jesus."

That's not exactly the way I preached it, but I didn't have a chance to comment. Jim leaned forward and placed his mouth just inches from my tummy. He cupped his hands around his mouth and placed them against my stomach — like a megaphone. I was half reclining in the chair and was not prepared for what was about to happen.

"You're forgiven!" he shouted. His voice grew louder as he shouted at my abdomen. "You're forgiven!"

I could feel the vibrations going through my body as he continued. I wondered if my lymph glands were listening, my liver, even my kidney. As it continued, I grew peaceful. Each time he shouted I wanted to say, "Don't stop. Keep going." He did, shouting over and over for three or four minutes. Finally, exhausted, Jim sat back on his haunches in front of the chair. It was a strange but powerful ministry. But it was a marvelous climax to a God-ordered day.

That night, however, everything came unglued in my spirit. After almost four sleepless nights, Jackie dropped into a deep slumber while I found my mind invaded by thoughts from the underworld. Gone were the victories of the morning as I had undergone the biopsy so easily. Gone was the peace of the afternoon as I lay in the hospital bed cushioned from pain by the prayers of others. Gone were the wonderful victories of the evening as the pastors and staff prayed over me and cast out the darkness that had sought to control my life. Instead my mind became the devil's playground as he glided among my thoughts, bending them toward destruction and death.

I lay awake most of the night planning my funeral. Thoughts of doom and despair rolled in like storm clouds, darkening all spiritual light.

I could see my body lying in a casket, my cheeks sunken from the effects of cancer, my lips cold and white. I could hear the wails of the grandchildren who loved me so. The wracking sobs coming from my three beautiful daughters. My sons, sitting in front of the casket, staring hopelessly into a future without their daddy. My wife, crumpled on the floor, devastated by death. Unable to function. I could hear the moans and convulsive sobs of my friends, the despair and anguish of my flock. I had preached healing, but it had not been mine to receive. God had let me down, and surely He would let them down also when crisis came their way. Over and over the words of Zechariah echoed through my mind: "Strike the shepherd, and the sheep will be scattered, and I will turn my hand against the little ones."

I turned, trying to get the thoughts to go away. But the room was filled with darkness as the demons tantalized me deeper into despair.

What should I wear in the casket? Would it not be better just to bury me in a T-shirt so sons and sons-in-law could have my clothing? Why do people bury good clothes in the ground? Would one of the boys want my wedding ring? My watch? My pocketknife?

Who would write my obituary for the magazines? Steve Strang? I remembered the pain I felt when I had to write the obituary for my close friend and fellow editor, Al West, who had died of leukemia at age thirty-eight. The obituary I wrote for missionary Adger McKay became a major magazine article. Would Steve be as sensitive as I was when I wrote the obituaries for my friends Catherine Marshall and David du Plessis? He had once mentioned, in a magazine editorial meeting, that we should have some obituaries already written and in our files for aged or sick saints who might die unexpectedly. That way we could get them into print at the last minute. Maybe Steve or someone on the staff, someone I didn't even know, had already written my obituary. It was sitting in a file folder under "B" in the publishing office, just waiting to be pulled out and used. Should I get up in the middle of the night and go downstairs and write it now? That way, at least, the facts would be straight.

I reached over and touched Jackie's warm body. What if my death drove her insane? I was the sole breadwinner. We had no life insurance. Even though the house was almost paid for, she wouldn't have enough income to pay the taxes. All our income depended on what I produced. When I stopped writing, the checks would stop coming in. We had no investments. The church might carry her for a few months, then she would be on her own. Could the children afford to pay their taxes and hers as well? What if they lost their jobs? What if they lost their faith? What if...? The list was endless, and at each pause I could almost hear the devil scoffing. See, I told you it was all a sham. Nothing works. The liberal theologians are right. God does not really intervene in the real affairs of men. You may go to heaven, but you're going prematurely. You are going to die. Soon.

72

Dawn finally arrived. I sat on the edge of the bed, haggard and confused. Jacob had wrestled with an angel all night long. I hadn't even wrestled with Satan. I had just lain there and let him spike me with a million thoughts of death.

Jackie was still sleeping. I walked downstairs and back to my study. There was a white sheet of paper hanging out of my fax machine. A message had come for me during the night. I ripped it off and looked at it.

It was from George Cowan, the prayer director at Wycliffe Bible Translators. "This is the message that is going out this morning on Wycliffe's 'Take 59' computer program."

I was aware of the Take 59 program. Almost every desk in the Wycliffe headquarters, as well as the desks in all the regional offices around the nation, was hooked to a central computer system in Huntington Beach, California. From there the messages went to the more than five thousand missionaries all over the world. Each morning when the workers sat down at their desks, they would find a message on their computer screen: "Take 59." That was followed by a different prayer request each day, reminding the worker to take fifty-nine seconds and pray for the request which appeared on the screen.

The prayer request that morning was for me. "Jamie Buckingham has been a good friend of Wycliffe Bible Translators for many years. Last week he was diagnosed with severe cancer. As you pray for him, pray the promise of Isaiah 26:3, 'Thou wilt keep him in perfect peace whose mind is stayed on thee.' "

I stood in front of the fax machine, staring at the message.

No! I almost said out loud. That's not the kind of prayer I need. I need for you to pray I will be healed.

Clutching the request in my hand, I walked back upstairs. Jackie was just stirring under the sheet. I sat beside her. She turned on her side, put her arm around my waist and began to pray out loud. I lay down beside her and listened as she prayed, the dark thoughts of the night still clinging to the corners of my mind like cobwebs in an old barn. They snared her prayers and would not let them pass.

She sensed something was wrong.

"I was awake most of the night," I said. "All I could think of was death."

"You've got your head and your heart mixed up," she said softly. "Your heart believes. Your heart has faith. Your heart knows God is a God of miracles, and He is going to heal you. But your head — your mind — is listening to Satan. Satan doesn't speak to your heart — that's where God reigns supreme. He speaks to your mind. He will especially speak to your mind because you are a logical, rational person. You analyze things. That's the reason it is so important that we fill our minds with God, with the Word of God, that we keep our minds fixed on Him. If not, your mind will become Satan's playground, and he will convince you, rationally, that you will die. Once you buy into that, you're gone."

I reached down and picked up the folded fax message, which I had dropped on the floor beside the bed.

"Now I understand why God wants His people to pray that my mind will be fixed on Him. Read this."

She propped herself up in bed, clutching the flimsy fax paper. "We shall, from this moment on, fix our minds only on God and His Word," she said with determination. "Regardless of what the doctors say, we will listen only to You, God. We believe You have prepared a way for us through this wilderness, and we will walk it with joy — looking only unto You."

It was a bench mark from which she never strayed — even in the darkest hours when death seemed so close.

NINE

ON THE POINT
OF A SPEAR

WEDNESDAY WAS JULY 4. JACKIE AND THE CHILDREN had planned a picnic in the backyard. We had recently converted an old horse stable into a picnic pavilion, and this was the first time to use it. All the children were coming, plus a few friends from the church.

I felt strange among them — abnormal among the normal. Everyone was so healthy. So alive. Outwardly I looked healthy, but inside was something dark, clawing and grabbing, determined to spread its foul tissue into the vital organs of my body. I was different from the others. They knew it too.

The young men had arranged the tables under the pavilion. The little children were running and laughing around the area. Some were in the swimming pool, playing and splashing. The women were helping Jackie arrange the food on the table. The men were sitting, talking, glancing around to make sure the children were safe.

I sat with them, dressed in shorts and sneakers. They mercifully steered the conversation away from "my condition," although I knew it was in the minds of each one — not only my sons and sons-in-law, but the other men who had joined us for the outing.

It was Paul Boutin, our neighbor across the street, who finally hit the matter straight on. Paul and Debbi had been part of the church for years. She headed our dance ministry. Paul, a meter reader for the power company, was a close friend and one of our active backyard basketball players.

"My life has changed since last Sunday," he blurted as we finished eating. Six of us were sitting in lawn chairs in a semicircle. His eyes were glistening with tears. "I don't know what's happening to me. I've known God for a long time, but this is different. I've never prayed as much, never felt so close to Him as I do now."

"What do you mean?"

"I don't know how to describe it. But this thing with you has shaken me all the way to my foundations. It started a couple of years ago when Debbi's parents were killed in that automobile crash. That was the first time I'd thought much about death. But this is different. This time I'm thinking about God — all the time — and it's wonderful."

His voice choked, and he dropped his head, unable to continue.

My son Tim picked it up. "Dad, a lot of us feel the same way. God has just moved in on our family and on our church. Life's never going to be the same anymore — for any of us."

I sensed he was right. I knew we were all merely actors on a stage, reading lines written by the Author — lines which were often created just moments before we read them. I knew that behind the scenes were shadowy figures moving scenery, arranging sets, preparing for the next act. I never had insight into what the next act would hold, but I was confident God was in charge.

"If the Lord had not been on our side," David had written in Psalm 124, "the raging waters would have swept us away." Looking back on my life I knew how accurate that was. There had been many crisis points, junctures in life where if God had not been on our side the raging waters would have swept me away. At each of those junctures I had been afraid, sometimes terrified. Yet God had been on our side. Through miraculous interventions He had carried us through the torrent — not only to safety, but to heights never dreamed of ahead of time. Would He not do the same this time? Surely there would come a time in the future when I would be able to sing with David in the latter verses of that psalm, "We have escaped like a bird out of the fowler's snare; the snare has been broken, and we have escaped. Our help is in the name of the Lord, the Maker of heaven and earth."

As the picnic was breaking up and parents were collecting their children, I felt Tim's brawny arm around my shoulder. "Kathy and the kids and I are all believing for a miracle. That kidney biopsy they took yesterday is going to show the cancer is all gone."

It was the second time he had said it. His eyes were sparkling with genuine faith, making me want to believe with him.

But it was not to be as we desired. That afternoon the doctor called. Jackie and I were sitting in the den listening to praise tapes when the phone rang. I could feel my throat tightening as he began to talk.

"I called the pathologist this morning. They had just finished looking at the slides. The biopsy confirms the diagnosis. You have renal cell carcinoma. It is either a stage three or stage four. Stage three means it has spread beyond the organ to other organs in the vicinity. Stage four means it has spread throughout your body. I've scheduled a bone scan for Friday morning to see if it has spread into your bones. Report to the outpatient center of the hospital at 7:00 A.M., and they'll tell you what to do."

I hung up the phone and turned. Jackie had been listening in on the extension. Her face was blanched. She rushed across the room and threw her arms around my waist — holding me tightly. "You are not going to die. The devil is a liar. I don't care what all the tests show — you are going to live. God has told me so, and He does not lie."

"I hate it for Tim," I said. "His faith has been so strong. What will this do to him?"

"God is leading Tim just as He is leading us," Jackie said. "Bruce has already been there. He saw God heal Michele after the doctors said she had multiple sclerosis. Now it's Tim's turn to find out you can trust God — even when things seem to be going bad."

My brother John arrived late that afternoon. He had called the day before from Birmingham and said he felt he should fly his plane down and spend the night with us — just to encourage me. I met him at the airport.

It was good to see him. I walked with him back out on the hot tarmac where his twin Beech was parked. It felt good to smell the aviation gas and feel the heat rippling up off the pavement. I missed flying. I helped him tie down the plane, then we headed home. We had talked almost daily, and I told him of the results of the kidney biopsy. He assured me the doctors were taking all the right steps.

"You still need another opinion," he said. "I've not seen the CT scans, but you need to consider surgery."

"They ruled out exploratory surgery," I said.

"No, you don't need that. The CT scans show what's wrong. But if there is any chance of having your kidney removed by surgery, you ought to consider it."

"The doctors all say the kidney is inoperable. The urologist who looked at it said it was three times its normal size and was rooted to the walls of my abdomen.

He said to remove it would kill me."

"Maybe so," John said. "This first week they run all these tests. You go through this flurry of activity. Then things begin to calm down a little bit. Let's wait and see what God has in store."

"You're the first doctor I've talked to so far who has even mentioned God," I said.

He laughed. "I'm not here as a doctor. I'm here as your little brother. I'm also here, hopefully, as God's representative to encourage you to keep on fighting — no matter how severe the prognosis."

That night after John had gone to bed, Jackie and I sat alone on the side of our king-sized bed. My friend and neighbor, Curry Vaughan, had stopped by that afternoon. We had known Curry and Nancy for almost twenty years, and our families had grown close. He had committed himself to walk with me through this dark time, no matter what the cost.

"I have a word for you," he had said that afternoon, standing in our kitchen. "Last night as I was praying for you, God directed me to Deuteronomy 8. As I read it I felt this was God's word for you at this time."

He opened his Bible and read it to me:

"Remember how the Lord your God led you all the way in the desert these forty years, to humble you and to test you in order to know what was in your heart, whether or not you would keep his commands. He humbled you, causing you to hunger and then feeding you with manna, which neither you nor your fathers had known, to teach you that man does not live on bread alone but on every word that comes from the mouth of the Lord" (Deut. 8:2-3).

We had prayed together. As he was leaving he made an offhand remark about communion.

"You and I know there is healing in the broken body of Jesus. Maybe you and Jackie should start taking communion together."

It was an idea that rooted instantly. John French, my partner for the prison videotape ministry, had called earlier from his vacation home in Michigan. He had suggested the same thing. Out of the mouths of two witnesses....

That night Jackie brought a glass of juice and a cracker up to the bedroom. We were sitting on the side of the bed, praying over the elements, when we heard the downstairs door in the kitchen open. It was Tim.

"Come on up," I called down the stairs.

He came into the bedroom. His face was anguished. "Sandy told me about the biopsy," he said.

"Sit down between your mom and me," I said. "How do you feel about it?"

"At first it hurt real bad. Then I got angry."

"Angry at whom?"

He dropped his head. I reached up and ran my fingers through his curly blond hair. He was struggling with the words. "I guess I was angry at God."

"That's OK," Jackie said softly. "He understands."

"I felt like He let me down," Tim blurted out. "I've never had faith like that before. I didn't even know what faith was. But I believed, Dad — I really believed. The boys and I would get on our knees several times a day. When Kathy and I sat down to eat, we took a long time to pray for you. I was praying for you all the time when I was working: driving the truck to the job, digging ditches for the sprinkler systems, on my knees working with the pipes. All I've done is pray. And God gave me this big faith. We all believed the biopsy was going to show God had done a miracle — but He didn't."

"Do you think you can still trust Him?" Jackie asked gently.

"I don't know. I want to. But why did He give me all that faith, then let me down?"

"Tim," Jackie said, putting her arm around his broad shoulders, "God's doing a lot more than healing your dad. It hurt me too when we got the news. It hurt bad. But my faith hasn't wavered, and I don't want yours to waver either. God is still a good God. He is in total control. His Word says He wants your dad to live and not die. Let's stand on that together — regardless of how bad the news seems."

As she talked, I remembered the words of a little chorus Jack Taylor, one of the columnists for *Ministries Today*, had taught our church the last time he preached at the Tab. "His Word is working mightily in me," the chorus began. What we see and what we feel on the outside don't matter when the Word is working inside of us.

"Our faith is not in circumstances, Tim," I said, rumpling his hair. "Our faith is in God."

"I guess I'll just have to start over again," he said, looking up.

"Stay with us for a while and take communion with us. We're going to be doing this every night until I'm healed. I'm glad you're here this first time. We'll start over together."

The phone calls from around the nation began the next morning, shortly after I took John back to the airport. Years before I had written Pat Robertson's biography, *Shout It From the Housetops*. Pat had remained a friend. Steve Strang had called Pat and told him the news. Now Pat had gone on the air to ask the Christians of America to pray for me. The results were awesome.

The next day Paul and Jan Crouch also issued a nationwide call through the Trinity Broadcasting Network in California. Christian radio stations all over the country picked it up, asking their listeners to pray. Even without my knowledge, a massive base of prayer was forming as people around the nation — most of whom I did not know — began interceding, asking God to heal me.

Two more things of great significance happened that day. Two copies of Dodie Osteen's little book *Healed of Cancer* arrived in the mail, sent from two different friends. Dodie was the wife of my old friend John Osteen, pastor of the Lakewood Church in Houston, Texas. John had preached the night, twenty-two years before, when I had received the baptism in the Holy Spirit in Washington, D.C. I had met his wife a number of times but did not know of the wonderful miracle she had experienced. I devoured the little book the hour it came — reading it through before lunch without stopping. It told how she had been diagnosed with a fatal liver cancer and sent home to die. Instead she had fought, prayed and filled herself with the Word of God. Instead of dying she had lived — and was still living abundantly. The second half of the book contained some of the healing scriptures that had helped her. They would become a foundation for our lives from that day on.

The second significant event was a visit from our old friend Wylene Hughes. Wylene, a former secretary at our church, had been part of our lives for more than twenty years.

"I've brought you two things," she said laughing. "One to feed your spirit, the other to feed your tummy."

She uncovered two huge apple pies, still warm and oozing with goodness. "These are guaranteed to make you feel better," she chuckled.

Then she handed me a stapled sheath of papers. "Five years ago Ed Gray was dying of cancer," she said.

I knew Ed and his wife, Flo. They used to live in Melbourne and attend the Tabernacle Church. They had retired and moved to the mountains in northern Georgia.

"The doctors told him he didn't have a chance. He went to the Bible and indexed a whole bunch of healing promises. He wrote them down and began to claim them for himself. On the basis of the Word of God alone he was healed — and remains healed."

She handed me the stapled papers. "Last year Ed sent me all those verses. I didn't know what to do with them. Now I've typed them out and personalized them for you. 'I am the Lord who heals you, Jamie.' I've prepared a bunch of copies and am giving them to everyone in the church who is willing to pray them for you. Here is your copy so you and Jackie can pray these verses every day — standing on God's Word to heal you."

She reached out and kissed me on the cheek. "Thanks." And she was gone.

Those scriptures, along with the ones in the back of Dodie's book, would become our spiritual meat and drink — our life source. In fact, they still are.

Friday morning at 7:00, Jackie and I pulled up in front of Holmes Hospital. We took the elevator to the fourth floor of the north wing where the nuclear medicine department was located. The technician gave me a shot of radioactive liquid and told me to report back for the bone scan in two hours, after the isotopes had spread through my body.

We were back at 8:30. Laura Watson and Sue Hitt were in the waiting area. They were part of the intercessory prayer team from the church that had committed to pray for me while I was taking the test. Inez Thompson and Gordon Strongitharm, two of our pastors, were on their way. Others, they said, were downstairs in the chapel.

It was like a dream, like flying in the fog. I was there, talking, listening, but I seemed to be somewhere else too. Sue was talking to Jackie, saying that her husband, Corky, wanted to come up also. Sue and Corky were both Jewish. Sue, who had been dying of multiple sclerosis, had been miraculously healed. She had then accepted Jesus as her Messiah. Corky was still unwilling to declare Jesus as God's Son. Yet he seemed strangely attracted to me, and I often had lunch with him — just as a friend. I was trying to focus in on the ladies' conversation, but earthly things just didn't seem important — even when the talk centered around prayer.

The nuclear technician was at the door. They were ready. The scan would take about forty minutes, she said. I lay on my back on the table as the scanner slowly passed over my body, starting at my head and moving down to my feet. The technician had told me it would then reverse itself and pass under the table from foot to head — checking to see if any of the radioactive material in my veins had invaded my bones. I had read somewhere that if there was an invasion, it would show up as a "hot spot" on the scan.

The scanner produced a steady ticking noise as it passed slowly over my body. Someone had told me that if the ticking increased, it was a sign the scanner had discovered a hot spot. I decided not to listen, quoting over and over, "Thou wilt keep him in perfect peace whose mind is stayed on thee."

"OK, time to get up." It was the cheery voice of the technician. I had fallen asleep on the table. Smiling to myself, I sat up and slid off the table.

So that's what perfect peace is, I thought, going to sleep as the storm rages around you. A mental picture of the scene described in Mark 4 — Jesus asleep in the stern of the fishing boat as a storm raged across the Sea of Galilee — flickered through my mind. "Thank You, Lord!"

"We need to take a gamma ray scan," the technician said. "There is an area in your left side that is blurred. We want to see what shows up on the other scan."

Again I wasn't there. I heard her words, but it didn't make any difference. Under other circumstances I would have felt the panic building in my stomach and throat, but I knew Jackie, Laura and Sue were in the waiting room praying for me. Others were praying: my children and grandchildren; those down in the chapel; many at the church office and around the community; friends around the nation. Why should I fear?

Waiting for them to set up the gamma ray scan in the room across the hall, I noticed a feeble-looking man lying on a gurney in the hall. I walked over to him. He was a mere shadow, just bones covered by jaundiced skin. One leg had been amputated, and he had tubes running out of his body into bottles suspended on poles above the stretcher. I looked into his emaciated face. He was Oriental — perhaps Korean. Totally uninhibited, I reached out my hand, placed it on his fragile shoulder and started praying in the Spirit. Quietly.

"He can't understand you," a nurse said as she stepped out of a nearby doorway. "He speaks only Korean."

"It's OK," I winked. "I wasn't praying in English."

I looked down, and the old man was smiling, great tears flooding his eyes. With one bony hand he reached up and touched my arm. He nodded. He may not have spoken any English, but one thing was certain — he understood.

I squeezed his shoulder gently and went into the room where I was to have the next scan. The technician wanted me to stand against a drum-shaped piece of equipment that would take pictures of my hip and kidney area. I could see the vague shapes flashing on a large monitor across the room. When it was over and I started out of the room, I noticed an older woman sitting in a wheelchair just inside the door. Her head was drooping. She was in obvious pain.

"May I pray for you?" I was astounded at my boldness. Never in my life had I approached a total stranger and prayed for them. Yet within the last ten minutes I had done it twice.

She slowly raised her head. "Are you a priest?"

"No, just a follower of Jesus."

"Oh! Yes, please. I hurt so much."

I put my hand on her head and prayed softly. "Lord, in obedience to Your command to lay hands on the sick...."

"Oh!" She flinched under my hand. "What was that?"

"What was what?"

"I feel so much better."

I reached down and kissed her cheek then headed back toward the waiting room. Something — Someone — had taken control of my mind and body. I was not doing natural things. I had often wondered what it would be like to move through a hospital like this, laying hands on the sick and praying for them to be healed. Now it was happening; only it had taken my own sickness to get me here. I felt I was the point of a spear — the shaft being the prayers of all those who were interceding for me. I was compelled, moving here and there at the direction of Someone else.

Back out in the hall I saw a doctor standing in the little office marked Nuclear Medicine.

"Is there any way I can get the results of my test now?"

"This is you," he laughed, nodding to a clear film with a skeleton outlined on it. It was on his light box. "It's you without your flesh on."

He pointed to the area in the skeleton's left side. I had trouble believing it was my skeleton. It looked like the bones I had seen in anatomy books. "Something's going on right here," he said, pointing with his pen. "There may be a cancer in this lower rib, or it might be something else."

"I had a kidney biopsy day before yesterday."

"That's probably it," he said. "I'll look at the gamma scan, but that checks out with what I see. Your doctor will give you a call and let you know."

Corky Hitt, Sue's husband, was in the hallway. Short, balding, he was a typical Jewish merchant. Always ready with a wisecrack. Always ready with a deal. I had seldom seen him serious. This morning his face showed deep concern. He grabbed my arm and pulled me to one side.

"Ya know, I got this really healthy body. Now my teeth aren't too good, but the rest of me is healthy as hell. So if you need a kidney, I got two. I want to give you one."

I felt tears coming to my eyes. I looked down at my short friend and saw his eyes were moist too. In his own way he was expressing love. Genuine love. Putting his arm around my waist, he pulled me around in front of him so I was facing him and so no one in the hall could see what he was doing. He reached up and took the gold star of David which hung around his neck and rubbed it on the front of my shirt. "God don't want you dead. He's gonna heal you, 'cause I'm praying for you."

His eyes brimming, he quickly pulled away and was gone.

That afternoon my doctor called. The bone scan, he said, was negative. The cancer was stage three. It had spread into my lymph glands and possibly other vital organs but had not spread throughout my body. He said he would set up an appointment with an oncologist — a cancer treatment specialist — Monday afternoon.

That night Oral Roberts called. I was lying in bed, weary from the day's activities. Jackie handed me the phone and sat down beside me, praying softly in the Spirit while I talked. Oral Roberts was weeping. Partly for me, partly because he was in pain in his shoulders. We talked for almost an hour. He wanted to pray for me, he said, but before he could do it he needed for me to pray for him. "I've spent my life praying for people to be healed. Now my shoulders are worn out from reaching out and laying hands on millions of people. Tonight I need strength. No one knows just how much I hurt."

After we hung up I asked Jackie to hand me a pad and pen. I jotted down the most significant things he had said.

"Medicine and prayer are not in conflict. Submit to your doctors as unto the Lord, but seek Him at every place of decision. Doctors hate disease more than most Christians do."

"God has given me faith to believe this is not your time to die. But I cannot give you that faith. The Holy Spirit will have to give it to you."

Jackie looked at what I was writing. "Faith is a gift of the Holy Spirit," she read. "I have it. Now it is time for you to receive it also."

"But how do I get it? I've had faith to believe for so many others. I remember calling Norm Foor (a member of our church) after the doctors told him he was dying of cancer and saying the same thing to him that Oral just said to me. He got well and lived a wonderful life for a number of years. I had faith to believe for you when the doctor said you had breast cancer. I've had faith to believe for the church when all the critics said it was doomed. Each time God has been faithful. But how do I get faith to believe for myself?"

I could feel the tears welling up in my eyes.

She reached over and squeezed my hand. "It's a gift, and God wants to give it to you. All you have to do is ask for it."

She was right. "Lord, You said You would give good gifts to those who ask. You'll not give a snake if I ask for a fish; You'll not give a stone if I ask for bread; and You will give the gift of the Holy Spirit if I ask. I have received many gifts from Your Spirit — now I ask for faith, faith to believe Your Word."

"It's yours," Jackie whispered. "It will flood in on you like a mighty river, washing away all doubt. Do you remember last year when we walked through Wadi Kelt from Jerusalem toward Jericho? You told me how you had been down in the deep canyon once before, hiking through the Judean wilderness, and the sand in the bottom of the wadi was dry. Then suddenly there was a rainstorm on the mountains around Jerusalem. The water poured off the mountainsides and collected in the head of the canyon. You said you were barely able to get out before the entire wadi was flooding — rushing down toward Jericho and the Dead Sea. Your wadi may be dry right now, honey, but there is a flood on the mountains. Soon the channel will be full. Just wait and see."

Saturday morning we went fishing. Gene Berrey had called the night before and asked if we wanted to get out on the water for a few hours — just for a

84

change. Gene lives on the Indian River, the saltwater inland waterway that runs the length of Florida's east coast. His eighteen-foot boat was docked behind his house. All we had to do was drive across the causeway, join Gene and Jane in the boat, motor out to one of the little islands in the river, and we would be in another world. It sounded good.

Florida had just passed a new law requiring a license for all saltwater fishing from a boat. Jackie and I stopped by a tackle shop on the way to Gene's house to purchase the license. When we got to the Berreys', Gene asked to see my license.

He looked at it, grinned, then reached out and hugged me.

"What's that for?" I asked.

"You've just been told you have incurable and inoperable cancer, and you go out and buy a one-year fishing license. That's faith."

Suddenly I realized the option I had been given at the tackle shop. The clerk had asked if I wanted a thirty-day license or the one-year license. It had never crossed my mind that I might die. Without thinking, I had bought the one-year license. Now Gene had called that "faith." God was already answering my prayer.

It was almost noon when we got home. A message to call the doctor was waiting for us. He would be in his office until 1:00 P.M. He answered the phone himself. He was excited.

"I've just talked to Dr. Rosenberg at the National Institutes of Health in Bethesda, Maryland. He heads up the National Cancer Institute, and they are interested in your case."

"What do you mean, 'my case'?"

"They are doing extensive research on new methods of treatment. Your case presents an interesting challenge, meaning you would probably qualify for one of their new protocols. NIH is government-funded and would pay all expenses, even your flight expenses back and forth."

"I'm not sure I want to be a case."

He ignored my comment and continued to talk about this being a special opportunity. "They only accept a few cases. Each case has to fit tight criteria. However, after I explained your diagnosis, he found it significantly challenging. They want you to have a CT scan of the chest, however, to make certain the cancer has not spread into your lungs. I've scheduled you for 5:00 this afternoon at the hospital. If it's clear, you have a good chance of getting into NIH. It's really prestigious, you know."

My head was reeling when I hung up. This would be my second CT scan in a week, plus the kidney biopsy also done under the CT scan, plus the bone scan.

I was a puppet. Only I wasn't sure who was pulling the strings.

That afternoon Jackie and I once again made our way through the long corridor of the ground floor of the hospital. It was quiet. Most of the side doors were closed since it was late Saturday afternoon. I rang the little bell at the desk in the radiology reception room, and a man finally came out. "Come on back. They're ready for you."

Once again I was lying on the table, my arms over my head, an intravenous tube in my arm pumping special liquid into my system to help the machine see the contrast between the diseased parts and the healthy parts. The table was moving slightly, and I could hear the voice of the technician as the machine made pictures of my lungs.

"Breathe."

"Don't breathe."

"Breathe."

Then I heard another voice. Clear. Distinct. It was not a voice like the technician's. It came from a different source. It was not audible through my ears, but it was as clearly understood in my mind as if it had been spoken. It was the voice of God.

"What Satan meant for evil, I will turn to good."

The table moved slightly. The technician's voice sounded again through the speaker inside the CT scan machine.

"Breathe."

"Don't breathe."

"Breathe."

I could hear the machine whirring each time I held my breath and a circle of lights inside the hole of the donut flashed around, indicating the picture was being taken. But the voice I had heard in my heart overpowered all other sensations. He spoke again.

"Now you will see My mighty hand at work in your life."

It was the first time, in the midst of all this crisis, that I had heard God speak. I knew it was He. I felt joy, deep joy, and peace. He had not deserted me in my time of trouble. He was there.

Back home Jackie sorted through the mail that had come that morning. She opened a small package that contained a little notebook.

"This came in the mail this morning," she said. "It's from the Community of Jesus."

The Community of Jesus was a community of Spirit-filled people located on Cape Cod. It had been founded by two women — known simply as Mother Kay and Mother Judy — about twenty-five years before. Made up of several hundred people who had built their houses around the various community buildings, it had the trappings of a Protestant monastery. A number of the young men and women had taken lifelong vows and entered into orders as part of community life. They wore robes (or habits) and were committed as are monks and nuns to a life of obedience, poverty and chastity. The others who belonged to the community had private ownership of their houses and worked in secular jobs — but were in strict submission to the community authority. Mother Kay had died the year before and leadership was continued by Mother Judy and Betty Pugsley, a master musician who had led the community in mastering, among other classics, the ancient Gregorian chant.

Jackie handed me a small, loose-leaf, six-ring binder with a number of blank pages and three pages at the front with writing.

The cover was hand-painted with the inscription "Words and Promises for You."

The front page was a note from the Mother Superior at the community: "On the next two pages are two words of Scripture received for you this past Sunday — which we thought you might like a copy of. We're sending them along in this small notebook and would like to send others in the coming weeks. Our prayers are with you."

It seemed innocuous until I turned the page. There, in beautiful calligraphy, were the words from Psalm 118:17 (KJV): "I shall not die, but live, and declare the works of the Lord." Under it was a notation: "Received by a sister in prayer on Sunday, July 1." It was the same verse God had given to Jackie that same day.

Other pages were to be sent to me — thirty-two in all. Some were prophecies, some were scriptures the Lord brought to mind as these precious people prayed for me — often through the night hours. I entered all the pages in the little book, along with the special words God would begin giving me the following week. But none was more precious than that verse from Psalm 118:17, which was to be the verse I would hang my life on as we walked step-by-step into that mysterious summer.

TEN

SUNDAY II

MY SUNDAY MESSAGES DURING JULY WERE MORE than acclamations of my faith. They chronicled my spiritual journey as well.

Despite the mysterious growing pressure in my upper abdomen, I felt invigorated being in the two morning worship services. The songs had taken on an entirely new meaning as I sang them. The Bible seemed alive. The people were warm, caring. Seated on the front row during the worship time, I felt, on several occasions, the people behind me reaching out and placing their hands on my back — praying. Tears were hard to control when I felt it happen.

That morning I began my message by giving them a brief report of the week's activities, including the experience I had praying for the Korean man on the hospital gurney in the hallway. Before going further, I gave an altar call. I asked those who were sick to come forward so I could pray for them. Almost two hundred people responded. Jackie joined me on the platform. She started at one end of the line, and I began at the other, going from one to another, laying our hands on each one and praying. Only then did I preach. What follows is an edited version of the sermon that morning.

Helpless But Not Hopeless

This is the dawning of a new day. Nothing is going to be the same in my life, in my wife's life, in the life of this church. If you like old things, now is the time to bail out. God is saying, "I am going to touch you in a new way. As you open your heart to Me, My heart is opened to you. My kingdom is yours."

With this new revelation will come a new understanding of the person of God the Father — and a new understanding of His kingdom on earth. We are not going to have "church as usual" anymore. Conventional things, traditional things, are falling away as we come face-to-face with God's plan.

This week I have faced, perhaps for the first time, my own mortality. I'm returning from that encounter to tell you that God is good, He is faithful, He is the Healer, and He is in control. I am more convinced than ever that God has chosen me to touch Him, to be with Him, then report to the body of Christ what He is like. I am not sure how that is to be done, but I feel this sense of mission welling up inside me. It frightens me, for it is different. But I am excited about the future.

The final reports on the biopsy came in Wednesday. They confirmed all the earlier reports. At this stage the doctors have given me no hope for life — much less long life. In short, from a medical perspective things are hopeless.

But this week I have discovered something. There is a difference between hopelessness and helplessness. We are helpless, but we are not hopeless. Our hope is in God — who is eternal.

Despite the fright, this has been the finest, most glorious week of our lives. (I am speaking in the plural, because Jackie and the family have walked every step with me.) We have met God in a way we didn't think we could meet Him this side of heaven. In fact, as I was standing there during the worship service, praising Him with my arms up, I began to say, "Now! Now! Just take me now. I have never been so ready as I am now."

Obviously He didn't. But that is how close I've come to Him over these last eight days.

We cut off our TV eight days ago. There seems to be no logical reason to spend our time watching it. We glance at the newspapers. There are few things I'm interested in other than prayer, studying the Bible, holding my wife's hand, and being with my family and friends. I've stayed away from the church office, for there is no business going on there. The pastors, for the most part, are spending their time on their faces before God. The same is true with most of the church staff, who have spent the entire week praying. Jackie and I have been spending our time together — at home, in the car, waiting in the hospital — doing the same thing. I want her to tell you about it.

Jackie's Sermon

This has been the toughest week of my life, and of our thirty-six years of marriage. Yet it has been the most glorious week as well. I have prayed for years that Jamie and I would come into the relationship that we've had over these past eight days. God has met us in such a deep way. Words can't express it. You just have to experience something like this in order to understand. But, believe me, it has been marvelous.

I am standing on the word that God gave me from the very beginning — "this is not unto death." I received that word by faith, and God has given me faith to believe it. I am holding to it. I am not listening to the doctor's reports. I am not focusing my mind on bad reports. I am focusing my attention on the Lord Jesus Christ. He is our Sustainer. He is our Provider. He is our Healer and our health.

At night when Jamie is asleep, I have the privilege of putting my hands on my husband, who is a precious man of God. I honor him. I revere him as the Scripture tells me I should. As I pray for him during the night, I am praying new strength into his body, not the old strength that Jamie Buckingham used to go on, but the strength of Jesus Christ. And I have the privilege of standing firm. We are standing firm in what God has given to us, what He has placed in our hearts. As I touch him with my fingers, they become the channel through which the answers of all your prayers flow into his body. These are prayers coming not only from this church, but from all over the world. God has a mighty work for him to do.

As I pray, I see light. Jesus is the Light. There is no darkness within this body. And where the light of Jesus is, there cannot be any darkness. I claim the light and life inside him. We stand on that.

God gave me a special little blessing the other night as I was praying. He said, "Jackie, you have prayed for Jamie all these years. You have stood in the gap. You have prayed believing. I hear your desire. I know the desire of your heart. I'm not going to take him home. He's not going to get off that easy. He's going to have to stay here and walk it out."

Yes, He did say we would have to walk through the fire. But He also said it would not kindle upon him. Then, once through, great and mighty things would happen. I believe that.

Last year when Jamie was working on Bill Nelson's book on the American space industry,[1] he told of making a research trip to the Johnson Space Center in Houston. He was there to experience firsthand the training the astronauts go through prior to a shuttle flight. One of the things he did was learn how to walk through fire. The space center fire crew took him out to the fire pit, a shallow pool with only a few inches of water in it and a coating of inflammable fuel on top. He said when they ignited the fuel, it burned so ferociously it seemed impossible to get close, much less go through. But the fire chief showed him how to use the hose, first putting up a shield of fine mist which enabled him to get right up to the fire. Then, by directing a powerful stream of water from the nozzle, he was able to separate the fire and walk through it without being burned. The lesson, he said, was to keep going forward, never turn back, stick with your partner — who is holding the other side of the nozzle — and never turn loose of the hose.

That's where we are now. A terrible fire is burning, and it seems impossible to go through. But we are moving ahead; we'll never turn back; we're walking with all those who are praying with us, and we'll never turn loose of Jesus.

We need you to continue to stand firm with us. Don't focus on death, discouragement or despair. Focus on life and hope.

God has shown me that Jamie's experience is to be a light of hope for others all over the body of Christ. Oral Roberts told us the other night that God wants to birth something new among the body of Christ. He said he felt Jamie is one of the pushers, one of those chosen to help the birth take place.

So stand with us, church. Stand firm. Stand on the Word of God. It has become alive in our hearts as we have devoured it, prayed it and let it nourish us. We thank each of you for your love and prayers. Keep it up, because God wants to do something great in your lives as well as ours.

My Turn Again

Pray for my healing. Otherwise you will have to hear her on Sunday instead of me. (Applause)

Pray for Jackie, because she is indeed the touch point right now for so much that's going on. It really has been the finest week of our lives.

Curry Vaughan came by the other day with a word God had given him. He said the Lord had spoken to him from Deuteronomy 8: that God brings wilderness experiences on us to humble us and to test us, to see if there is any sin in us, that we might move on to the greater things He has for us.

This has been a humbling experience. It's been humbling because of the helplessness I've felt to know that others are having to hold us up through this tough time.

I'm more and more aware of the tremendous need for prayer. The body of Christ has been ripped apart because of our attitudes toward each other. Our unwillingness to pray for each other. The way we have judged each other. What would happen if we came together and began to pray for each other rather than ripping each other apart? What would happen if we started rebuking Satan away from people rather than judging people and cursing them in the name of Satan?

What if we stood together and said, "I don't care what you believe, you are my brother or sister, and we will walk together"? What would God do in our midst if we took that stance? What would happen throughout the kingdom of God? We have allowed Satan to rule this earth and destroy good people through our critical spirits and harsh judgments of each other.

Friday night, in the middle of the night, I felt God was speaking. I didn't hear Him, but the thought was so strong: "If you're healed, start acting like it. Don't just sit around like a hermit." We got up the next morning and went fishing with Gene and Jane Berrey. It was a blessed time out there on one of the islands in the river, soaking in God's sun, breathing God's salt air, wading through the shallows and kicking the little crabs. As I was there — back among the living — a new resolve began to build. I've got a fight ahead of me, but by God's strength we're going to walk through this thing, and God is going to get the glory.

Jackie has reminded me several times that the only legitimate way to pray is to find out what Jesus is praying and to pray with Him. In my text this morning I read where Jesus is in heaven, seated at the right hand of God, interceding for us [Rom. 8:34]. If that's so — and it is — then I need to find out what Jesus is praying and join with Him in agreement in that prayer. That is the only legitimate prayer. Everything else is wishful thinking.

I praise God for those who are wishing good things for me: people who say "good luck" and all that sort of thing. That's great, and may God bless you for it. But luck will not heal me. The only thing that counts is finding what Jesus is praying and pray it. Jesus said, "I only do what the Father tells me to do. I only say what the Father tells me to say." Here in Romans 8 we discover we really don't know what to pray for. But if we'll let the Holy Spirit fill us and pray through us with "groanings that we can't utter" — then we'll be praying in the will of God.

Yesterday morning as we were motoring back up the river, I was sitting in the stern of Gene's boat with the wind blowing through my hair and the sun on my back. I began a monologue with God. Here's how it went.

"Lord, I'm going to bring my case before You. I ask You to let me live so I might touch You with one hand and touch Your people with the other. Let me live so I can hear You with my ears, and speak Your Word with my mouth. Give me, please, enough strength and enough comfort that I can hear what You are saying and put it onto paper and share it with the entire body of Christ.

"Father, I can't do that if I'm hurting too badly, so I need strength and I need ability to get it done. All other things are immaterial to that. But please give me enough time and enough comfort so I can be Your mouthpiece and Your fingertips."

Oral Roberts told me that while he had faith to believe this was not my time to die, God would have to give me that faith for myself. He said it couldn't come from him or from my wife. It would have to come from God.

Faith is one of the nine gifts of the Holy Spirit. I began to ask God for faith, and gradually I've found it building inside me. But it has come in strange ways.

Last Wednesday the doctor called and said the pathologist's report on the biopsy showed I really did have cancer. I had prayed, and my children had prayed, that the report would show no cancer. Instead it proved the cancer really is there. Now I realize I was not praying what Jesus was praying; I was merely wishing. Now God has said, "Jamie, if I took the cancer away right now, it would be too quick. I have more work to do in you and this church. It's going to take more time. Be patient."

So whatever is going to happen will be a process. Miracles are instantaneous. Healing is a process. This, I believe, is going to be a mixture of both. I do not know how, but God is a God of all means and methods.

This is sure: I am not planning on dying soon — regardless of what the doctors say. I'm still planning for a future. I've got a hiking trip to Israel that I'm supposed to lead in October. Unless there's a big war that breaks out in the Middle East, I'm planning on being there. I am not going to cancel out on life. We will get what medical help seems right, but we're praying for God's direction at every step as well.

Friday morning when I went in for the bone scan, the nurse asked me to fill in a data sheet. One of the questions was: Do you have cancer? I thought for a moment and resolved, I refuse to say I have cancer. Cancer is trying to have me, but it is not mine. It belongs to Satan. In the space provided I wrote: "The doctors say I do."

God has been telling me I have been a filter for other people's knowledge. I have traveled the world as a giant filter, observing and hearing what others have said or written. Like a spiritual kidney or lymph gland, I have filtered these things, trying to reproduce only that which is pure. However, in the process I have collected a lot of garbage and poison. Now I need a backwash. A cleansing.

Not only that, I need to change my methods. Instead of listening to what people are saying, I need to be listening to God. Instead of reading what people are writing, I need to read what God has written. My filter system has overloaded and broken down. It needs to be purged and never again exposed to the kind of poison that causes cancer — of the soul or of the body.

I'm looking at a God who heals. I'm encouraging you to do the same thing. Every one of you has your own set of problems, and there are more coming down the road. Let me give you some guidance right out of the fire: Keep your mind fixed on God. If you do, He will give you perfect peace.

Eight years ago I felt that God told me He was going to give me another fifty years of creative and productive life if I cooperated with Him. I haven't kept my end of the bargain. I have been walking in my own strength — not God's. Now I've repented, and marvelous things are beginning to happen in my life, in the life of my family and in the leadership of this church. I don't like being the focal point. I'd much rather sit on the sidelines and report it. But God has said He does not want me as a spectator in what He is doing. He wants me in the thick of it. That's where I am. That's where I'll stay as long as He gives us grace.

At the close of the service Michael Thompson, our worship leader, stepped to the pulpit. Beginning the next morning, he announced, at 6:00 — Monday through Friday — and continuing for as long as necessary, the men of the church were to gather in the auditorium for one hour of prayer. It was time to go to war.

As we were leaving the building that morning I was stopped by Vince Anderson and his wife, Jung Hi, a Korean. She was weeping.

"That man, that Korean man you prayed for in the hospital...that is my Korean daddy. He is in a nursing home...he is dying...he did not know Jesus. Yesterday he told me in Korean he had accepted Jesus."

Her voice broke, and she threw her arms around me, holding tightly. "He now knows Jesus. He is ready to die. Thank You, thank You, God."

I held her as she wept. Looking up I saw Vince's handsome face. He too was weeping — his arms around both of us.

"Thank You, thank You, God!"

Jamie's mother, Elvira Buckingham (Mother B.)

Mother B. and Jamie

ELEVEN

TEARS: A TELESCOPE TO HEAVEN

My SISTER, AUDREY, HAD CALLED ON FRIDAY. SHE was insistent I drive to Vero Beach and tell our mother what I was going through. I balked.

"She's almost ninety-three years old, Audrey. She comprehends very little. She has her own set of problems, far bigger than mine."

"Jamie, you don't understand. You're not a mother. If it were my son, regardless of how old I was, I would want to know. I would need to know."

"I've talked to Clay and John about it," I argued. "Neither of them thinks I should tell Mother B."

"They don't understand either. But if you talked to their wives they would. And if you talk to Jackie, she'll agree with me."

Audrey was right. I dreaded the encounter but knew it had to happen. Every first Sunday night of the month for the last ten years I had driven to Vero Beach to speak at Central Assembly. We always went by to see my mother at the Baptist Nursing Home before the service. This was the first Sunday night of the month, and it seemed right to go early and break the news. Buddy Tipton, the pastor at

Central Assembly, had already learned of the cancer attack and had called.

"We don't want you to preach this Sunday. We want to have a church-wide prayer meeting and pray for you. We are believing God for a miracle."

Mid-afternoon, with T.J. and Kristin — Tim's ten-year-old son and Robin's ten-year-old daughter — in the back seat, we headed down the interstate to Vero Beach. All kinds of thoughts were racing through my mind.

Several years after my father's death, I had the heart-wrenching task of moving my mother into the Baptist retirement center in Florida. She was sticking with my dad's plan when he donated the property to the center. She took only a few things with her, urging us children to divide up the rest.

After the big pieces of furniture had been shipped out, my two brothers, my sister and I wandered through the old house. Familiar keepsakes littered the floor. Everything had a memory attached — different to each of us. We decided to take turns choosing.

I wanted but one thing: the tattered "prayer book" Mother and Daddy had used every morning for many years. Actually it was an oversized photo album with seven pages — one for each day of the week. Each page contained the pictures of those they prayed for that day.

My dad had made a little stand so the album could be propped open on the breakfast table. Each morning before eating their meager breakfast they prayed for their friends. I took the old book and sat on the steps, looking at each page.

Monday they prayed for their local Gideon chapter — an organization dedicated to the distribution of Bibles.

Tuesday they prayed for the people in the Billy Graham organization — and for Billy's crusades.

Wednesday they prayed for Tom and Betsy Smoak, then missionaries with Wycliffe Bible Translators in Colombia, South America. I recalled sitting at breakfast with them, listening as my mother's voice broke with emotion as she prayed for the six Smoak children by name.

Thursday they prayed for two elderly women who had given their lives as missionaries to mountain people in Appalachia.

Friday they prayed for old friends.

Saturday a family picture helped them remember all their children and grandchildren.

Sunday, even after they were too feeble to attend services, they prayed for their local church and for the staff and residents at the retirement center.

Mother eventually went to that same center. The book had been left behind.

I had taken it home. It remained in my study, closed. The stand, however, was on our breakfast table. It held *our* prayer book — complete with pictures of those

Jackie and I tried to pray for daily.

Mother finally had to leave the retirement center for the adjacent nursing home. Her mind was no longer clear. Often, when I visited her, I'd find her sitting in her wheelchair, staring vacantly into space. She told me once she missed her prayer book, but her eyes were too bad to see the pictures.

Now, driving south along the interstate, I was struggling with how to tell her what the doctors had found. Her mind, like her body, was so fragile. I hated to involve her in the heartbreaking emotions I knew the news would bring. Yet I felt I had no choice.

The grandchildren were playing in the back seat, coloring pictures and talking.

"I don't want to tell her details," I told Jackie. "Let's just talk in generalities."

"She may want to know more," Jackie warned.

"Her mind's not clear," I countered. "I think I can handle it."

We spent the remaining miles praying. The children joined in. We drove through old downtown Vero Beach, past McClure's Drugstore where Jackie had worked as a soda jerk after school, past the place where Jackie's mother had her dress shop, past the Buckingham-Wheeler Insurance Agency where my father had been a silent partner. His office had been in the back of the building. Now my high school chum and college roommate, Jim Thompson, owned the agency. Memories! A lifetime of them!

We turned off Fourteenth Avenue and headed east, past the old building that once housed the *Vero Beach Press Journal*. It was a weekly paper back then. Later I wrote a column until the paper went daily, and I didn't have enough time. Another high school chum and college roommate, John Schumann Jr., was now owner and publisher.

We crossed the old Florida East Coast Railway tracks. I smiled, remembering the time John Schumann, Jim Thompson and I had discovered the tires of a car were the same width as the railway tracks. The three of us had taken my dad's pickup truck, eased it up on the tracks at a crossing and taken off down the coast — oblivious to the fact that a train might have been roaring toward us from the opposite direction. We did not meet a train. We met something far worse. When we got to the next crossing, Wallace Gossett, the local police chief, was waiting in his police car. His "Follow me, boys!" was like a death sentence. We had escaped with a stern warning that if it ever happened again a worse thing would happen — he would tell our parents.

Jackie gripped my hand as we turned into the old homestead road. Here I had grown up as a child. The big redwood house was now sitting vacant. It was occupied only in my dreams. It always represented home when I dreamed. We pulled up behind the nursing home which now sat where Daddy's Valencia oranges used to hang heavy on the trees — waiting to be picked. The children wanted to play outside in the big oaks. We agreed. It was going to be tough enough without having them exposed to the ordeal.

Inside the door, Mother B. was sitting in her wheelchair in the hall, lined up with five or six others — all staring at the opposite wall. We rolled her around to the little chapel. I sat in a chair facing her, feeling her parchment-like skin over those thin, brittle bones as I held her hands. I knew we had agreed I should tell her only generalities. But holding her hands and looking into her watery eyes, I began to cry. I blurted it out. All of it.

I felt those bony fingers reach up and touch the tears running down my face. Suddenly she wasn't a ninety-three-year-old woman anymore — and I wasn't a fifty-eight-year-old man. She was my mother, and I was her little boy.

She squeezed my hands. "Glory isn't such a bad place, son. I've been praying every day asking God to take me there. I had nothing to live for."

With a twinkle, she added, "Now I know why He's left me here. To pray for you."

Almost as an afterthought, her mind, once so brilliant as a teacher, suddenly dipped into her receding reservoir of memory, and she quoted verbatim from Henry Ward Beecher: "Tears, son, are often the telescope through which men see far into heaven."

I could almost hear my daddy, standing in front of the fireplace in the library of the big house, quoting from Kipling's "L'Envoi."

> When earth's last picture is painted, and the tubes are twisted and
>   dried,
> And the oldest colors have faded, and the youngest critic has died,
> We shall rest, and faith, we shall need it — lie down for an aeon or
>   two,
> Till the Master of All Good Workmen shall set us to work anew.
>
> And those that were good shall be happy: they shall sit in a golden
>   chair;
> They shall splash at a ten-league canvas with brushes of comets' hair;
> They shall find real saints to draw from — Magdalene, Peter, and
>   Paul;
> They shall work for an age at a sitting, and never be tired at all!
>
> And only the Master shall praise us, and only the Master shall blame;
> And no one shall work for money, and no one shall work for fame;
> But each for the joy of the working, and each, in his separate star,
> Shall draw the Thing as he sees It for the God of Things as They are![1]

We talked on for a while. I was the one in a fog. Mother's mind was as clear as it had been in her youth. It was time to go. I took her hands once again in mine to pray. "Jamie," she said in her broken voice. "Remember this. Do not give God orders. He is a good God and will only do good things to you."

In the car driving back across town toward Central Assembly, Jackie had her Bible open in her lap. "Your mother's right. We're not to give God orders. But we are mandated by God to give orders to Satan. He has no right to destroy your body. You are the temple of the Holy Spirit, and we are to resist him with everything in us — in the name of Jesus."

That same sentiment was reflected in the service that night. The church building was packed. Buddy introduced me as usual, and Jackie and I came to the microphone and shared just a few words of update. Then Buddy stepped back to the microphone.

"Tonight there won't be any preaching. Instead we're going to go straight into the throne room of God in behalf of God's servant. If you want to kneel quietly, you may. If you want to come to the altar and cry, you may. If you want to stand and shout, you may. However the Holy Spirit directs you to pray, you may."

He asked me to sit in a chair in the middle of the platform, and the pastors and elders of the church gathered around me — laying hands on me. The entire auditorium exploded in a cacophony of prayer. Some were cursing Satan and his cancer. Some were pleading with God for my healing. Some were standing and shouting praises. Some were walking back and forth, gesturing with their hands, interceding. The men on the platform were praying loudly. Then, as Jim Bartholomew had done on Tuesday evening, I was aware that Buddy Tipton was kneeling before me — his face next to my face. I opened my eyes and saw him weeping. I was weeping too. I felt my face begin to contort and wanted to cover it with my hands. But the men around me were gripping my arms and hands, holding them up in prayer. They were weeping too, and I forgot about making a spectacle. I just sat there and cried, letting the moisture from my eyes and nose run down my face and splash onto my shirt and lap. Buddy reached out and embraced me, holding me close. I felt his love, his deep friendship, and knew I was being held by a brother.

That night, driving home in the car, the grandchildren asleep in the back seat, Jackie once again reached over and gripped my hand in the dark.

"Something is about to break open," she said. "The refiner's fire has burned out the dross. Now it is time for God's glory to be reflected in your life."

"I miss my daddy," I said softly.

"I miss him too."

"When I was fired from South Main Street Baptist Church in Greenwood, he

101

never asked why — although he may have suspected. All he did was come to us and hold us up during that dark time. I thought the world had ended. I was sitting alone in our bedroom that Thursday morning after that awful Wednesday night business meeting. You remember what it was like. I had gone out in the yard that night and ripped open my shirt, pleading with God to send lightning from heaven and split my chest. Neither of us had slept that night, afraid the dawn wouldn't come — afraid it would. Then, the next morning, Daddy called. All he did was bless us. Love us. Say he would stand beside us. Before he hung up he quoted a portion of John Greenleaf Whittier's 'Eternal Goodness.' After all those years in business, he never forgot his love for literature."

The words returned, and I spoke them softly to Jackie — and to myself.

> I see the wrong that round me lies,
>   I feel the guilt within;
> I hear, with groan and travail-cries,
>   The world confess its sin.

> Yet in the maddening maze of things,
>   And tossed by storm and flood,
> To one fixed trust my spirit clings;
>   I know that God is good!

> I know not what the future hath
>   Of marvel or surprise,
> Assured alone that life and death
>   His mercy underlies.

She picked up the last two stanzas and quoted them with me — in unison.

> And so beside the Silent Sea
>   I wait the muffled oar;
> No harm from Him can come to me
>   On ocean or on shore.

> I know not where His islands lift
>   Their fronded palms in air;
> I only know I cannot drift
>   Beyond His love and care.[2]

TWELVE

WHISPERS OF DIRECTION

In the great drama of life there is always one player who seldom appears on stage, yet who always plays the leading roll. James Russell Lowell described Him in *This Present Crisis*: "...And behind the dim unknown, standeth God within the shadows, keeping watch above his own."

God, I knew, was the major actor in this drama being played out on the stage of my life. I was but a minor actor. In fact, most of the time I felt I was but a piece of furniture, moved here and there by busy stage hands at the direction of the manager. Others played larger roles, and they were one by one making their entrance. But it was God who owned, directed and played the leading role in this presentation.

Yet up until this time — with that one exception when I was lying on the gurney waiting for the CT scan of my chest — I had not heard Him speak. Even then it was more of an echo, a word given from another time and place, which finally reached me.

Monday morning was different. Sunday night, after we returned from Vero Beach, Jackie asked if I was going to get up and go to the early-morning men's prayer meeting. I knew I had no choice, even though my energy level was waning. Therefore that night, before we dropped off to sleep, I set the little alarm on my wristwatch to go off at 5:00 A.M. Three of the men on the property — Bruce, Tim and Jon Moore — were going also. Jon, my son-in-law, wanted to ride with me. Bruce and Tim would drive separately and go to their jobs after the meeting.

I woke before dawn. It was still dark outside. I lay in bed half dozing, waiting for the alarm. Then, as clearly as if He had been sitting on the side of the bed, I heard God whisper. He spoke only a few words, but they were so distinct I knew I would never forget them.

"Rest in Me. I will direct you."

I did not know it then, but He would speak additional words at the same time and in the same manner for the next five mornings — Monday through Friday. Each word would have special significance for the day about to dawn. Only in retrospect do I understand. At the time, as precious as the words were, most were without meaning — for I was unable to catch them in the framework of the future for which they were intended. God was calming me, preparing me for the hours just ahead.

I got up and felt my way to the bathroom where I turned on the lights and wrote the words in the back of the little notebook from the Community of Jesus — as I would do for the next five mornings. It was the only journaling I would do.

As I think about it now, I remember a phone call from Len LeSourd, my old editor at *Guideposts,*

"Jamie, you've got to make notes on all that is happening."

"Len, you know me. I learned from you. I make notes on everything. My notebook and pen are as much a part of my life as my watch and glasses. I see stories in everything and am constantly writing them down. But this is different. I remember sitting with you and Catherine up at John Sherrill's one night. She said a good writer had to be a spectator, not a participant. Once he got emotionally involved he would lose his objectivity. Well, I'm emotionally involved — right up to my eyebrows. I'm no longer a spectator. I'm a participant. I'm involved in a bloody warfare, Len, a spiritual warfare. Every morning before we get out of bed, Jackie and I recite Ephesians 6:10-18 — putting on the full armor of God. By the time I get out of bed I've got a sword in one hand and a shield in the other. I have to slash and hack my way past Satan and his demons just to get to the bathroom and brush my teeth. I wish I could journal what is happening, but I'm too busy trying to stay alive to write anything down."

But I did write down what God had said that morning.

There were more than three hundred men in the semidark church auditorium when I arrived. Many were on their knees. Some were lying prostrate on the floor. A few were walking around the room. The rest were sitting quietly, some reading their Bibles, some with their heads in their hands. Several were kneeling at the altar.

I was struck with the intensity in the air. There was no loud noise, only the soft hush of whispered prayers. I glanced around the room. This was my family — my extended family. I loved my friends out across the world, many of them involved in large ministries. But as King David had his strong men, these were mine. I knew most of them. They looked different, though. Then I realized why. They were in their work clothes, not the clothing they wore to church or to social gatherings where I usually saw them. An hour from now some would be sitting behind their desks managing large companies; others would spend the rest of the day working outside in the broiling July sun. I stood at the back, looking around. I was deeply moved.

I walked slowly down the aisle and knelt at the altar. Four or five others were there. Some had their Bibles open. How should I pray? I put my Bible on the step in front of me and let it fall open randomly. My eyes fell on Jeremiah 33:3: "Call to me and I will answer you and tell you great and unsearchable things you do not know."

Suddenly I was weeping. I did not know why. I tried to stifle it but could not. I crawled to the platform and lay flat on my stomach, stretched out on the carpet. One hand was touching the base of the Plexiglas pulpit. I had made special effort to get a transparent pulpit. Now I wished I had one of those massive wooden pulpits — so I could hide behind it. For almost a quarter of a century I had led this flock. Now I was no longer able to lead. Like a military officer, I had been wounded in front of my men. Struck down. I could only lie before them.

My weeping grew harder. I had no idea why I was crying. I felt the carpet under my face growing moist — soggy from my tears. But I couldn't make them stop. I pulled my glasses off and turned my face toward the back wall. I hated for the men to see me this way, but I had no choice.

I heard the voices of the men in the auditorium. I recognized the voices of some of the young pastors in our community — young men with smaller churches not affiliated with the Tabernacle Church. They were crying out to God, asking Him to save me from death for the sake of their churches, as well as for the sake of the Tabernacle.

"O God, for Your name's sake, don't let him die." It was the voice of Michael Thompson, our worship leader. He was pacing back and forth across the back of the platform, weeping almost as hard as I.

Other voices joined in. Gradually the sound grew louder until it was a roar. It must have continued for half an hour. When the crescendo subsided, so did my weeping. Exhausted, I lay flat on the carpet, my eyes closed.

I felt hands on my back, my shoulders, my legs, arms and feet. Many of the men were coming by and touching me, praying softly, before they left for work. I lay there until it was over. Soaking it in. Receiving.

Outside the sun had risen. The men were starting their cars and driving off to their work places. I paused and talked to Curry Vaughan.

"I was out jogging yesterday afternoon," he said, "and I passed Dave Weldon on the road. He asked about you."

Dave Weldon was a young physician, an internal medicine specialist, who lived across the street from Curry — just a block from our house. I knew he was an elder at Zion Fellowship, the small charismatic fellowship Curry had founded after he left the Tabernacle. Curry was no longer there, but he had continued his relationship with many of the people. Dave Weldon was one of them.

"He said his church prayed for you yesterday. He said he's available to help any way he can. Here's his home number if you want to call him."

On the way home, chatting with Jon, I heard another voice speaking. "I told you I would direct you."

By the time we had reached the house I knew what I was supposed to do. Jackie was in the kitchen fixing breakfast.

"Before you ask about the meeting," I said, "I need to call Dr. Weldon."

"Why?"

"If I'm going to win this battle, I need a doctor standing with me who will not only understand the power of all this prayer coming my way, but will pray for me himself."

She agreed. I told her what Curry had said, then called Dr. Weldon's house.

His wife, Nancy, answered. I introduced myself.

"Oh, we've been praying for you," she said.

Hearing her words was like hearing Jesus speak to the raging sea: "Peace, be still." I felt a deep calm inside. I had made the right move. I realized God was providing me with a Christian doctor. Nancy said her husband had already left to make rounds at the hospital. She would call his beeper and have him return my call as soon as possible.

After breakfast Jackie started opening the mail from the previous week. One letter in particular touched my heart. It was from my old friend DeVern Fromke, whom I had not seen in years. Soft-spoken and intimate with God, DeVern had shunned the publicity that surrounds most writers and traveling teachers. In earlier years, when our church was small, he often came and taught. As we grew larger, he stopped coming. Although he was one of the deepest and most articulate teachers I knew, he seemed almost embarrassed by having a large crowd come hear him. In fact, he had returned our last honorarium to the church, saying it was too large.

Jackie read his letter out loud as I sat and listened.

"I am not often watching TV, but when the word came through Sheila Walsh on 'The 700 Club' of the doctors' diagnosis of your condition, I wanted to rush to the phone and assure you of my love and prayers....

"The next day I was meeting with the elders here in Central Indiana — and again there was a surge of the Spirit calling forth intercession. That night at the Broad Ripple Fellowship, as we prayed for you and your family, there was much assurance that God will have His perfect will accomplished....

"Jamie — what can I say? In these recent weeks God has been doing such a deep and devastating work of ploughing in my life. All my pride in the knowledge of spiritual things has been exposed, and I am realizing just how needy I really am. But God is merciful and so faithful. Are we — you and I — awake and ready to receive what He wants to do? I tremble, as I know you are now trembling. But, remember, while being in the hands of a living God is fearful, it is the only safe place on earth.

"Nita and I are standing with you and your whole family. Jesus is Lord!"

We sat silent a long while.

The phone rang. It was Dr. Weldon.

"Do you want me to take your case?"

"I've got to have a Christian doctor," I said, "one who will understand that medicine is not my source of life — only God."

"Call your other doctor. Tell him you are changing physicians. It's done all the time. I'll send for your records this morning. I'd like to see you in my office at 4:00 P.M."

The time in Dr. Weldon's office at Melbourne Internal Medicine Associates was uneventful except for one thing. He prayed for me. I knew I had made the right decision.

"I've looked at your scans," he said. "I want you to talk to one of the oncologists in our clinic. He knows who you are and will see you right away. His name is Joe McClure. He has a Ph.D. as well as an M.D. and has served as a cancer specialist at the National Institutes of Health."

Dr. Joseph McClure was warm but factual. He wanted Jackie to sit in for the consultation.

"The treatment you receive depends on what you want," he said. Looking me straight in the eye, he asked, "What do you want?"

"I want to live," I said simply. I realized it was the first time the question had been put to me as if I had a choice. It felt good to say it.

He grinned. "Then you have four options. One, you can do nothing. That's the cheapest way, for it will cost you nothing. If you have a book you want to finish, if you have a couple of sermons you want to preach, you probably have time. Then it will be over. Quickly."

I interrupted. "Is there a possibility that a cancer such as I have will go into automatic remission?"

"That sometimes happens, but it's rare. Very rare."

He paused. "Number two, I can treat you with chemotherapy. It will not cure you, but it may put the disease into remission. I think I can handle that without the side effects being too harsh.

"Third, I can administer one of the new immunotherapy drugs: interferon, interluken or a combination of IL2 and chemo. There have been some instances of these drugs actually curing cancers like this — but there is no guarantee. You would need to go to a hospital like Shands at the University of Florida in Gainesville to have the protocol set up, but I can administer the drugs here. However, they are very expensive, and we're not sure of the side effects."

He got up and walked across the room. Turning, he looked back at the two of us. "However, I want to present a fourth option, and this is the one I want to try to talk you into." He paused, then continued. "Because of who you are, a man with many contacts around the nation, you are going to be besieged by people who will say, 'Why did you stay in Melbourne for treatment? Why didn't you go to a well-known medical center like the Mayo Clinic, or one of the big teaching hospitals?' I can do everything here they can do as far as treatment, but you need to be able to come up with an answer for your friends. Therefore, I am going to advise you to go to a teaching hospital or a national treatment center."

"Where?" Jackie asked.

"Dr. Weldon says your brother is at the University of Alabama in Birmingham. That is one of the finest hospitals in America. So is Shands in Gainesville. I've sent patients to Memorial Sloan-Kittering in New York, which is one of the best in the world. So are Stanford University in California and M.D. Anderson Cancer Center with the University of Texas. Go home and think about it. Then let me know."

Thirty minutes after we had walked into his office we were back in our car.

"He didn't tell us a thing," Jackie said.

"He told us just what God wanted him to say," I responded. "This morning God spoke to me and said that I should rest in Him, and He would direct my path. He just has."

"What do you mean?"

"We're not to stay here. I don't know where or when, but God wants us to go somewhere else for some other reason. Surely there's more to come. We'll just need to keep on resting in Him."

"How do we do that?"

"One day, one step, at a time. I guess if we put our feet down and the ground doesn't break through, it means we can take another step."

That evening before we left for our home church meeting, Jackie came into the bedroom where I was lying on my back, staring at the ceiling.

"Let me read you something you wrote a long time ago." She had in her hands a copy of *Tramp for the Lord*, the book I had written for Corrie ten Boom back in 1974. The ten Boom family had harbored Jews from the Nazis during World War II in Holland. They had a special hiding place in their home where Jewish families came and stayed. They had been caught and arrested. Corrie's father and sister had died in a concentration camp. Corrie had almost died in Ravensbruck. After the war she had traveled the world sharing God's Word.

Jackie sat down on the side of the bed and read what I had written, just the way Corrie had told it to me.

> When I was a little girl I went to my father and said, "Daddy, I am afraid that I will never be strong enough to be a martyr for Jesus Christ."
>
> "Tell me," Father said, "when you take a train trip from Haarlem to Amsterdam, when do I give you the money for the ticket? Three weeks before?"
>
> "No, Daddy, you give me the money for the ticket just before we get on the train."
>
> "That is right," my father said, "and so it is with God's strength. Our wise Father in heaven knows when you are going to need things too. Today you do not need the strength to be a martyr; but as soon as you are called upon for the honor of facing death for Jesus, He will supply the strength you need — just in time."[1]

It was a statement of faith. I wondered: Was I ready to trust Him, not just with money for a train ticket, but with my life?

(Top) The basketball gang: (standing) Tim Buckingham, Marion Ranzino, Jamie Buckingham, Jon Moore, Bruce Buckingham; (kneeling) unidentifed, Paul Boutin, Dr. Randy Wisdom

(Right) Jamie's brother, Dr. John (Laddie) Buckingham and his wife, Shirley

THIRTEEN

HAVING FAITH
AND FEELING SICK

IT CAME AS A DAWN SURPRISE. JUST AS I WAS WAKING the next morning, I heard His whispered voice again. I recognized Him immediately. This time He spoke three short sentences.

"Do not fear.

"Things are not as they seem.

"I will watch over you."

I lay quietly, waiting. But there was nothing else. I repeated what I had heard. Then I repeated it again out loud.

Jackie reached over and took my hand. I didn't know she was awake.

"Did He say that to you?"

"I think He did. But how can I tell? Maybe it's just me wanting to believe it so much my subconscious flashes the message to my conscious just to fool me."

"Paul talks of 'the God who gives life to the dead and calls things that are not as though they were.' "

"Where's that found?"

"Romans 4:17. Dodie Osteen used it as one of the Scripture verses that helped

111

her understand what was happening in her body. Just because a thing is visible does not make it real, any more than being invisible makes it unreal. Maybe that's what He meant when He said, 'Things are not as they seem.' ''

"Did you sleep?" I asked her.

"I don't think so. I felt like I was hovering over you throughout the night, fighting off the demons, waging spiritual warfare. You are not going to die. You are going to live and declare the works of the Lord."

I moved against her warm body. She scooted toward me. I touched my hand against her cheek. It was moist. I reached over and felt her pillow. It was wet. "I should have stayed awake and prayed with you," I said, ashamed.

"You don't know what an honor it is for me to spend all night long interceding for you. For years I wept for you because I did not think you loved me. Now I weep for you because you do love me. This is my call — to stand in the gap for you until the battle is won. Then we shall move on, together."

I held her close, interrupted only by the sudden and insistent beeping of the tiny alarm on my wristwatch. It was time to rise and pray with my men.

"Don't forget," she said as I was leaving the darkened bedroom, "your brother is flying down again today from Birmingham. He's going to spend the night with us. I'll meet you at the airport at noon."

The atmosphere in the semidark auditorium was the same as the morning before. I had driven in by myself. Alone in the cab of my pickup, I had spent the twenty minutes praying out loud as I drove the dark streets from our house to the church building. The other men on the compound had driven their own cars, knowing I would have to stay on for our regular Tuesday morning staff meeting.

Standing in the back of the auditorium, I realized the crowd was even larger than the day before. I took a seat on the front row. Once again I opened my Bible, this time to the Psalms, and began to read where the book had fallen open. Suddenly it happened again. Tears bubbled from my eyes like little springlets in the desert sand. Was this from God, or was I just on the far edge of an emotional breakdown? Jackie said it was because I had grown tender toward the things of God. I hoped it was that and not that I was dropping off the edge into la-la land.

I crawled up the two little carpeted steps which surrounded the platform and once again prostrated myself — face down — on the carpet behind the pulpit. Here, every Sunday morning, my feet stood. Here, time and time again, I had opened the Bible and proclaimed boldly that Jesus was Healer, that through His death at Calvary He had purchased not only our salvation, but our healing. Where was He now? Where was He now that I needed Him so badly?

This time I knew why I was weeping. I was weeping in desperation. I heard myself saying over and over, "Please...please...please."

I was ashamed. There were others in the church so much worse off than I. I had a loving family around me. I had people all over the world praying for me. I had a nice home and health insurance. Never in the history of our church had this many men gathered to pray for one individual — but they had gathered for me. What of those who had none of these things? What of those who were dying — alone? Gradually my focus changed. Instead of pleading for myself, I was pleading for them. I was doing what Jackie and I had been doing for almost two weeks, interceding for others. I heard myself calling the names of men and women, boys and girls in our church who were going through critical times.

Finally I had cried myself out. I lay on the floor, my arms spread over my head, palms down against the carpet. Silent.

Then I heard a man praying, pleading in a loud voice. He was weeping harder than I had wept. "O God, I'm so sorry. I'm so sorry."

That's all he said, but he kept saying it. Then I heard a man, on the far side of the room, sobbing. "Lord, I love her. Please forgive me for what I've done to her. Give me another chance. Please, God, please, send her back to me."

Others picked up the chorus. The auditorium rang with confessions — many of them shouted in utter abandonment. It became a cacophony of sound, yet somehow I knew God was not only sorting it all out and hearing each prayer, He was pleased. Mightily pleased.

At the staff meeting that morning we dispensed with the normal routine. We started by receiving communion together. Then, instead of passing out an agenda, Don Williams led us directly into a time of extended prayer. I realized the church office had virtually shut down to all business. The men and women were spending most of each day in prayer — not just for me, but for the church.

My brother John had just finished tying down his twin Beach when I arrived at the airport after the church meeting. I met him in the lounge at the FBO [fixed base operator]. His son, Brian, also a pilot, had flown down with him. After giving me a hug, John said, "I've got a surprise."

He nodded down the hall. There was my sister, Audrey. "She flew in from Missouri last night then flew on down with us this morning."

Audrey was crying when she hugged me. "You're going to live," she said. "My entire church back in Fredericktown is praying for you."

"So are a lot of others," I said, holding her tightly.

Jackie met us, and we had a long lunch together at a nearby restaurant. It was filled with reminiscences, good times from childhood. John and Jackie had been in the same high school class. I was one year ahead and Audrey four years back. Now, more than forty years later, we were sitting together laughing, remembering. It was the best therapy God could have ordered.

That afternoon John talked doctor-talk to me. "I've prayed a lot about this," he said. "I just can't seem to shake the feeling that there is something we're missing. This just isn't the normal kind of case. There are too many abnormalities about it — things that don't fit into any mold. I want to get all your records, including the pathologist's slides of the tissue they took from your kidney, and take them back to Birmingham. We have some of the finest doctors in the world at the University of Alabama School of Medicine. They've agreed to look at everything and give a second opinion."

I thought of Dr. McClure's words less than twenty-four hours before as he encouraged me to go to a teaching hospital. This wasn't that, but it was a step in that direction.

We spent the rest of the afternoon gathering up the various records. I called Dr. Weldon's office. They said they would have the scans and reports ready when we came by. We would have to go to the hospital to pick up the bone scan pictures and the pathology slides. The slides, in particular, had to be signed for.

"They are legal evidence," John reminded me, "in case of a lawsuit."

We were in my den. John was sitting in an old wooden rocking chair near the fireplace. Behind him on the wall was the huge eighteenth-century grandfather clock that had once hung in the big redwood house in Vero Beach when we were youngsters. Its brass pendulum was swinging methodically. I wondered if John remembered how the clock sounded at night after we were tucked in bed and all the lights were out.

"What kind of lawsuit?" I asked.

"In case you don't have cancer and sue the doctors and hospitals for false diagnoses, those slides will prove you do have a cancerous kidney — just as the CT scans will show you have cancer in your lymph glands."

"What if God takes it away?" I asked.

He pulled his glasses down on his nose and looked over their rims, just the way I imagined he had done thousands of times when his patients had asked stupid questions and he needed to lecture them.

"You know how much I love God and His Word," he said matter-of-factly. "But I'm concerned that you keep blaming this cancer on the devil and praying for a miracle to take it away. I'm not sure that cancer, or any disease, comes from the devil. Cancer is a fact of life. One out of three — Christians and non-Christians alike — comes down with it. Christians and non-Christians alike are sometimes cured, sometimes not. I just don't believe disease is spiritual. It is physical. Jesus came to save our souls. What happens to our bodies is part of a natural process over which even we doctors have little control."

He paused, not wanting to tread heavily on things he knew I held sacred. Yet he felt obligated as my brother and as a medical expert to express what he believed. I was at peace, listening — but not agreeing. He continued softly.

"I believe in miracles. I believe Jesus performed miracles. I've seen miracles, but they've all been in the spiritual realm. I've seen lost people saved. I've seen broken families mended through the power of Christ. I've seen wicked people become good. I've seen stingy people become generous. But documented physical miracles are rare. I've never seen a crooked leg straightened simply through the power of prayer. I've never seen a blind man see or a deaf child hear just because someone prayed for them."

He paused again, as if gathering strength to continue. "Nor have I seen cancer cells disappear through prayer. You need to know that. It would be unfair if I didn't say it to you."

"But you're praying for me." It was a simple statement, reflecting what he had told me over the phone.

"I've never prayed as hard for anything or anyone in my life. I pray for you throughout the day. Shirley and I get on our knees at night and pray for you."

"What are you praying?"

He sat back in his chair. His voice, almost embarrassed, broke as he answered. "I'm praying for a miracle — the miracle I've never seen."

That evening was Tuesday, so the basketball gang gathered. John and I walked out the back door. The big overhead lights were on, and I could hear the sound of bouncing balls as the fellows warmed up. Bruce, Tim and Jon were there. So were Randy Wisdom and Mick Payne, a U.S. Army officer stationed at Patrick Air Force Base on special assignment.

I introduced my brother John to the group. He and Randy pulled aside to talk doctor-talk — about me, I suspected. I picked up one of the balls and shot a few goals. As soon as I did, I could feel that mysterious pressure building just below my rib cage in the center of my abdomen.

"What do you think?" I asked the two doctors standing on the side of the court talking — Randy in his shorts and basketball shoes, John in his street clothes. "Do you think I can play?"

"You've never been able to play before," Randy deadpanned. "Do you think having cancer will give you some supernatural ability to play now?"

I threw the ball at his leg — the one with the blue brace strapped around his knee. He jumped back, laughing, and kicked it into a palmetto clump.

"Come on, Dad," Bruce shouted. "Get your shoes and shorts on. I'll guard you."

"You're the one person I don't want to guard me," I said, laughing. "You'll take advantage of me just because I've slowed down. I'd rather guard Dr. Elbow.

That way I won't have to worry about sweating, because he never runs."

I headed back into the house to change into my shorts and shoes.

"Are you sure it's OK?" Jackie asked.

"I've got two doctors down there. If I die on the court, at least they'll know how to notify the next-of-kin."

"You're not going to die," Jackie said sternly. "And this next-of-kin is going to take John and walk out to Sandy's house. I don't want to be around when you get punched in the one good kidney you still have left."

Dressed and ready, I went back outside to join the others.

"Do as much as you feel like," Randy cautioned. "If you get tired, slow down or stop — just keep your elbows out of my side."

But the game wasn't the same slam-banger we usually had. The other men, I could tell, were watching out for me. On several occasions Paul Boutin, who could hit 90 percent of his bank shots from side court, would throw the ball to me rather than taking his shot.

"Shoot!" he would holler.

I noticed that as soon as I got the ball all the action stopped. Instead of rushing to block the shot, everyone would step back one step and wait for me to shoot. If I drove for the basket, instead of running into the usual forest of swinging arms and battering knees, the path would open mysteriously before me, and I would find myself with a clear layup. But far more ominous was the fact that just that little bit of exertion brought on the scary, but now familiar, feeling of exhaustion. I played only one game, then backed off.

I looked around. Dave LeBeau, a member of Bruce's home church, had arrived. Dave had gone with me to Israel back in January when I had taken our pastors, elders, my sons and sons-in-law and a couple of young men in the church. His presence meant the three-on-three game could continue without me.

"You guys go on without me," I said. "I'm really slowing this thing down, and no one is getting any exercise."

"Hey, look at it this way," Tim said. "Nobody's bleeding either, like we usually do."

I punched his arm and told them I needed to visit with my brother; he was flying home early in the morning. The truth was I needed to go inside and sit down. I was worn out.

That night as Jackie and I lay in bed, she reached over and took my hand.

"God is not going to let you die. Not yet. He said He's going to make you walk out all these wonderful promises you've been making. He promised me this afternoon, as I was praying, that He loved me so much He was going to keep you alive just for my sake."

FOURTEEN

DON'T FORGET NOT TO WORRY

DO NOT WORRY!"

It was all He said on Wednesday. Just a tiny whisper from heaven moments before the alarm went off. I lay in bed, waiting to see if there was more. But that was the only message. Was something about to happen which would cause me to worry? How do you not worry? Telling a man who has been told he's going to die not to worry is like telling a homeless person to stop being poor. Nevertheless I felt encouraged. God knew something I didn't know and was warning me not to get upset about it. I got up, jotted the message down in my little book and promptly forgot about it.

I should have remembered. I was heading into a bad day.

John and his son, Brian, came in with me for the early-morning prayer meeting. They sat in the back of the auditorium while I went on down to the front. Afterward I introduced them to a few of my friends, then we headed to the airport so they could get an early start. Audrey was supposed to meet us at the airport at 7:30, and they would be on their way.

I went with them out on the tarmac to prep the plane. I missed flying. While we waited for Audrey, I remembered my first lesson. It was in 1958 from Ed Seymour, an ex-alcoholic who had become a member of our Southern Baptist church in Greenwood, South Carolina. I recalled the morning he had stopped by the church parsonage where we were living. He wanted me to drive with him out to the airport in his battered old 1948 Chevrolet. When we got to the little Greenwood Airport, he took me around to the big hanger. A yellow J-3 Piper Cub was sitting on the tarmac in front of the open doors.

"Get in. I'm going to teach you how to fly."

Ed (we all called him Mr. Ed) had been a basic training flight instructor during World War II. He was crusty, almost crude. His years as an alcoholic had taken their toll. He was missing most of one ear where he had rolled off his couch one night and fallen on top of his bulldog, who had bitten his ear off. I was fresh out of seminary, the pastor of a large Southern Baptist church in a small South Carolina mill village. Flying an airplane — with Mr. Ed at the controls — was the last thing I wanted to do. Before I knew it, however, I was strapped in the front seat of the little cub. Mr. Ed was standing outside under the wing giving me some basic instructions.

There were only four controls: two rudder pedals on the floor, a control stick that came up in between my legs and a small throttle mounted on the left windowsill.

"Put your heels on the brakes and hold them tight," he said. "I'm going to spin the prop, and I don't want this thing running over me or taking off and flying until I can get in."

He had my attention. I set the throttle as he told me, then turned on the switch. He walked around the wing tip to the nose, grabbed the prop in both hands, shouted "Clear!" and pulled down. Nothing happened. He repeated the procedure, and this time the little sixty-five-horsepower engine sputtered, then roared to life. Moments later my instructor was strapped in the back seat, and we were moving down the taxiway, not in a straight line but traversing. The nose of the plane stuck up in the air, meaning it was impossible to see through the windshield until we had enough speed to pull the tail off the ground.

I felt the stick wiggling between my legs. "Keep your feet lightly on the pedals," Ed shouted from the back seat, "and hold the stick lightly. Don't grip it. Let me fly the plane, and you just feel everything I do. That's the way you learn. If you freeze up, if you get frightened and take the controls away from me, you'll cause us to crash."

He added the classic pilot's phrase: "An airplane crash can mess up your whole day."

I laughed nervously and held the stick — gently. Moments later I saw the throttle move all the way forward and heard the engine roar. We were rolling down the runway. I felt the stick move forward. When it did, the tail wheel came off the runway, and we were speeding along on two wheels. I could feel the rudder pedals moving right and left, correcting for the slight crosswind. Then I felt the stick slowly move back toward my belt buckle, and suddenly we were flying.

"You did great," Ed shouted from the back seat. "You'll make a good pilot because you followed instructions perfectly."

All that came to mind as I stood on the concrete watching as John checked the oil dipstick under the cowlings of his Beach Baron. He drained gas from both wing tanks to check for water condensation. He was ready to go as soon as Audrey showed up.

We walked back to the lounge. Ed Seymour's words from thirty-three years before kept running through my mind: "If you freeze up, if you get frightened and take the controls away from me, you'll cause us to crash."

"Dear God," I prayed silently, "help me to walk through this without freezing up and going into a panic. I just want to follow Your instructions and learn from You — never again try to fly without You."

We waited an hour and a half; Audrey still had not arrived. I was getting antsy. I finally called home. Jackie answered and said she would try to track her down. Half an hour later she called back. There had been some kind of mix-up. Audrey was waiting for John at the Vero Beach Airport. Someone was driving her to Melbourne. She would be there in forty-five minutes.

It was almost 11:00 A.M. when John, Brian and Audrey finally took off. I walked back to the hot car and sat looking at the steering wheel. Doubt and anxiety, twin sisters from hell, had crawled in the car with me — one beside me, the other in the back seat. Both were whispering.

Remember, he's your baby brother. The emphasis was on "baby."

He's a good man, but he's not a real specialist. He's just a country doctor who lives in town and makes mission trips to help poor natives. What's he know about cancer?

He couldn't even get the instructions right to pick up your sister, now he's taken off with all your medical records. He's going to bumble this, and you're the one who's going to pay. You've made the worst mistake of your life. In fact, this could cost you your life.

By the time I got home I was an emotional basket case. The twins got out as I pulled into the driveway, but they had already done their damage. My mind was filled with despair and doubt.

"I stood there and watched him fly off with my life in his hands," I told Jackie. "What if the doctors up there misread the scans? What if he gets busy and forgets to take them to the office? What if he leaves them in the plane and the sun destroys all the X-ray film?"

"Jamie, he's your brother. He's a fine doctor. He flew all the way down here just to help you. You can trust him, even with your life if necessary."

Then she paused. "Did God whisper something to you again this morning?"

I had to stop and think, so filled was my mind with doubt and unbelief. I nodded my head.

"What did He say?

"He told me not to worry."

Jackie giggled. It irritated me. The more irritated I got the more she giggled until tears were running down her face. I tried to keep my mouth from grinning, but it was impossible. The next thing I knew I was holding her and laughing with her.

When the laughter subsided, Jackie said, "God told me something to tell you also."

"Oh?"

"He said you were to eat. You've been losing weight because you've lost your appetite and aren't exercising. God told me to start feeding you. He said to fatten you up because you were going to need it later on."

"What's that mean?"

"I have no idea. I don't know what anything means. I just know we're supposed to do what He tells us to do day by day. That's all we have."

It took about thirty minutes for the depression to return. By midafternoon I was back in the slough of despond. Jackie, seeing my private battle, insisted I come in the den and listen to a tape. Ed Gray, the fellow from north Georgia who had sent the list of healing scriptures, had also sent a tape. I slouched on the sofa and listened as Ed's voice, with that familiar twang, came through the speakers. I was touched. He had a personal message for me, reminding me of how the doctors had told him he was going to die in just a few weeks. He had gone to the Bible and found these verses. Every day he read them, meditated on them, claimed them as God's promises for his life. That had been five years ago, and he was healthier now than before he had cancer. The rest of the tape was Ed's halting voice reading the healing promises of God. I sat, listening. Faith welled up inside me.

The moment the tape was over, however, despair came rushing back into my mind. Faith, not a resident but only an invited visitor, fled.

About suppertime Jon, my daughter Robin's husband, came through the back door. Jon and Robin and their four little girls lived next door. They had met while Robin was a student at Oral Roberts University and married before she graduated. They had stayed on for a year while Jon taught in the health and recreation department, then moved back home. Jon was working out of his home as a sales representative for his brother's direct mail firm headquartered in Tulsa. He had a sheet of yellow paper in his hand as he came into the breakfast room.

"The strangest thing happened a few minutes ago," he said, scratching his curly head and looking at the sheet of paper. "I was sitting at my desk praying for you, and suddenly I had a vision. I've never had a vision before, but this one was real. I saw this thing growing before my eyes, then it changed and took on another form. Finally it faded. I grabbed this paper and drew the image sequence of what I had seen."

He held the paper out for me to look at. On it he had drawn four circles. The background of each circle was black. The inside of each circle, he said, was a brilliant white light. In the lower corner of the first circle was an ugly black form, shaped something like a bloated kidney bean. In the second circle the black form had moved to the center of the circle and was now a black circle surrounded by brilliant white light. In circle three the smaller black circle was now a light gray. In circle four it had faded to almost nothing, with the white light engulfing the entire area.

As Jon showed me the drawing, Jackie looked over my shoulder.

"That's your kidney," she said, pointing to the ugly black form in the first circle. "And this is what God is doing to it as it is exposed to the light of the Word and the prayers of the saints."

She laughed again. "God told you not to worry. Now He's even sending you pictures to encourage you."

But it wasn't enough. All I could think about was those medical records flying off in that twenty-year-old airplane. I started up the stairs, planning on skipping supper and going to bed early. As I passed the front door on the way to the stairs, the doorbell rang. I opened it. A man was standing there with a huge vase of beautiful flowers. Behind him in the driveway was his florist truck.

"Somebody must love you an awful lot," he grinned. "This is the most expensive arrangement we have in our shop."

I carried it into the kitchen. Jackie closed the oven door, wiped her hands on a towel and opened the little card.

She read: "Jamie, I love you with all my heart. Caroline and I are fasting and praying for your healing. Mike Evans."

"Now God is not only speaking to you and drawing you pictures, He is sending you flowers through people you make fun of with your writing."

"I don't make fun of Mike," I defended myself. "We've been through too much together for him to take me seriously. It's just that he sends up some balloons that are just too tempting for me not to poke at in one of my columns."

But Jackie was right. Over the last several years I had allowed my satire to become too pointed. Mike, a Jewish/Pentecostal evangelist who had a way of getting himself interviewed on national television as an expert in many fields, was one of my favorite targets. Yet we were friends, and I dearly loved him. Why did I allow myself to write sharp criticism of him in the form of humor?

I thought back to the time Mike was in the hospital in New York with a heart attack. I was the only one he had called. Later he had asked me to come up to his Stony Brook retreat center on Long Island to speak to more than one thousand messianic Jews who had gathered.

That night there was a demonstration against us. About twenty young men and women from the militant Jewish Defense League had broken into the auditorium just as I started to speak. They had loosed more than one hundred white rats, hoping to cause panic when the rodents scampered across the floor of the crowded auditorium. Five young men carrying razor-pointed umbrellas had jumped the stage and tried to grab the microphone away from me. When I wouldn't give it up, one of them had pulled a knife. I thought he was going to stab me, but instead he tried to cut the microphone cord. Then, on cue, a camera crew from CBS appeared. They had been told by the Jewish Defense League that there was going to be a riot. But there was no fight. Instead, Mike had stood in the midst of the turmoil and started singing: "Jesus loves *you*, this I know. For the Bible tells me so." The angry youths finally left.

I thought of the time Mike had accompanied me into the Sinai on one of my camping/research trips. We had come across a Bedouin camp where a small child had been terribly scalded on its head. We had a medical doctor with us, Angus Sargeant from High Point, North Carolina. Angus had examined the child and said there was nothing he could do. The burn had infected and caused a huge scab to form, covering most of the top of the child's head.

Mike stepped forward. "We must pray for the child, and Jesus will heal him."

The child's father, a Muslim, was holding him and wearing a magnificent hajh, a curved Bedouin knife. Undaunted, Mike reached out and laid his hands on the little boy's fevered body — praying loudly in Jesus' name for healing.

The next day we returned to the camp and discovered that during the night the scab had fallen off. Underneath was new skin. The child was healed — attested to by the doctor who was with us.

Why would I want to take my paper sword and slice away at a man like that? But I did. Now Mike and Caroline had sent the most expensive flowers in the shop — a symbol of their love and concern.

"God's dealing with you about your judgmental spirit, isn't He?" Jackie asked.

I gave her a crooked smile. "I'm like the Charlie Brown character who once said, 'I take my religion seriously. I get into arguments almost every day.' "

"The very ones you've judged are the first ones God has sent to minister to you. "

"Did you know I got a call from Benny Hinn this afternoon? He offered to drive over from Orlando and pray for me."

"You've taken some shots at Benny, haven't you?"

"But I like Benny. I'm grateful for the ministry God has given him."

Jackie reached over and put her hand on my arm. "Just as long as you are willing to listen to God before you put things on paper. He has a lot of servants, you know, and they don't all look like you."

"Benny wasn't the only one who called. So did Frances Hunter."

This time Jackie laughed out loud. "Everyone you've poked at with that pointed pen of yours is rushing forth to minister to you."

"She was so genuine. She said she and Charles wanted to get on a plane and fly to Melbourne tomorrow, pray for me, then get on a plane and fly back to Houston."

"What did you tell her?"

"The same thing I told Benny. That I didn't want anyone to come pray for me unless God sent them. That I was not going to seek anyone out and didn't want anyone to come and lay hands on me unless they had a mandate from the Holy Spirit. I wanted their prayers, but they were to come here only if God sent them."

She nodded, approving.

"Frances is sending me the rough draft of the first chapter of her latest book, which describes her own healing from a terminal disease," I added.

"You've got a lot of friends out there, sweetheart. You need to start treating them the way they treat you."

I pushed my food around on my plate. I had lost what little appetite I had. For the second time that evening I told Jackie I was going upstairs to bed early. It had not been a good day.

Or had it?

I couldn't sleep. I sorted through the various tapes that were stacked up on my night stand — most of them sent to me from friends and unknown prayer partners around the nation. We were saturating ourselves with the Word of God.

I was scrambling through these tapes, trying to find one I would like, when Jackie came up. She had just received a new *Hosanna!* praise tape. She put it on the player, but nothing seemed able to break through the darkness.

At 9:30 the phone rang. It was Gordon Strongitharm, one of our staff pastors. One of his pastoral duties was to carry the beeper and answer the emergency calls that came into the church office after hours.

Jackie took his call, jotted something down and then hung up.

"Gordie just got a call from a Dr. Ralph Johnson, a medical doctor in St. Petersburg who is trying to get hold of you. Gordie seemed to think you should return the call."

"Now?" I said from the bed, where I was propped up on pillows.

"The doctor left his home phone number. You can wait until tomorrow, however."

But something was sputtering inside me. It felt like the old Model-A Ford we once had around the house when I was a boy. To start it someone had to twist the crank. Then the engine would sputter, backfire, cough and finally catch. I now had that same feeling in my spirit. Something was trying to get started.

"No, I think I'm supposed to return this call now. This hasn't been a good day for me. I'm ready for a messenger from God. Maybe he's it."

"God has already sent you a number of messages today," Jackie reminded me.

"I know. I've given the devil a key to my mind, haven't I?"

She smiled and handed me the phone.

Dr. Johnson answered on the first ring. "I was praying you would call back," he said jovially. There was a ring in his voice that gave me confidence.

"Who are you?" I asked.

He gave me a rundown on his practice — actually a testimony of his life. He was a radiation oncologist who had been director of the department of radiation therapy at the National Institutes of Health, the prestigious hospital that wanted to treat me as an experimental case. However, he had begun to drink and finally resigned. In the process he lost everything. Wife. Position. Money. He moved to Florida and opened a small cancer clinic associated with the Bayfront Medical Center in St. Petersburg. His drinking got worse. He was losing his ability to function. Then, in a remarkable series of incidents, he had an encounter with Jesus Christ. He had stopped drinking instantly. Shortly afterward he had remarried. Now he was baptized in the Holy Spirit, and he and his wife were part of the Suncoast Cathedral, a large Assemblies of God church in St. Petersburg. He continued with his work at the Bayfront Cancer Clinic but spent a large amount of time giving free medical treatment to the homeless and several times a year made medical mission trips overseas.

I laughed. "I think I can trust you."

"What do you mean?"

"I have problems trusting people who don't walk with a limp," I said. "It sounds like you have one. Now tell me how you found out about me?"

"This morning when I got up, I was standing in the shower and said, 'God, just zing me with something special today.' I've never prayed like that before and didn't think much about it until a few minutes ago when I got a phone call from a missionary nurse named Jackie Wickes. I met her last year when we were both in the Caribbean on the hospital ship *S.S. Anastasis*, sponsored by Youth With a Mission. Jackie had asked for my card. I seldom carry cards, but I had one and gave it to her."

"Our church supports Jackie," I interjected. "She's a single mom who gave up her nursing job after her kids were grown and has been with YWAM ever since."

"Someone from your church had told her about your condition," Dr. Johnson continued. "She said God had directed her to call me. She scrounged around and found the card I had given her a year ago. She felt I would have a word for you that you would receive only from a medical doctor."

"Well, do you?"

He laughed. "You'd better tell me about your situation first."

I explained everything, closing out with the fact that my brother John had left this morning with my medical records.

"You've done exactly the right thing by letting him take them to Birmingham," he said. "Do you have his phone number? I want to call him."

"Now?"

"It's only 9:00 P.M. in Birmingham," he answered. "I want to make a couple of other phone calls, and then I'll call you back tomorrow."

I gave him John's home number and hung up. Jackie was standing at the foot of the bed, looking at me. "How do you feel?"

"Better," I said. "Much better. For some strange reason I think I've just heard from a messenger from God — and I don't even know the man."

FIFTEEN

FINDING
REAL FAITH

I WOKE UP ON THURSDAY CHUCKLING. IT FELT GOOD.

"Are you OK?" It was Jackie's soft voice from the pillow beside mine.

"God just spoke to me again, just as He has every morning this week."

"What did He say?"

"He said, 'See, I told you.' "

"That doesn't make any sense."

"It does to me," I said, turning toward her, our noses almost touching on the pillow. "Yesterday morning he told me, 'Do not worry.' I worried anyway. All that confusion at the airport. John flying off with my medical records. Somehow I saw that as my last thread to life, and it seemed to be unraveling. Then last night Dr. Johnson called, and things fell into place. Now God says, 'See, I told you.' All that worrying was unnecessary. He really is taking care of me."

"It sounds like He was chiding you," Jackie said.

"I guess so, but it was so gentle. You know what it was like? Remember last week when Kristin came screaming into the house? She had come home from school, and her mother wasn't home. She came running over here, frightened.

You told her not to worry, that her mom had gone to the store and would be back in a few minutes. She didn't believe you. No telling what was going on inside her head as she listened to her fears instead of you. Then in a few moments Robin came driving up. You held Kristin and said, 'See, I told you.' And she laughed and hugged you and ran home happy. That's what the Father sounded like this morning when He whispered to me."

She smiled. "Then be happy. I believe with all my heart He has already healed you. All we need to do is walk it out in faith."

After the early-morning prayer meeting, I stopped by the church office to check my mail slot before heading home. It was stuffed with mail, just as our mailbox at home. I deeply appreciated all the wonderful get-well cards from my friends. I even appreciated the letters saying, "If this is your time to die, I'm praying you'll die peacefully." (Thank God, I received only three of these, although Jackie hinted there were more that she fielded and kept me from seeing.) But what I cherished most were those genuine words of prophecy God was giving to people on my behalf. I knew that love, as much as I needed it, would not heal the cancer. Thus, when the prophetic word came, I embraced it.

In the back of my mail slot was a small note from Audree Evans. Audree's husband, Hugh, and his son Hugh Jr. had been attending the early-morning prayer meetings.

It was thirty minutes before the church office opened for business, and the building was silent. I sat in the chair of church secretary Phyllis Smith and read quietly. Audree had been in the service the Sunday before when Jackie and I had prayed for the sick in spite of my own weakness and discomfort. She had written this word for me on Monday, July 9, and dropped it by the office the next day. It was in the form of a short story.

> There was a man of God who received word that the King wanted him to come to his throne room for an audience. Now it was common knowledge that the King would only receive people in his throne room who wore white. This great man of God saw that his robe was stained (soiled), so he called his friends and fellow men of God to come help him cleanse his white robe. They gathered together by the hundreds, the thousands, to assist this beloved man. However, as they moved about the river bank, the ground became soft and muddy. They slipped and slid, and soon all their robes were stained and soiled.
>
> The man of God was very upset at first. He needed their help, but they had more problems than he did. Forgetting his own robe, he began helping others wash their robes.

Just before time to appear before the King, there was a knock at his door, and a package containing the whitest, brightest robe was delivered to the man of God. Along with the robe came this message:

"My subjects were unclean until the day you assembled at the river and, in spite of your own problem, sought to help them. Because of your love for my people, I give you this new robe.

"P.S. I've cancelled our meeting. You didn't know it, but we met at the river. I was one of the commoners you helped to cleanse."

I sat for a long time, going back over the various messages that had come through the mail. Finally I came to a note from Inez Thompson, our seniors' pastor and my friend for more than twenty-five years. She told me about the time she had been diagnosed with cancer. Her message was about faith.

God is in control, Jamie, and His word to us is we are to praise Him in all things. We are not to look on the circumstances; we are to stand on His Word, which says we are healed by the stripes of Jesus. No matter what appears to be happening — we are to praise Him.

Yes, there is an enemy, Jamie, and we are to stand firm against him. But as a church we are also to recognize the mighty power of God, remember the enemy has been defeated and walk in that victory. Refuse to give to the devil precious time that should be used in praise. Let's just brand him for who he is, a defeated foe, and move on in victory with our Lord Jesus Christ. We are victorious. You are healed. Let us proclaim it.

I found myself talking back to her letter.

"Inez, I believe all you've written. But it's all theoretical. How can I proclaim myself healed unless I believe it in fact? All my life I have held to intellectual honesty. How can I say a thing is — unless I believe it is? I know what the Bible says. I know if I talk poverty, I'll have it. I know if I say I'm dying, I'll die. Yet I do not believe there is any formula I can repeat which will guarantee my healing. Simply saying I am healed will not heal me."

My mind flashed back to my grievous experiences with the wives of two dear friends. Bill Sanders's wife, Martha, had died of cancer. Bill, a former Southern Baptist like me, was pastor of Tulsa Christian Fellowship and a longtime friend. Martha Sanders loved Jesus and believed with all her heart that He wanted her healed. Yet she died of cancer.

Then Chuck Farah's wife, Joanne, was struck with cancer also. Chuck was not only Bill Sanders's co-pastor at Tulsa Christian Fellowship but was professor of biblical theology at Oral Roberts University. My first trip to the Sinai had been with Chuck and Joanne. She was a great faith person. The world's most famous faith-healers had prayed for her — yet she died. I remembered being with her just two days before she died. Chuck had turned his entire house into a nursing home for his wife. We sat and talked of heaven. She was so frail and weak. She knew she was dying. To have stood at that time and proclaimed her healing would have been ridiculous. There just wasn't anything left to heal. The only conclusion I was able to draw was the one Kathryn Kuhlman used to say: "For the Christian, death is the greatest healing." Yet I could not say it was God's will for Martha Sanders and Joanne Farah to die from cancer.

I was confused.

Suddenly I was praying. "There are just too many unanswered questions, God. I want to believe. I want this faith for myself. I know faith is a gift of the Holy Spirit and it is right for me to ask for it. But it is still not mine. I only believe it in theory — not in practice. O God, help my unbelief!"

I left the church office and went back home. Within an hour my brother John called from Birmingham. "Two of our top radiologists and a urologist looked at your scans yesterday afternoon," he said. "Our pathology department also looked at the slides. They confirm the diagnosis from Melbourne. It's definitely renal cell carcinoma and has spread to your lymph glands. They don't think the kidney is operable."

Before I could ask any questions he continued. "Dr. Johnson called last night. Twice."

"Twice?"

John chuckled. "He's something else. The first time he called to ask what our people had determined from the scans. He then said he had some ideas and that he would get back in touch with me. Thirty minutes later he called again. It seems he had just read a paper on cancer therapy published by a Dr. David Swanson.

"David Swanson is a professor of urology at the M.D. Anderson Cancer Center in Houston, part of the University of Texas Medical School. It is one of the world's finest cancer clinics. He is one of their top surgeons. Dr. Johnson called Dr. Swanson, told him of your situation and then called me back to ask what I thought. The chief of medical service at M.D. Anderson used to belong to our church here in Birmingham. So this morning I called him, then talked to Dr. Swanson. I've made an appointment for you next Wednesday at 7:15 A.M. I have the phone numbers for you to call to make the arrangements."

There it was. Just like that. Not even a "Why don't you think it over?" Someone else was now running my life. A doctor I had never met had done a late-night investigation, and my brother had made an appointment for me in a strange city in a strange hospital. These were things I had always taken care of. Now I was out of control. Yet somehow I knew God was the One pulling the strings behind the stage. Is this what faith was? Letting go and letting God?

That afternoon a special envelope arrived. This one came from friends in Utah from the Order of Aaron. This group of former Mormons had formed a commune in the desert, and they felt a special call to serve the Lord with music. Their symphony orchestra was one of the finest in the West.

Many letters filled their envelope. One letter, from Doug and Karma Childs, had special meaning to me. Doug had included a poem written by his sister, Carol Trost. It was titled "Faith."

Faith's blossom is not plucked in pleasant field,
    Not so; it groweth on the craggy height
Where cruel thorns will rend before they yield,
    And oft the peaceful vale is lost from sight.
Faith does not bloom where placid rivers flow,
    'Neath gentle sun, or mild summer shower;
Lo, on storm-blasted mountain see it grow,
    And you must brave the storm to pluck the flower!
Yet with what joy your heart will overflow
    When you, with bloodied fleet, triumphant stand
Upon the summit where faith's flowers grow,
    And hold the sacred blossom in your hand!

That night my brother Clay called from Pennsylvania. He had just gotten home following an evening Bible study.

"I saw a bumper sticker this afternoon," he said, "and thought of you. It said: 'Alone. Unarmed. Trusting God.' " He laughed.

"Is that faith?" I asked. "I'm having to redefine everything I ever believed. I've done pretty well with some of it, but I'm having a real struggle with faith."

"Don't be so uptight," Clay said gently. "Just remember: Faith isn't believing *in* God. Faith is believing God."

I knew I had my answer.

SIXTEEN

THE LEAVES ARE GREEN, BUT THE ROOT IS CURSED

BE STRONG IN THE LORD AND IN THE POWER OF HIS might."

I knew I should have recognized it as a Scripture verse, but in that early-morning time when my brain was still foggy, I was having trouble placing it. (Later I remembered it as the opening verse from Ephesians 6:10-18 that Jackie and I were quoting daily as we "put on the whole armor of God.") It had come that Friday morning, as all the other words that week, as a whisper — waking me to the new day.

I lay quietly on my back, my eyes closed. I had come to expect these whispered words upon waking. This time I felt there was more to come. I spoke out loud, paraphrasing young Samuel in Eli's temple. "Is there anything else, Lord? Speak, for Thy servant is listening."

For the first time since the whispers began, He spoke again. Jackie was awake beside me. She had heard me speaking but did not hear His reply. Yet it was as clear to me as if she had whispered it herself.

"Cooperate with Me, and I will heal you."

I felt a wonderful surge of elation.

"He said if I cooperated with Him, He would heal me," I told her.

She propped up on one elbow, looking down at me in the gray darkness of early morning. A full moon in the low western sky was shining through the pine trees. Its light filtered through the window onto her face. In a few moments the moon would disappear, and the sun would cast its rays from the east.

"Cooperate. That's the same word He used eight years ago when He told you He would give you another fifty years of life," she said.

"I didn't do a very good job back then," I said. "This time He has a piece of clay totally yielded to the Potter's hand."

"Don't be proud of your humility," she warned gently.

Driving to the morning prayer meeting, I struggled with something else. God had not said I was healed. He had said He *would* heal me if I cooperated with Him. Like all of God's promises, it was in the subjunctive mood. If I would then He would. It was in the future tense — yet to come.

By the time I got to the church the elation had been replaced with fear. Jon was riding with me, but I paid little attention to what he was saying. He was talking about Robin and the children; the dog was pregnant again; we needed more chlorine in the swimming pool; he and Paul Boutin had finally gotten a price estimate on pouring a full-sized half-court in the pasture, meaning we wouldn't have to keep playing on that odd-sized court behind the garage.

What difference did it make? If I was going to die, I wouldn't be there to play basketball anyway. Sure, God had said He would heal me, but not unless I cooperated with Him — and I just didn't have enough faith to make that work.

The prayer meeting was a daze. I walked around the inside of the building trying to pray. All I could think of was that God had said He was going to heal me, but it still wasn't mine. The promise was out there in the future. Still unattainable.

As the prayer service drew to a close, Ben Slaughter, a businessman and sometimes church soloist, came to the platform. "I think we're all supposed to lay hands on Jamie. It's time to declare him healed in the name of Jesus."

The men surged to the front. I came to the platform and lay, face down, behind the pulpit — the position I had found myself in almost every morning that week. The men filed past me, touching, praying. Some paused longer than others. Some were weeping. Others were shouting. These were not the same men who had started the week. Something had happened in them. They were a different breed. Their repentance had been real, and faith had taken root. Now I was praying they would impart it to me also.

Back home I called Hanna Shepherd, my travel agent. It had been two weeks since that Saturday morning when I told her to cancel all my summer travel. I made reservations to fly to Houston on Tuesday afternoon. My appointment was on Wednesday.

I hung up and sat staring at the phone. Houston. I had attended conferences there. I had changed planes at the airport dozens of times. I had spent two days at the Johnson Space Center with Congressman Bill Nelson researching his book. But it was one of the few major cities in America where I had never spoken. I had no close friends there — pastors I felt I could call to help me. Sure, I knew Charles and Frances Hunter, but not well enough to ask for practical help — like how to find a hotel near the medical center or how to get to the hotel from the airport.

I also knew John Osteen, the pastor of the huge Lakewood Church. John had preached the night I had received the Holy Spirit back in 1968 in Washington, D.C. Across the years we had called each other occasionally. Jackie and I had read Dodie's book twice since we'd received it the week before. But I didn't feel I could call John either. "John, this is Jamie. I'm arriving Tuesday afternoon at Houston Intercontinental, and I'm scared to death. Will you come hold my hand?"

Yet sitting there that morning I felt compelled to call him. I felt foolish, but I looked up his name in my Rolodex file, found his home number and dialed it. His answering machine answered the phone. I started to hang up, then thought I should at least leave a message, letting him know I was coming to town so he could pray for me. I had just started to speak when I heard his Texas twang overriding the answering machine tape.

"Jamie! I'm here. Hang on until the machine cuts off."

Moments later he was on the line. "Dodie and I have been praying for you. All the people at Lakewood are praying for you."

Without waiting to hear why I was calling, he began to preach faith to me. All I could do was sit at the desk, the phone rooted to my ear, and listen. He was speaking directly to my problem of unbelief, quoting Scripture nonstop. Finally I broke in.

"John, God spoke to me this morning."

"What did He say?"

"He said, 'Cooperate with Me, and I will heal you.' "

"That's wonderful! Why don't you start praising the Lord?"

"No, you don't understand. He didn't say I *was* healed. He said He *would* heal me. Future tense."

"I know you're a writer, and you deal with tenses. But, remember, with God there is no past tense, no future tense. God did not tell Moses His name was 'I

135

was.' Nor did He tell him His name was 'I will be.' God's name is 'I AM.' God is always in the present tense. If He said He *would* do a thing, then that means it's already done. He's already signed the contract. It's done, Jamie, not only because He said it to you, but because He has said it in His Word — and His Word does not lie."

He was excited. Almost shouting. I could hear him inhaling as he picked up the theme of faith once more.

"You need to ask God to give you a date and a time when you can say for sure: healing is mine. Just as you have a birthday, you need a healing day. I am praying that this day, July 13, will be that day."

Although I never did get around to telling John why I called, his words started a fire in my heart. I knew he was right. Now all I needed to do was appropriate it. Make it mine.

I walked with Jackie to the mailbox at the end of the driveway. I could tell, day by day, that my energy level was dropping. Whatever it was in my upper abdomen seemed to be slowly suffocating me. Yet none of the doctors had found anything in that area. Maybe it was my diseased kidney pressing against the other organs in my body. Perhaps it was the lymph glands. Just as Jackie had heard that she should feed me and keep my weight up, I knew I needed to exercise to keep my muscles in shape. But exercise was now limited to walking. Anything else seemed to cause almost instant exhaustion.

In the mail that morning was a handwritten letter from Tom Winfield, one of the employees at Strang Communications. I tore open the envelope and read it as Jackie and I sat on the low parapet on the side of our driveway entrance. The week before, I had rewritten my Last Word column for the July issue of *Charisma* — the one Steve Strang had asked me to write on "the future." I had described my situation and told my readers about the cancer diagnosis. I had closed it saying I was submitted to whatever future God had for me. I had faxed the column to the home office in Lake Mary, Florida. Steve had duplicated the column for all the employees to see before it went into print. Tom had read it and reacted:

> I read your column, and the closing line bothers me: "Our times are in His hands." There must be no doubt about God's intent, Jamie. Jesus healed because "God was with him" (Acts 10:38). The intent of Jesus Christ is the same now as it was then.
>
> You need to read *Healed of Cancer* by Dodie Osteen. When it was over, without a single medical treatment, she said, "The Word of God set me free, and today it keeps me free." She made her stand on the written Word. Given only a few weeks to live, she fought for her life.

She got into the healing scriptures. She would not leave the house before she spent an hour or two praying these scriptures to God. She did not die, and in eighteen months every trace of cancer had left her body.

Many prayed for Dodie, but the symptoms persisted. One night, in bed, the Lord spoke to her heart. He said, "Now it's just between you and Me." She made some critical decisions. One: I don't want to die. My husband needs me, my church needs me, and my children need me. Two: I am going to fight. I know God does not want me to have this cancer.

So she began her personal fight to save her life. She took her stand on the scripture "By his stripes I am healed." She fed her faith and overcame demonic opposition. She cast down fears and imaginations by daily intense sessions in the Word — turning to those scriptures that applied to her. She held her position of faith until it was over.

My prayer for you is: "O Lord, strengthen him to stand on Your Word."

I was thoroughly chastised. First John Osteen. Now Tom Winfield — quoting John's wife to me. When we got back to the house I sat down at the kitchen table and opened my Bible to Acts 10:38 — the verse Tom had mentioned in his letter. It was from Peter's sermon at the house of the Roman centurion Cornelius. I read it out loud while Jackie juiced a bunch of carrots for my daily glass of fresh carrot juice.

"…[Jesus] went around doing good and healing all who were under the power of the devil, because God was with him."

Jackie was standing at the sink cutting celery to go in the juice.

"Calvary!" she said.

"What?"

"Calvary!" she repeated. "Everything stops and starts at Calvary. Sickness stops there. Healing starts there. Jesus really did pay it all."

Words to those wonderful old hymns I had memorized as a boy in the Baptist church flooded my mind. Hymns about the cross, about Calvary, about the blood of Jesus.

Years I spent in vanity and pride,
   Caring not my Lord was crucified,
Knowing not it was for me He died
   On Calvary.

Mercy there was great, and grace was free;
   Pardon there was multiplied to me;
There my burdened soul found liberty,
   At Calvary

                — William R. Newell

My eyes flooded with tears. I got up and walked around the counter to where Jackie was standing at the sink. I put my arms around her waist. She had her hands in the sink, fingers covered with celery strings. I put my moist face against her neck and held her tight. I whispered the words of another hymn:

Jesus paid it all, All to him I owe;
Sin had left a crimson stain, He washed it white as snow.

She nuzzled me with the side of her head. "God is not going to let you die. He is just going to draw you closer and closer to Himself. He has something special for you, something only you can do. That's why He's going to keep you here. But He can't use you as you've been. What He's doing to you now is changing you into His likeness — so you will love the things He loves and hate the things He hates. Then He will use you in a mighty way, but only for His glory."

She rinsed her hands, wiped them on a towel and turned to face me. "He not only wants you to stand on His Word for your healing, but He also wants you to fall in love with Jesus again the way you did that night on that island in Scroon Lake when you gave your heart to Him."

How easily I remembered what I had so easily forgotten. It was the summer between my junior and senior years in college. I had been a BMOC — Big Man on Campus — at Mercer University. Jackie, wearing my engagement ring, had joined me there my sophomore year. I was in love with her and in love with myself. President of the student government, cadet colonel of the ROTC unit, president of my ATO Greek letter fraternity — I was enjoying life to the fullest. But I also knew there was a call of God on my life, a call I was struggling against.

That summer Jackie and I spent a week at Jack Wyrtzen's Word of Life Camp in New York. Several years earlier Jackie had given her life to Christ at a youth revival in Vero Beach. I, even though active in Christian organizations, was still grappling with the intensely personal aspect of commitment.

The closing night of the week-long Bible camp there was a campfire service on the shore of the lake. Gil Dodds, an Olympic-class athlete who at the time held the world's record for the indoor mile, was speaking. Gil was a soft-spoken, committed Christian.

Jackie and I pulled away from the throng of young people who had grouped around the fire. We walked back up the hill and reclined on the grass looking down at the fire, listening as Gil gave an invitation for all those wishing to commit their lives to Jesus to come forward. Nearly everyone, it seemed, got up and stood around the fire.

The group of young people moved on down the shore of the lake, singing softly. Jackie and I were left alone on the dark hillside. It was there God spoke to me about Jesus.

"Look at the sparks from the campfire," I thought I heard Him say. "That's the way you are. You will ascend high and burn brightly. But soon you will be nothing but a cinder and fall to earth.

"Or," He continued softly, speaking to my heart, "you can become like one of My stars."

Lying on my back, I looked up. High above the dancing sparks of the campfire were the glittering stars in the night sky. A verse I had learned as a boy ran through my mind: "Those who are wise will shine like the brightness of the heavens, and those who lead many to righteousness, like the stars for ever and ever" (Dan. 12:3).

I turned to Jackie and took her hand. "I am giving my life to Jesus," I said simply. "I will follow Him wherever He leads." I was crying, but not ashamed. I was in love with the Master.

Now, as the Holy Spirit had restored my love for Jackie, He had also restored it for Jesus as well. We stood for long moments in the kitchen — the three of us — holding each other.

Eventually I pulled away and walked back to my study. It was time for me to start writing what the Bible said rather than resigning to the prognosis of the doctors. I sat down at the word processor, slipped my Last Word disk into the slot and pulled the July column up on the screen. There was still time, I knew, to do a last-minute rewrite. I reread it. Tom Winfield was right. Instead of closing it with a ringing affirmation of faith, I had let it fizzle into a whimper of resignation. What kind of help would that be to my readers — many of whom were in similar crises?

I erased the last two paragraphs, then started to write.

"Either the Bible is true, or we should shut down all churches, curse God and die."

I grew bolder as the little green words materialized on the monitor in front of me. Why not just say it. Let it all hang out. Live or die on the Word of God. After all, in eternity, that's all that's going to stand anyway.

"Jackie and I have decided to stake our lives on His Word, believing in faith: 'I shall not die, but live, and declare the works of the Lord' (Ps. 118:17, KJV)."

I closed the file, then punched the print key. I attached a note to the typesetter that I had rewritten the last two paragraphs and ran it through the fax machine. Somehow, just writing it and sending it off meant something. I had not just said it; I had now taken a stand on it.

By midafternoon I was feeling punk. The house was quiet. I lay on the sofa in the den, staring at the wall that was decorated with plaques from all my book jackets.

"What arrogance!" I said to Jackie.

"What do you mean?"

"See all these book-jacket plaques hanging up here? It's just more evidence of my ego. It's time to rip all that stuff off the wall."

"Stop it!" she said sternly. "You've run yourself down enough. All you see is the wrong you've done. You've forgotten all the good things God has done through you — and those books are part of it. You need a few reminders, a few memorials to remind you — and the children — of the grace of God in your life. You can pull down all those spears and arrows you brought back from the Amazon if you want, but the book jackets stay."

"Even when I try to be humble I fail," I muttered.

"You're not feeling well," she said. "Let's look at one of these videotapes Oral Roberts sent us from the Charismatic Bible Ministries convention three weeks ago."

"I really don't think I can take someone shouting at me about faith," I said. "My gut hurts."

"Let's listen to Oral's closing sermon," she said. "He won't shout at you. And if he does, you can turn him off."

She popped the videotape into the VCR and lay down on the other sofa to watch with me. I was only half listening but knew I should be interested.

The musicians sang for a few moments. Then Oral was on camera, retelling the story of how Jesus healed Peter's mother-in-law. It was classic Oral Roberts — a simple Bible sermon with five or six points taken directly from the Scripture. I was half-dozing, picking up only phrases here and there, when I heard Oral say: "If Jesus says you're healed, you are! Get up! Everybody get up and say, 'I'm healed!' " Suddenly I was awake. Wide awake!

The tape, of course, was almost a month old — and he was speaking to an audience on the ORU campus. But that afternoon the word was meant for me.

I came off the sofa shouting, "I'm healed!" Jackie leaped out of her chair at the same time, shouting, "Hallelujah!" For the next thirty minutes we walked through the house shouting thanks to God and proclaiming my healing — based on the promises of the Bible.

Fortunately, no one else was home at the time, nor did anyone knock on the door. But it would have made no difference. When you're dying and you're talking to your God, you don't care who's puzzled or offended by your behavior.

That night we had dinner with Gene and Jane Berrey. Jane, a nurse, met us at the door. I grabbed her, hugged her tightly and whispered in her ear, "I'm healed!"

I heard her gasp. She pushed back and looked me in the face. "How do you know?"

"God told me this afternoon. He said it was done at Calvary. This afternoon I decided to accept what He has done for me. That means I'm healed."

She broke into tears and grabbed me again, hugging me. Then we all started acting crazy again.

Outwardly nothing had changed. The cancer was still in my body. But as the fig tree cursed by Jesus remained flush with leaves but was dead from its roots, I knew I was healed even though nothing had changed in my body. I didn't know what God was going to do, but for the first time I believed He was going to do something good.

Jamie and Jackie's children: Bruce Buckingham, Robin Moore, Bonnie Ranzino, Tim Buckingham, Sandy Smith

The Buckingham clan: Jamie and Jackie with their children, children's spouses and grandchildren

SEVENTEEN

ALIVE AGAIN

I WOKE EARLY SATURDAY MORNING. I LAY SILENTLY. Waiting. Waiting for God to speak as He had each morning of the week. There was nothing. I knew I could make up something, but that would not suffice. Each morning He had whispered to my heart just as I was waking. This morning He was silent.

I thought: "And on the seventh day God rested."

I arose early anyway. We had a meeting of the church board of directors scheduled for 8:00. None of the men had said anything to me, but I knew there were a lot of anxious questions. What would happen to the church if I were to die? Who would take over? What were my wishes? Would the church fold up?

There had been a surge in both attendance and finances during the first two weeks of July — normally our slowest month of the year. But was this merely temporary? A lot of people who had drifted away and were attending other churches had started coming back. Were they coming out of curiosity? Out of support for me? Or had God spoken to them, and they were responding with genuineness?

The board, which was the legal entity of the church, needed answers — and assurance.

I sat at the end of the conference table and looked around me. These were people who knew my spirit and would die for me. They were my loyal, longtime friends. I looked on them as my extended family. I loved them all.

I started the meeting by giving them a frank evaluation of my health and my spiritual pilgrimage. I told them of the appointment in Houston. I no longer doubted God's intention; I just feared His processes — including having to go to Houston. They listened intently, then interrupted the meeting to gather around me and pray.

The group was somber but deeply committed in mood. We discussed a few matters of business, then it was time to elect officers. For the first time in several years we had a vacancy. Jim Bauman, our former church administrator, had long served as vice president of the board. The previous year Jim had left the church staff to go back into business full-time. Feeling he could not give the office of vice president the proper attention, he had resigned. That morning the men elected my good friend and next-door neighbor, Brooks Watson, to replace him. I left the meeting feeling a burden had been lifted off my shoulders.

That afternoon the family gathered for a barbecue. Tim, our family chef, had mixed his usual outstanding barbecue sauce. The little children splashed in the pool while the food was cooking. Then we gathered in the picnic pavilion to eat. It was a fun time, and no mention was made of my "situation." That was good.

After we had eaten I stayed outside for a while, playing with the grandchildren. Buddy Tipton, pastor at Central Assembly in Vero Beach, had showed up the night before with a bright yellow canoe in the back of his truck. He knew I had been wanting one to replace my old canoe, which had finally rotted out. He had found this one in Vero Beach and brought it up as a gift. One day, I promised myself, I was going to make that canoe-camping trip I had wanted to make ever since I was in college. I had often talked about it with Gene Berrey, an old canoeist also. We wanted to take our sons along, put the canoe in at Okmulgee River at Macon, Georgia, and paddle all the way downstream to Savannah on the coast — camping on the sandbars and paddling through the Okeefeenokee Swamp. Buddy's gift brought that dream just one step closer. I needed things which gave me hope for the future, something to plan for.

The grandchildren, excited about the canoe, wanted me to take them out on the little lake in the pasture. We paddled until they got tired, then I went inside. Their parents had arranged for baby-sitters to take care of them so the adults could gather to pray.

Inside I sat with my five children and their families. We talked a lot about healing, about miracles, about their expectations for the future. The barbecue feast had been a celebration of what God had done that we didn't yet see, but believed. I realized all of them were walking in a high degree of faith. They simply refused to let Satan have victory in this. Then we spent about thirty minutes praying. First they laid hands on me. Bruce, the eldest son, anointed me with oil. My girls hugged my legs and feet and prayed through their tears — as Mary had done at Bethany when she anointed the feet of Jesus.

Jackie and I had to leave for a few minutes. We had promised the folks at the Emmaus Road Community, just a mile down the road, that we would join them briefly that evening. The little community was meeting to pray for me. They wanted me there in person. We promised the kids we would be back within half an hour.

The Emmaus Road Community met in Del and Jean Likens's house. Nearly all were members of the Tabernacle. Years before, after we moved onto Hield Road in what was then rural Palm Bay, several families from the Tab had gotten together and bought twenty acres of property a mile west of us. They divided it into one-acre lots and ran a community road down the middle. Over the past several years a handful of "non-Tab" families had bought vacant lots and moved in. They were part of the neighborhood — but not part of the community. I wondered just how long any community could last.

I looked around the Likens's living room. It was filled with old friends. Del had just retired as a school teacher, but Jean continued on with her nursing.

Al and Saundra Reed, Jim and Charlene Bauman — both families had been part of the church staff and our lives for years.

Joe and Clair Eauclair lived across the street from the Reeds. Clair played violin in our church orchestra.

I had met Reg and Lily Fife — both from England — in the early 1970s when he was working as a publisher for Norman Grubb's Christian Literature Crusade. When they retired, they had joined us in Melbourne. The Tab had literally built their house for them.

Doug and Gloria Armstrong sat quietly to one side. A year before I had conducted the funeral for Gloria's twenty-year-old son.

Richard and Mary Ann Levy were taking care of Mary Ann's father, who was dying of cancer. Richard was an officer with the Melbourne Police Department, and Mary Ann had a quiet prophetic ministry.

Mel Honeycutt, a retired Air Force colonel, hugged me when I came in. Mel and Linda had raised their children in their two-story house at the end of the road. Now all but one were grown. Like the rest, they had been part of the Tabernacle for many years.

Del served communion — just as we had when the community first formed.

Then they asked us to sit in the center of the room in two chairs — just as we had prayed for others so many times across the years. It was a sweet time with old friends.

"We're anointing you with oil," Del said, "not to die — but to live. You go back to your family. We're going to stay on for a while and pray."

Back at the house the television was on. It was the first time it had been on in two weeks. I felt a small surge of anger at its raucous intervention. I remembered Jesus' words to His sleeping disciples in the Garden of Gethsemane when He withdrew to pray. "Could you not watch with me one hour?" Then I realized that just because Jackie and I were moving in one spiritual realm, we shouldn't expect the rest of the family to do the same.

"Hey, Dad, come on in," Bruce shouted from the den. "You can't read the Bible all the time. You need to be part of the human race."

He was right. My pendulum had swung so far into heaven I was in danger of being no earthly good.

Reluctantly, I went into the den. Bruce, Tim and Jerry, Sandy's husband, were sprawled out on the floor. The others were lounging in chairs. They were watching an old Three Stooges movie, laughing uproariously.

"Watch him! He's getting ready to do it again!" Just about that time one of the stooges would whack the other one with a frying pan. Bruce was laughing so hard he was shedding tears. Tim was pounding on the floor with his fists.

Suddenly I was in it with them. How long had it been since I'd laughed like that? My stomach was hurting, but I couldn't stop. I remembered reading how Norman Cousins, former editor of *The Saturday Review*, had laughed himself to health following his cancer attack. Well, my health was coming from God, not from my laughter, but because He had healed me I was free to laugh. It felt good. Cleansing.

The movie was finally over, and I sat weak, laughed out, in my chair. I thought of the picture of Hook's *Laughing Jesus* that we had put it in the kitchen. It had been a gift from Jack Taylor, pastor of Anchor Church in Fort Worth, Texas. Jack had said we needed to laugh at the devil. Well, we hadn't laughed at the devil that evening — but we had enjoyed life. It felt good to be part of the land of the living again.

146

EIGHTEEN

SUNDAY III

I SAT THROUGH MOST OF THE SINGING DURING THE worship period. Part of it was to conserve my strength. The rest was to conserve my emotions. It seemed that every song worship leader Michael Thompson had chosen applied to me. On several occasions I had to fight back the tears as we sang of God's greatness.

My preaching that morning was simple. After giving an update on the events of the week, including my plans to travel to Houston on Tuesday, I told about how Jackie and I had watched the tape by Oral Roberts and claimed healing. Then Satan had attacked my faith. Following is a brief digest of my message.

My Sermon

I knew the miracle was mine. I knew the healing was mine. Then, in the midst of all that praise, a thought came into my mind like a dart.

"You're going to destroy this church. If you get up and tell people you are healed, they are going to get all excited. They will say, 'That's wonderful!' Then you are going to die, and this church is going to scatter in a thousand different directions. There will be a ripple effect around the world as people's faith is shattered.

"Not only that, you are going to destroy your family. Your children are going to hear you say you are healed, and hope will spring up inside of them. They are going to believe what you are saying about God. Then you are going to die of cancer — right in front of them. Soon. And they will lose faith and turn from God."

A final thought came: "Why don't you just go ahead and die peacefully. Other Christians do that. Why do you want to fight — knowing everyone loses the battle against cancer? Just die easy. Make it easy on yourself, easy on the church, easy on your family."

But this time I knew where those thoughts came from. "Satan," I said out loud, "I rebuke you in the name of Jesus."

Faith is believing in an invisible God. It's believing an invisible God does things we don't see, but they are done just the same. Many of you are struggling as I have been — battling impossible odds. But our God is God of the impossible who calls things that are not as though they were.

I'm careful about what I'm about to say. But this Word is all I have. If this Bible is not true, we can disband this church right now. We can say, "Folks, we're going to close the doors. Don't come back. We're going to sell the building to the city for a recreation building. All this church stuff is foolishness. All this giving of our money, singing songs and praising God is crazy. Forget about church. Forget about God. Eat, drink and be merry, for tomorrow you die."

I can no longer play church games. I've got to stand on this Word. I've got to live it out. If the Bible says God is Healer — He is Healer. Otherwise the Bible is a lie, and I'm a fool to believe any of it.

Faith is believing God. And God has revealed Himself through this Bible. This morning I take that stand. On the basis of this Word I am healed. I will not die, but live and declare His works.

I am not walking in some kind of illusion. This is not denial. This is reality. I do not believe God wants to take me home using cancer. He's got better methods. He can take me like Elijah, in a whirlwind and a chariot of fire. He can take me like Isaac, who lived a full life, blessed his sons, pulled the covers over his feet and went to be with his fathers. He can take me like Enoch, who "walked with God and was not because God took him." He can even take me like Samson, going out in a blaze of glory.

I told my children last night, after they finished praying for me, that I was ready to go right then. I'm surrounded by my family. I've lived a full life. Why not now? But I know God has more,

Just returned from Mount Sinai, Moses spoke to the perplexed people at the base of the mountain: "Now what I am commanding you today is not too difficult for you or beyond your reach. It is not up in heaven, so that you have to ask, 'Who will ascend into heaven to get it and proclaim it to us so we may obey it?' Nor is it beyond the sea, so that you have to ask, 'Who will cross the sea to get it and proclaim it to us so we may obey it?' No, the word is very near you; it is in your mouth and in your heart so you may obey it" (Deut. 30:11-14).

In other words: act on the Word. Obey it. Boldly state that you will believe it.

"See," Moses continued, "I set before you today life and prosperity, death and destruction. For I command you today to love the Lord your God, to walk in his ways, and to keep his commands, decrees and laws; then you will live and increase, and the Lord your God will bless you in the land you are entering to possess.

"But if your heart turns away and you are not obedient, and if you are drawn away to bow down to other gods and worship them, I declare to you this day that you will certainly be destroyed. You will not live long in the land you are crossing the Jordan to enter and possess.

"This day I call heaven and earth as witnesses against you that I have set before you life and death, blessings and curses. Now choose life, so that you and your children may live and that you may love the Lord your God, listen to his voice, and hold fast to him. For the Lord is your life, and he will give you many years in the land he swore to give to your fathers..." (Deut. 30:15-20).

I have heard his challenge: I choose life.

Walking out of the church building that morning, I realized the die was cast. Like Julius Caesar, I had crossed the Rubicon River and implicitly declared war. There was no turning back.

Michael Thompson called me that afternoon. "You may not remember, but I had scheduled Mike Williams, a black preacher from Joy Tabernacle in Houston, to preach next Sunday. But I don't think we need any guest preachers right now. The people need to hear you. I called him this week and asked him to cancel."

I had indeed forgotten about Michael Williams. Michael Thompson had met him at a children's education conference. He was greatly impressed with him and wanted him to come to Melbourne. I had met him once before and agreed our people needed to hear him speak.

"Do you have his phone number?" I asked. "I hate to cancel him, but you're right. I think I'll call him and just explain the circumstances."

"I've already called, and he understands. But I'll give you the number just the same. Maybe you'd like to call him after you get to Houston in case you need a friend."

I didn't wait. I called him right away.

Michael Williams's rich voice came through the phone: "I was just praying you would call. What time do you arrive on Tuesday? What airline? I'll meet you."

A great weight lifted. We would not be alone. I had a friend in Houston.

NINETEEN

ONE PERSON'S PRAYER
AVAILS MUCH

I WORKED IN MY STUDY ALL MORNING ON MONDAY. There were last-minute calls to the hospital in Houston; calls to secure reservations at the Marriott Hotel adjacent to the medical center; calls to Birmingham to make certain my medical records had been overnighted to Dr. Swanson; calls to Saundra at the church office to check on my insurance; calls to Don Williams to make certain all the last-minute staff problems had been solved. Then I spent the rest of the morning and early afternoon working on finals for *Ministries Today*.

Charles Green called that afternoon. Charles was pastor of Word of Faith Church in New Orleans, a large, independent church. His son, Michael, the minister of music, was one of our columnists for the magazine.

"Our entire church is praying for you," he said. "But as I was praying for you this morning I had a vision. I've never seen anything like this before, but it was so striking I knew I had to call you.

"In the vision I saw a large church congregation. The pastor had just come to the pulpit and told the people of your situation. He called them to prayer. As the people began to pray, I saw a tiny but brilliant stream of light — like a laser beam — coming from heaven. It came through the roof of the church and outlined one nondescript person sitting in that huge congregation.

"I asked the Lord what it meant. He said that it was imperative for many people to pray for Jamie. But it would not be the prayers of the many who would save you — it would be the prayers of one unknown person of faith that would break through to heaven. As far as I know it is someone who has never met you, but someone who loves you and is praying in great faith. And you will never know who that person is until you get to glory."

I was staggered by the vision. It confirmed letters I had received in the mail that morning — some from people I knew, some from folks I'd never met. Several had quoted James 5:16 (KJV), "The effectual fervent prayer of a righteous man availeth much." As Moses had interceded for the nation of Israel, so would the heart of God be opened to the prayers of one person who truly believed.

I thought about a letter from a young man in Kirkland, Washington, who was a new Christian and a member of Doug Murren's Eastside Church: "I heard you preach when you were out here in February," he wrote. "I had just become a Christian, and what you said meant much. Then last Sunday when Pastor Doug announced that you had cancer, I felt like I had been hit in the stomach. I went home and told my wife, and we both cried the rest of the day. I woke up during the night, crying and praying for you. Then I felt God say that I should fast for you. I've never fasted in my life, but yesterday I started fasting. It's tough, because I work outside and need food. But God has helped me, and He has assured me He would heal you if I did my part...."

That evening God reminded me one more time of the power of prayer. Just before we left for our home group meeting, I went into the kitchen to see if Jackie wanted me to carry anything out to the car. The phone rang.

"This is Dania Smoak."

My mind flashed back almost thirty years before when I had met Tom and Betsy Smoak, Dania's parents. Tom was flying planes in the jungles of Colombia for the Wycliffe Bible Translators. Jackie and I had loved their six children — including Dania, who was badly crippled.

"God told me to call you and pray for you," Dania said. And without any further remarks she began to pray. She prayed passionately, boldly, with great authority. I could only stand, phone to my ear, and listen as this young woman whom I had not seen in almost ten years bombarded the gates of hell, then came humbly before God's throne on my behalf. On two occasions during that fifteen-minute prayer the power of God was so strong I had to grip the back of the kitchen chair to keep from falling to the floor. She finally finished. I could hear her weeping on the other end of the line.

"I shall continue to pray until you are healed," she said. Then she was gone.

I sat down in the chair I had been holding onto. Jackie came in from the other room and stood behind me, her hands on my shoulders.

"I was listening on the extension," she said softly. "God answers prayer — especially prayers like that."

Then she said it again, words she repeated to me over and over during the ordeal: "You shall not die, but live and declare the works of the Lord."

On Tuesday morning Jackie and I left the house at 7:00 to attend the regular staff meeting. It was the first time she had ever sat in on a meeting unless the wives of the other pastors were present. I knew, however, that regardless of what might happen in the future I would never again try to conduct ministry apart from her. I also knew her presence in the staff meeting was confusing. The staff was a well-defined group. Each had his or her own job to do. Having Jackie in the room caused an awkward atmosphere. Everyone loved and respected her; they just were not sure what was going on. Was I getting ready to die and appoint Jackie pastor of the church? If I lived, would she be the co-pastor? Was she there to protect me, in my weakening condition, from any criticism the staff might throw at me?

Don Williams, our staff coordinator, was loving and understanding. He quickly found her a chair and placed it at the head of the conference table beside mine. I made a simple explanation to the staff.

"God has done something new in my life. After thirty-six years of marriage I feel welded to Jackie. I cannot imagine ever again being part of anything she cannot be a part of also. She is not here as co-pastor of the Tabernacle Church. She is here as my wife. But if you get me, you get her also. We are one. I want the same for each of you pastors. I know some of your wives work, and others have small children. But from now on the doors to these meetings will be open to all spouses. The leadership of this church will no longer be singular. From now on it will be plural."

I knew it was a foreign concept. But much was changing, not only in me, but in the church as well.

Jimmy Smith served communion then read a passage from a new book by Francis Frangipane called *The Three Battlegrounds*. The passage he selected was for me. Afterward he handed Jackie the book, suggesting she take it with her to Houston to read. We excused ourselves early. We had a busy day ahead.

As we got ready to go, Don Williams asked us to wait in the conference room for a moment. He then asked the staff — all of them — to meet him in the hall.

Moments later Don called for us. The staff had lined up on both sides of the hall all the way to the door leading out into the parking lot. They were standing with hands extended, fingers touching, forming an arch for us to walk under — like an arch of swords formed for a bride and groom at a West Point wedding.

We bowed our heads and, holding hands, walked slowly down that line of outstretched hands of blessing and healing. By the time we reached the door we were both in tears. Don was the last man in line. He kissed me on the cheek as we went through the door. His face was wet. We sat in the car praying for each staff member by name and for the protection of God on the church as we left for Texas.

On the way home we made one stop. One of the staff members had been visiting a retired pastor who had recently joined our church. He was recovering from cancer surgery and had requested to see us.

We didn't stay long. He had just returned from Tampa, where he had gone through exploratory surgery. The surgeon found cancer in and around his pancreas. They had simply stitched him back up and sent him home.

When we walked in he was sitting in a recliner dressed in pajamas and robe. His face was gray, much different from the robust color I remembered.

"I'm ready to go," he smiled. "I have served Jesus all of my life. I've preached about heaven for forty years. Now it's my time."

"But don't you believe God wants to heal you?" Jackie asked.

"That would be wonderful," he said. "I believe in healing. I've seen many people healed. At the same time I am not afraid to die."

We prayed for him, and he got up and slowly walked us to the door. "Look at me. I used to play tennis every day with men much younger. Now I can hardly walk. But God is good, and I love Him dearly."

In the car I sat with my head against the steering wheel.

"What's wrong?" Jackie asked.

"I think it was a mistake for me to go in there," I said. "I admire him for his courage and his love of Jesus. But there was a spirit there. A spirit of resignation. Now it's attacking me too. I don't want to be like that. I don't want to give up. I refuse to resign. I've got to fight this thing, not in my own strength, but in the power of His might. Pray for me."

Jackie prayed as we drove down the street, rebuking the spirit of resignation and calling for angels of encouragement to fill the car. By the time we pulled into the driveway I felt spiritual strength returning.

Back home, just before leaving for the airport in Orlando, the phone rang. It was Mary Derrington, a housewife and one of the children's workers in the

154

church. Mary was the one who had a vision concerning my daughter-in-law Michele just a few days before she was healed of multiple sclerosis in January.

"I know you are rushing to catch the plane to Houston," she apologized, "but I got up early this morning to pray for you. My husband was at the prayer meeting at the church. I was in the backyard just as the sun was coming up and suddenly had a vision. I saw the fingers of God go into your body. Then they withdrew. I was sure I would see them pulling the cancer out of your body. But there was nothing, just His fingers slipping into your side, then coming out again. Then I heard His voice, 'I killed that spider, and I'll pull down that web.' "

She paused. "I don't know what it means, but I knew I had to tell you."

Curry Vaughan was at the door. He had called earlier and volunteered to drive us to the airport in Orlando — an hour away. I told him of Mary's vision.

"I know what it means," he said. "God has killed the cancer in your kidney and is now pulling down the cancer's web in your lymph glands."

Then he grabbed me and shouted: "Hallelujah!"

"Early this morning," I told Curry, "God spoke to me again. It was one of those early-morning whispers I heard last week and had begun to believe I would never hear again."

"What did you hear?"

"He said, 'Walk out your healing.' "

Jackie grabbed my arm. "Well, the next step is Houston. Let's go."

Michael Williams was waiting for us when we stepped off the plane at Houston Intercontinental Airport. His big bear hug made me feel secure. Wanted. He drove us into the city, stayed with us while we checked into the Marriott, then came up to the room. His church, Joy Tabernacle, had sent a huge fruit basket which was waiting for us in the room.

"I need a pastor," I said.

He squeezed my arm. "Sit down. Talk to me."

"I'm not afraid of dying," I told him. "I've settled that. I don't believe it is my time to die, and I'm standing on God's Word that I was healed at Calvary. But I realize I'm walking on thin ice where it comes to my emotions. Yesterday I misplaced my billfold. I almost panicked looking for it. I was afraid I would burst into tears and fall in a heap on the floor. I didn't. But by the time I found it I realized just how close to the edge I am.

"Now I'm afraid of things I've always been able to handle. I don't know where the medical center is. I don't know how to get there. I feel like I did when I was a small child, sitting beside my daddy in the front seat of our old Ford Beechwagon. We would drive into a strange city at night in the rain. I would keep looking up at my daddy, wondering if he was afraid. As long as he knew where we were going, where we would spend the night, I was OK. I feel that way now. I just want to close my eyes, shut out all the strangeness and snuggle up against my Father. That's the reason I'm glad you're here. You represent God."

I saw tears come into his eyes, and he slipped out of his chair, knelt before me where I was sitting on the side of the bed and put his arms around my waist.

"You're gonna be OK, buddy."

"I believe that too," I said. "But you have no idea how good it sounds just to hear you say it."

Downstairs in the lobby Michael offered to drive us around to the entrance of the M.D. Anderson Center, just a few blocks away. However, he had already pointed the way — less than a ten-minute walk from the hotel — and my confidence had returned. He left, but not before inviting me to preach at his church the following night.

I accepted. I knew my only legitimate plea to God for leaving me here was to declare His works. I looked forward to this unique opportunity.

"I'll pick you up here at the hotel," he said. "Our folks just want to love up on you."

As soon as Michael left, Jackie and I walked out into the hot Texas evening. It was after six. The sun was just setting, but the temperature still hovered in the high nineties.

"Do you remember what it was like when we first moved to Texas?" she asked.

We had been married four weeks. We packed everything we owned in the back of our 1952 two-door Chevrolet and drove from Vero Beach to Fort Hood, where my brother Clay, then an army captain, was stationed. That night was the hottest night we had ever spent in our lives. Clay and Clara had no air-conditioning, their little army quarters cooled only by an evaporator fan. We slept with wet washcloths over our faces so we could breathe. The next day we had gotten up and driven to Fort Worth, where we were going to stay with my mother's cousins until we found an apartment and I had enrolled at Southwestern Baptist Theological Seminary.

We found a three-room apartment near the seminary, and I finally got a job working as a bus driver for the Fort Worth Transit Company. We lived in Fort Worth almost four years. Bruce was born there. I completed my theology degree and returned for an additional semester working toward a master's. I was ordained to the ministry at University Baptist Church. But despite all the wonderful memories of those first years of our married life, we could never think of Texas without remembering the summer heat.

We held hands as we crossed the street and wound our way through a back alley toward the tall, pink building that housed the M.D. Anderson Cancer Center. I didn't want to go to the front door, wishing to put it off as long as possible. I felt like a man who had been sentenced to prison but released by the judge on his own recognizance until the day he was to begin serving his time. Tomorrow I would report in, and the steel doors would clang shut behind me — maybe forever. I wanted to walk the streets of freedom as long as I could. But tomorrow would worry about itself. Each day has enough trouble of its own.

TWENTY

WAITING ROOM PRAYERS

THE TEXAS MEDICAL CENTER WAS ACTUALLY A conglomerate of many hospitals. The little chapel outside the clinic was part of the M.D. Anderson Cancer Center but was run by the Lutherans who owned and operated the hospital facility, known as the Lutheran Pavilion, next to the cancer center. The night before, we had walked by the chapel, a small, octagonal-shaped building set apart in a grassy area with a cross on top. I had wanted to rush in — but God was so real in my heart I didn't need to.

We prayed out loud as we made the ten-minute walk from the Marriott to the hospital. We were interceding for our intercessors, those back home we knew were praying for us at that moment.

"Today," I told Jackie, "we shall see people far worse off than we are. I pray God will protect our minds from despair and death. Let us walk today as Jesus among the suffering — bringing life to those who have no hope."

Our appointment at the front desk was for 7:15 A.M. It was a beautiful summer day. A cardinal swooped low then fluttered to a stop on the branch of a small tree near the bus stop. The shift had just changed in the hospitals, and white-robed technicians and nurses were hurrying home after spending the night with the sick and dying. We paused as a young man in a motorized wheelchair moved down the sidewalk in front of us. His twisted hand skillfully manipulated the knobs that directed his chair. He paused at a bump in the sidewalk. I started toward him to help, but realized he did not need me. Backing up, he sent the chair out into the grass, around the bump and on down the walk.

After checking in we sat in the lobby. Waiting. Holding hands. Praying softly. The man sitting in the chair beside me, an old cowboy, introduced himself.

"I'm from Muleshoe. Ever heard of Muleshoe?"

"My friend Jess Moody was born in Muleshoe," I said. "Actually he was born in Wedlock."

I couldn't help but smile as I thought of Jess, now pastor of a big Baptist church in California. Jess used to joke he was born in Muleshoe. Then he'd say, "Actually I was born just outside Muleshoe in Wedlock." Then he'd pause and say, "Well, actually I was born just outside of Wedlock."

"Yep, know where Wedlock is," the old cowboy said. "I got cancer of the prostate." He laughed. "Probably from riding too many horses. Been coming back and forth here for fifteen years."

Praise God for the survivors, I thought.

A young woman appeared. She introduced herself as Evelyn and took me to a small interview room. She asked questions. I told her I was a pastor. She said that, as a courtesy of the hospital, pastors were allowed to make a $250 deposit rather than the normal $500 deposit. I had forgotten places like that still existed. Praise God for Texas. She took my insurance information, gave me a folder with hospital information, then handed me a plastic card with my name and case number. "This will be your number as long as you are a patient at M.D. Anderson."

She asked me if I had any church ID. A calling card with my name and title would do. She needed proof I was a pastor. I was embarrassed because I had nothing to prove who I was. I was in a new world where no one knew me. I realized I had been living a secluded life in a circle of people who knew all about me. Now I was outside of that circle in a vast world of people and institutions foreign to me.

"When you get home, just mail me your card," Evelyn said with a smile.

It was the words "When you get home" that flooded me with relief — and hope. I was not going into prison or to the death chamber. I would one day go home. How sweet that sounded.

An hour later we were sitting in the waiting room of Station 42. A sign over the desk said Urology Department. Evelyn had brought us here, along with two other couples from downstairs who were also coming for consultation. One of them, a couple about our age, was from Muscle Shoals, Alabama. I talked with the husband on the elevator. He had just been diagnosed with prostate cancer. The other couple, in their late sixties, were too frightened to talk. When I asked the man what they were here for, he simply gestured at his wife, his face grim, his eyes blinking rapidly.

We found two seats together in the crowded waiting area. Most of the people in the room were middle-aged couples. There were two young Hispanic girls sitting in the corner. I didn't know if they were waiting on someone else or if one of them was here for treatment. Everyone looked relatively healthy. But I noticed when some of them got up to use the rest room, they moved slowly.

An elderly man came down the hall pushing a lunch cart. He stopped, and several employees appeared from various rooms and bought sandwiches and drinks. None of those waiting in the lounge seemed interested in food.

The receptionist at the desk had given us a long form to fill out. It was a survey, conducted by the center's research department, on my dietary and life-style habits. Jackie and I filled it out together. Some of the questions were:

- Do you drink coffee? How much?
- Do you use artificial sweetener? How much?
- Do you take the skin off the chicken before you eat it?
- Do you smoke? How much? How long?
- Do you drink alcoholic beverages? How much? How long?
- Do you or have you worked around asbestos?

The form was twelve pages long. We tried to answer all the questions as honestly as we could. I realized I didn't have any bad habits. We didn't eat pork, always took the skin off our chicken and had stopped eating fried foods. Why, then, did I have cancer? Maybe it was the red maraschino cherries I used to eat on top of ice cream sodas. I sighed. My answers would not help me, but they might help someone else down the road.

I returned the form to the desk. Jackie and I sat, holding hands, praying. We prayed especially for the people in the room. We started with the couple from Muscle Shoals. He had said he was a member of the Church of Christ when I told him I was a pastor. Then we prayed for the older, frightened couple. The nurse had already come and beckoned them into one of the back rooms. We went around the room. Some new people had arrived. Everyone seemed frightened. No one was smiling. Our hearts were broken for the deep suffering we sensed in the room.

I turned to Jackie.

"I'm so sorry you have to be here, going through this."

She gripped my hand tightly with both of hers. Her eyes filled with tears. "You don't understand. This is all I've ever wanted in life. To sit quietly with you. Holding your hand. Praying with you for others. I don't care what it took to get us to this place; this has been my only desire in life. And now God has given it to me."

Two hours later the nurse called my name. The time had gone by swiftly as Jackie had read to me from the book by Francis Frangipane. Jackie followed me back into a small examining room. The nurse weighed me, took my temperature and blood pressure, then asked me to strip down to my shorts and wait. Moments later a young doctor came in, introduced himself as Dr. Giannakis, Dr. Swanson's teaching fellow. With Jackie sitting in a chair beside the examining table, he listened to my heart and lungs, poked and probed my abdomen, felt my groin and neck for lumps, then did a rectal exam.

"You seem to be in good shape," he grinned. "Dr. Swanson will be in shortly. He's just getting out of surgery and needs to change."

Ten minutes later a slim, fortyish, bearded man appeared. I remembered how my brother John said he was one of the top surgeons at the cancer center. His handshake displayed unusual strength. "You seem to have a lot of doctors who are interested in you," he smiled. "I've talked to Dr. Johnson, Dr. Weldon and your brother."

"Not just doctors," Jackie interjected. "He's got people all over the world praying for him — and for you."

David Swanson smiled again but made no comment. He reached into a big brown envelope and brought out several large X-ray negatives. "These are the CT scans from Melbourne that your brother sent me from Birmingham. Our people here concur with their diagnosis, but we need to run more tests. I've ordered another chest X ray. Also I've scheduled you for an angiogram and a venacavagram tomorrow morning. It will take all day so don't schedule anything else. I want to see you again Friday morning for consultation. We'll determine then what we need to do. Get a good night's sleep and report downstairs at the desk at 8:00 A.M."

Michael Williams and his wife, Donna, picked us up at 6:30 P.M. in the hotel lobby to take me to the church to preach. "I hope you won't be uncomfortable with us," he said. "We're an all-black church with a few token whites."

We weren't disappointed. In fact, apart from my own church, I had never felt as loved and wanted as I felt at Joy Tabernacle that night. As I preached, I wound up declaring my healing to them, just as I had declared it to my home church.

They shouted in agreement and at the close of the service asked us to stand at the front. They wanted to pray for my healing.

I knew what was going to happen. About twenty of the congregation came forward to stand around us as the prayers started. The moment Michael's hand touched my head, my knees went weak. The power of God surging through me was soft, gentle, but overwhelming. I felt myself drifting backward, as if in a dream. Hands caught me and eased me down to the floor. I was vaguely aware that Jackie was beside me on the floor. The noise seemed to increase, but I was not there. I felt as if I were being transported above the little church building to a heavenly throne room where angels were joining in chorus with the prayers of the saints below. Gradually it subsided, and strong arms pulled me back to my feet. I had never been hugged by so many, nor had I ever kissed so many faces — men and women — as I did that night. God had given me a spiritual family in Houston.

The next day was spent in a fog. It began as God woke me with a whispered message: "I will walk with you."

It seemed there was more, but I was too confused to remember it.

We reported to the patient routing center, and I was taken to a treatment room. The two exams, the angiogram and venacavagram, were handled with careful precision. A technician numbed a small area in my right groin, made a tiny incision and inserted a needle into the big artery leading from my heart. Pictures were made with the CT scan machine as the needle threaded its way upward, injecting dye. When that was finished a second incision was made less than an inch from the first. Another wire was inserted, this one in the big vein — the inferior vena cava — that ran to the heart. More pictures, more dye. Then the gurney was wheeled to a small recovery area, and I was told to lie perfectly still on my back for seven hours.

"You must not move your right leg," the nurse said. "If the incision breaks open and you hemorrhage, you're in big trouble."

I looked up. She had a small dove pinned on her nurse's uniform.

"You're a Christian?" I asked.

She smiled. "I belong to a charismatic Episcopal church near here."

"You're not a nurse," I smiled. "You're an angel."

She squeezed my arm. "I know who you are. I'll be praying for you." Then she added, "I'll see if I can find your wife. She's not supposed to come back here, but I'll let her in if she stays only three minutes at a time."

Moments later I felt Jackie's hands on my shoulders. I could not see her, and the little room was too narrow for her to get in beside me without tripping over the IV tubes in my arm.

163

"You've got a visitor," she said.

I heard Rick Parker's deep voice. "Hi, friend."

"What are you doing here?" I almost shouted. "I just saw you Saturday morning in the director's meeting."

Rick was a businessman and a member of the Tabernacle's board of directors. He and Charlotte had recently moved to Fort Lauderdale, but he maintained his membership at the Tab because they planned on moving back within the year.

"I came out to see you," he said.

Jackie's excited voice was next. "He said he heard you say at the board meeting that you would be out here alone, that you didn't know anyone in Houston. So he flew out last night, found out where we were and met me here in the hospital. He took me out to lunch and wants to sit with me while you're here in recovery."

I was deeply touched. God had given me a church away from home to love me, an angel-nurse to watch over me and now a representative from home who paid his own way just to fly out and sit with my wife.

Sometime during the afternoon the nurse wheeled another gurney into the tight space next to mine.

"I'm sorry," the Episcopalian angel said. "We're out of space, and I need to squeeze her in here with you for a few moments until we can find another cubicle."

I glanced over. Lying beside me was a nice-looking woman about ten years younger than I. I thought she looked like a younger Catherine Marshall.

"You had the same thing I had?" I asked.

"I had an angiogram," she said. "I'm scheduled for brain surgery tomorrow."

We talked softly. Her name was Nancy. Her husband was on the administrative staff of the hospital. She was a Southern Baptist. She knew several Baptist pastors that I knew. She was frightened.

"My head hurts," she said.

"Do you mind if I pray for you?"

"Do you think that will help?" she asked.

"I'm betting my life on it," I smiled.

"It's OK with me," she said.

"Let me hold your hand," I said. I reached through the bars of my gurney, careful so the IV tube didn't get tangled, and took her hand. She gripped mine and squeezed it.

"Jesus, please take away Nancy's pain."

I heard her sigh. "It's gone," she said softly. Then she repeated it. "It's gone."

Moments later the angel-nurse returned. "I've found a place for your neighbor," she laughed. "I hope I didn't inconvenience you."

I closed my eyes and dozed off. I was at peace.

TWENTY-ONE

PULLING DOWN
THE SPIDER'S WEB

THE PHONE RANG TWICE BEFORE WE LEFT THE
hotel room Friday morning to walk over to the clinic again. Our daughter Sandy
called at 7:20 A.M. I had been awake off and on during the night. My lower
back ached slightly. Real? Imagined? The hurt was there, just enough to keep
reminding me of that ugly, deformed organ in my body. I had been awake for
about forty-five minutes, praying.

Sandy said Phyllis Smith, our church secretary, had called. Someone had
called the church office. Len LeSourd had suffered a stroke. I felt as if I had
been hit in the stomach. Jackie and I had just been praying for Len and Sandy.
What kind of out-of-control madness was this? I wanted to cry. Jackie was crying.

At the same time there was a strange sense of comfort. If Satan had struck
Len, at least I wasn't alone in this. Maybe this wasn't punishment for my sinful
life, but a genuine attack from Satan.

I dialed Len's number at Evergreen Farm in Virginia. Maybe someone there
could give me information.

"Jamie," Len laughed. "Word of my death is greatly exaggerated. I was in

165

Denver and went out to play tennis. I had a dizzy spell. The doctor said a seventy-year-old man should not play tennis in ninety-degree weather at an altitude of five thousand."

I fell back on the bed, laughing. God was still in control. But just as quick as the joy had come, that old feeling of despair reappeared. "You're in this by yourself. You're all alone. This is God's wrath for your selfish life-style. You will suffer long then die. It's not that this is too big for God, but God's not going to intervene in your case. You're on your own in the land of the dying."

The phone rang again. It was Jack Taylor from Fort Worth.

"I got up early," he said. "God has called Barbara and me into this battle with you. What is happening to you is mirrored in what is happening to the body of Christ. There are some gaping and dangerous holes in our practical theology that only suffering and pain will correct. You are right to claim healing, but the timing must be left to a sovereign God who operates in grace for our greatest good and His greatest glory."

I motioned for Jackie to hand me a pad and pen. I needed to start making notes.

"About ten minutes ago," Jack continued, "I felt I received a personal message from God concerning you. I've written it down and want to read it to you.

"Jamie, one of the enemy's chief tormentors is inside your body. I don't know its name, but it is in alien territory. You are not its captive. You are its captor. Investigate it thoroughly. When a piece of enemy equipment falls into our hands we do not throw it away. We take it apart piece by piece, discerning how it fits together, how it operates.

"Cancer is an enemy, having the very nature of the devil. It benefits in growth at the expense of healthy cells. Dismantle it; investigate it; analyze it — but don't bow to it. As doctors treat the physical with the best of medical science, you are to treat this with joy, laughter and praise. Torment the tormentor, curse the curse, speak the name of Jesus — His blood, the Word, your testimony.

"We are going to discover how to take authority over our attackers. Angels hate cancer and stand by to give chase at the bidding of God."

I asked him to repeat it again so I could check my notes. He said not to worry, he would send me what he had written. Then he added:

"A friend called yesterday to share something he had heard Pop Hagin [Kenneth Hagin Sr.] say about choosing to live. I believe many folks are going home because their theology has no options for supernatural extension of life. In essence God is saying, 'I don't mind your coming home; but if you choose to live another twenty, thirty or fifty years, it's yours.'

"I had two things happen to me while I was in the hospital in Little Rock following the bypass surgery. Both times I was given the choice to live or die. Once was in the cath lab during the angioplasty procedure and again one morning between the hours of 12:00 midnight and 3:00 A.M. I didn't take the choices lightly because I knew the easier thing would be to go home with Jesus. I have pondered what I might have decided had I known what would transpire during the next month of my life. Nevertheless, here I am."

He closed by adding, "God has entrusted you with a mighty stewardship, so He must have known you could be trusted."

I hung up and suddenly realized what was happening.

Every time Satan spoke, God spoke louder. It was up to me, I realized, which voice I chose to listen to.

Dr. David Swanson met us in the same examining room where we had seen him two days before. He had several sets of X rays in his hand. We chatted for a few minutes, then he held up the X rays: "Do you want to see these?"

"What are they?"

"Results from yesterday's tests."

I deliberately had not looked at any of the other scans. I was afraid if I actually saw what was going on inside my body my faith would be affected. But then I thought of Jack's call just an hour earlier: "Cancer is an enemy...dismantle it; investigate it; analyze it."

"Sure!"

Swanson grinned. "I thought you would."

He popped the X rays on the glass light box on the wall. With his pencil he traced the path of the wire. "Your arteries are clear. But you have a golf-ball-sized tumor in or on your renal vein coming from your kidney and up into the inferior vena cava — the big vein that runs from your lower extremities into your heart. It's hard to tell if it is outside the vein pressing in or actually a blockage inside the vein. That's what's been causing all that pressure under your rib cage."

"Could it break loose and move up into my heart?"

He shrugged. "It's unlikely, but it could."

He flipped the CT scans from Melbourne up on the light box. He pointed out my kidney. "It's at least three times the size of your good kidney and is rooted to the sides of your abdomen." Then he took his pencil and traced other shadows I could not understand. "These are your lymph glands. The only thing that would cause them to look this way is infection or cancer. It's hard to tell for sure on an X ray, but as large as these are, the most likely explanation is that the renal cell carcinoma has spread into the lymph system."

I stood looking. For the first time I had seen the enemy face-to-face. Before, he was merely rattling his sabers in the dark. Now he had stepped into the light,

167

and I could see him. Ugly. Deadly.

"What are the options?" I asked, my mouth dry.

He pulled the X rays down and shook his head. "I wish it were that simple. It's treatable, but the treatment is radical, toxic, and the results vary from person to person.

"Surgery is a possibility, followed by treatment. Or we can give you treatment followed by surgery. I've discussed this with my colleagues, and we are divided. Some recommend surgery. We might be able to remove the kidney but might not get it all — and surely cannot get all the lymph glands. Then your body would have to recover before we could administer treatment. It's a 'bloody' operation.

"On the other hand we can begin treatment now." He mentioned a number of chemical options: interferon, interleukin 2, TNF, interferon alpha plus other biological therapies. These, he said, could be administered by Dr. McClure in Melbourne, but a treatment plan would have to be established at some major teaching hospital first. Regular chemotherapy probably wouldn't work, he said.

"If he were your brother," Jackie interjected, "or your father, what would you recommend?"

He scratched his beard. "It's difficult for a surgeon to say this, but I would recommend treatment first, followed by surgery — if there is a response. Frankly, it's a tough call. I'm usually able to say to a patient, 'Do this or else.' But in your case I can't say that.

"There is no one right answer, and there are pros and cons to each approach. I think the biggest disadvantage of initial surgery is that I have strong doubts that a tumor this size can be cured by surgery alone. Then, once it's removed, if you give biological therapy, you have no way to tell if it is working.

"By giving biological therapy first, you can see if the tumor and lymph nodes are shrinking in response to treatment. If they are, then it is more rational to try such a big operation.

"Go home and think about it and let me know."

There was other talk as he rattled off various statistics including something called the "morbidity rate" for this kind of operation. My mind was reeling. I had tried to jot down a few notes, but the words were coming too fast and were too unfamiliar. He had shown a genuine personal interest, however. I was not just another case. I was a brother human being who was under attack from a deadly enemy. He wanted to help. Not only that, but all the resources of the M.D. Anderson Cancer Center were at my disposal. For that I was deeply grateful.

Walking out of the hospital to return to the hotel, I turned to Jackie: "Do you realize what he did? He put it right back in the hands of God. I want to stop by the room, call Michele and ask her to call Dr. McClure and set up an appointment for next Wednesday."

"Why do you want to wait? Today is Friday. Why not see him Monday?"

"I want to give God a chance to reveal His plan. Dr. Swanson said to go home and think about it. I translate that to mean go home and pray about it. If God doesn't show us something by Wednesday, we'll start treatment. I dread it, but if that is His plan, I'll drink the bitter cup."

She nodded and squeezed my hand.

We had planned on catching a cab to the airport, but there was a call waiting for us when we returned to the hotel room. It was from Curry Juneau, pastor of the Quail Valley Church in Missouri City, a suburb of Houston. I had known of Curry, a former professional football player, through Jack Taylor. I returned his call. He wanted to take us to the airport. We agreed. It was to be the beginning of another wonderful Houston friendship.

Sitting in the President's Club of Continental Airlines at the airport, Jackie asked me how I felt. The sadness had returned. I was trying to evaluate.

"Yesterday I spent all day among the sick, struggling to stay alive. Today I'm sitting here watching all these healthy people around me, as they sip their mixed drinks, caring nothing about suffering humanity. It's almost like I'm grieving for something I've lost, or am losing."

"What have you lost?"

"My health — maybe my life. All my life I've taken it for granted. I could walk and run, hike canyons and climb mountains, fly airplanes and ride bicycles, play ball and romp on the floor with the little people. Now my wonderful health is about to disappear, perhaps forever. Having cancer is not like breaking an arm while playing ball or falling off a bicycle and busting your knee. Things like that heal in a few weeks. Now I'm faced with the possibility of never being healthy again. This afternoon, walking back over from the clinic to the hotel, I thought of how simple it would be just to step in front of one of those big buses on Houston Street. No suffering...."

"Stop it," Jackie snapped. "You're listening to the devil. God's Word says He wants you healthy. Didn't He tell you, 'Cooperate with Me, and I'll heal you'? To be healed means a return to health. Expect it. Plan for it."

I squeezed her hand tightly. How I loved her!

On the plane she held my hand while reading passages from Oswald Chambers's *My Utmost for His Highest* and more from *The Three Battlegrounds*.

She paused, then closed the book. "God wants to deal with you about your exaggerations," she said. "You need to stop putting yourself down. You've been telling people that you never prayed before now. That you never read your Bible. That's not true. You may not have done it to the extent you're doing it now, but you were not an evil man. Don't downgrade God by saying all those books you've written, all those sermons you've preached, all those people you've helped didn't count. When you downgrade yourself you insult God."

I was listening. Intently. As long as we had been married Jackie had been preaching to me. I had accused her of trying to make me over in her image. As a result I had simply tuned her out. But this time it wasn't Jackie speaking. It was God speaking through her, and I was a soft sponge, eagerly soaking up all that was being said.

"People exaggerate to draw attention to themselves. You must draw attention to God. When you exaggerate your disobedience, you draw attention to self and don't glorify God."

I closed my eyes and put my head back on the seat. I could feel the presence of God in the plane as Jackie spoke.

"Who you are in Christ has not changed one bit. You are still a man of God. You are still called. Chosen. You may feel useless to the church because you've slowed down. But you are still ordained of God. Do not listen to the devil's lies, for he is telling you otherwise. He's constantly giving you death thoughts. God gives life thoughts. Choose life. Remember who you are!"

I realized that for the first time since all this began I was writing down what she was saying. Something had returned. I wanted to make notes. I wanted to write. I looked at the little yellow pad in my lap, filled with notes.

"It feels good to write," I said.

"I'm so glad."

"But from now on I will write with you. I'll write, but you will be my companion in writing. I shall run all my thoughts by you. If this ever becomes a book, it will be our book — not mine. In the past I've locked you out of this process. I never wanted you inside me. I would literally hide from you what I had written until it was finished. I let you see it only for approval and affirmation — not for contribution. Now we will do this, as we are to do all things from now on, together."

I rested for a while. Later I felt her hand on mine. She had her Bible in her lap, open to Mark 12:28-31. She was reading softly:

"One of the teachers of the law came and heard them debating. Noticing that Jesus had given them a good answer, he asked him, 'Of all the commandments, which is the most important?'

" 'The most important one,' answered Jesus, 'is this: "Hear, O Israel, the Lord our God, the Lord is one. Love the Lord your God with all your heart and with all your soul and with all your mind and with all your strength." The second is this: "Love your neighbor as yourself." There is no commandment greater than these.' "

She closed the Bible and once again reached over and took my hand. "You must first love God with all your heart, strength and soul. Only then can you love your neighbor. You've majored in loving your neighbor — women as well as men. Some of these relationships have been solid and healthy. Some have been twisted. Because your love for God was weak, some of these relationships in the past have gotten you in trouble. Your mercy toward others, which is a gift from God, was not tempered with a fear of God. Now God is calling you to Himself. Alone. When you fear God, you will never again fear what man — or demons — can do to you."

Steve Strang met us at the Orlando airport. He had called before we left for Houston and was insistent that he meet us and drive us home. He wanted to carry our suitcases.

"See," he laughed, "I even took off my tie in respect for you."

It was an in-house joke. All the men in the publishing house wore ties — just as Steve did. But when I drove over for editorial meetings I always dressed casually. Steve usually made a big to-do about it, but he respected me enough to let me dress the way I wanted. Now, by showing up in public tieless (which, I joked, was for him like showing up barefoot), he was letting me know just how much he really loved me. It was good to see him. I loved and respected him deeply and was moved by his desire to serve us by driving us to our home on the east coast, more than an hour away.

That evening I called my brother John and gave him the report from Houston. Dr. Swanson had promised to write him, but I didn't want to wait. I told him Dr. Swanson's choices.

"Whatever you do, don't put it off too long," John insisted. "Don't wait until Christmas. Don't even wait until next month."

"No, we'll reach some decision this week. If we don't hear from God by Wednesday, I'm ready to submit myself to treatment — whatever that means."

I didn't tell John, but I dreaded "whatever that means." I had seen people who were undergoing chemical treatment for cancer. Some, I was convinced, had died from the treatment rather than from the cancer. I didn't mind things like hair loss, but the other side effects could be hideous. I dreaded the thought of going from relative health to total debilitation — with no guarantee of healing.

During the night I woke feeling panic. I wanted to call Dr. Swanson. "Take this wretched thing out of my body, even if I die in the process."

But a deeper reasoning said, Give God a chance. Don't fear treatment. Claim

Mark 16:18: "When they drink deadly poison, it will not hurt them at all." No harm can come near you if you are following God's direction. The miracle has already been done. The spider is dead. The growth has stopped. Now let God pull down the web any way He wants.

TWENTY-TWO

A LAND WITH NO TRAILS

SATURDAY MORNING I CALLED MY MOTHER IN THE nursing home in Vero Beach. Sandy said she had called every day while we were in Houston, asking how I was.

The phone rang almost twenty times before she answered.

I told her what had taken place in Houston and that we were going to wait until Wednesday to make a decision. Her voice was weak when she replied.

"What are you going to do?"

"We don't know, Mother. We're trusting God to give us direction. We are seeking Him at every intersection."

"Oh, no," she responded, her voice much stronger. "You are walking in a land that has no trails. There are no intersections, for no one has ever walked this way before. You must seek God with every step."

I hung up the phone. Suddenly I was back in the Sinai. We had been traveling for three days and finally cut inland from the Gulf of Suez toward the Mountain of God, known by the Arabs as Jebel Musa. Our open-sided desert vehicle, with ten men inside, was bouncing along in the ruts of other vehicles which had gone before. We were making our way through a wide wadi, a dried waterway. Late that afternoon one of the men beside me in the back of the dusty truck pointed at the steep side of a mountain on the opposite side of the riverbed. He had spotted an abandoned turquoise mine, thousands of years old.

"There may be turquoise bits still in the mine," I said.

"Let's explore," the others suggested.

I asked the Israeli driver to stop and explained our group wanted to climb the mountain and explore the mines. I asked if he would leave the sandy ruts, made months before, and drive us closer to the base of the mountain.

He scowled, wrinkled his brow and shook his head. "No way!" he grunted. "Too dangerous."

During an earlier Sinai campaign, he told us, the Israelis had placed explosive land mines in that particular wadi, knowing it was the only way the Egyptians could escape through the rugged territory. They had kept a chart of the mine placements, intending to return and retrieve them after the war. However, at the height of the campaign, one of those rare cloudbursts flooded the Sinai. Torrents of rain fell on the desert mountains, pouring off the sides of the treeless cliffs and roaring through the ancient riverbed in destructive mayhem on its way to the Gulf of Suez. The land mines had been swept out of the ground and scattered all over the broad wadi. Some had exploded in the force of the water, but others were still buried in the trackless sand. Experienced drivers knew the only safe place was in the ruts made by a previous truck or military tank. In fact, just a few months before an Israeli colonel had been killed when his jeep ran over one of those old land mines and it exploded.

Our driver said the only way we could explore the turquoise mines would be to dismount from the truck and walk across the sand. But he — and his truck — would remain behind.

"Just walk lightly," he added, slouching down in the seat and pulling his cap over his eyes for a nap. "I'll be waiting here — if you get back."

Obviously I returned from my exploring safely. But I had done so only by realizing I was walking in a land that had no trails. Every step was critical.

I thought of all the possibilities before us. Not only were we faced with the two given by Dr. Swanson, but there were scores of others being presented by people — many whom we loved and respected — who were urging us to go this way or that.

Some had called and written about various therapies. Some said I should take coffee enemas and a diet of freshly ground liver juice. Several were recommending even more radical diets.

We had already changed our diet. Jackie had bought a juicer and was feeding me fresh carrot juice twice a day. I was on a heavy vitamin dosage. We had stopped eating red meat and were limiting ourselves primarily to beans, brown rice, grains and fruits. No more sugar. No more diet drinks. No more coffee — from either end.

But this didn't satisfy many of the diet enthusiasts. Some said we should not eat apples and bananas at the same time. Others said we should not eat fruit at all since it produced sugar, which cancer thrived on. Still others said we should eat only various Oriental foods.

We were familiar with many of the diets. Across the years people we knew who had cancer had gotten involved with radical diets. All but one had died.

More radical was the possibility of refusing all treatment. Does faith mean trusting God to heal us apart from medicine? I thought of Oral Roberts's word to me: "Cooperate with the doctors." This coming from the world's most famous faith healer.

Which way should we turn?

"Father, without Your direction we are doomed. One false step and I could step on a land mine and be destroyed. We shall move only as You direct, for this land has no trails."

Mickey Evans came by that afternoon. Of all the men I knew in the ministry, there was no one I respected more than Mickey. A rugged cowboy preacher from Indiantown, Florida, he had founded what I considered to be the best alcohol and drug rehabilitation camp in the nation. It was located in the gator-infested swamps between Indiantown and Okeechobee. Few men loved and knew God the Father the way Mickey did. His life was dedicated to the millions who made up what he called "the Fourth World" — those living in the shadowlands as society's castoffs.

When he came in our back door, he was crying. He hugged me and gave me a big bag of beef jerky. He knew how much I loved it from the hunting-camping trips we had taken together. I gratefully accepted it, knowing I would not eat it. We sat and talked "old times." Mickey had been the model for the leading character in the only novel I had ever written, *Jesus World*. I had apologized for having to kill him off before the end of the book. He had laughed and said he was honored to be killed in such a glorious manner. He had gone with me on two trips into the Sinai. We had flown together in his little airplane, hunted together, scrambled eggs and eaten fried gator tail together in the swamp. We had also prayed together. Mickey had come up several years earlier to officiate at Tim and Kathy's wedding in our front yard.

We prayed. Not long. Mickey just sat and cried, then got up and put his big arm around me, tears falling on his checkered cowboy shirt. Long ago he had discovered that real prayer is not words; it is a heart broken before God. His heart was broken for me, and I cried with him. We hugged, slapped each other on the back, and he was gone.

That night I told Jackie of Mickey's visit. She loved him as much as I did. I read to her what I had written down after he left.

"I surrender to You, Father, not to this disease. I give up to You. I do not give up to cancer.

"I shall resist the spirit of resignation, the calls to give up. I have given up to God, and He is a God who heals. It is Satan who binds, kills and destroys.

"From this time on I shall pray prayers of victory, not prayers of defeat."

We went to sleep listening to our old friend Terry Law reading healing scriptures from our tape player.

Jamie Buckingham at the Tabernacle, the church he pastors in Melbourne, Florida

TWENTY-THREE

SUNDAY IV

SUNDAY MORNING THE AUDITORIUM WAS PACKED for both services. I knew the people had been praying while we were in Houston. They were eager for a report. The following is a condensation of what Jackie and I said.

Jackie's Part

As soon as we got into our hotel room at the Marriott in Houston, I felt led to pray for the cleansing of the room. Mike Williams was still with us, and the three of us prayed that the Lord would remove any blackness that might be hovering in the room — for we did not know who had used the room before.

After Mike Williams left I took little pieces of paper and, while Jamie was in the bathroom, started writing down healing verses from the Bible. I stuck these on the mirror and around the room where we would see them. I felt it was important that we fortify ourselves with the Word of God.

I want you to know we are standing on the Word. Our eyes are on Jesus — on the Healer. We will listen to the doctors, but we're not going to take what they say as final. God is in control. He is a good God, and He wants to give only good things to His children. We are standing in that hope, we are standing on the Word, and we want you to stand there also.

You'll never know how much we love you all and how your prayers have sustained us. We know we got through this last week because of your faithful prayers. God is going to bless you, and you are going to see changes in your own lives.

When we got home on Friday, I was a little down. My mother had just gotten out of the nursing home and was there with us. Sandy had moved in and was taking care of her, but she had to leave when we got home to take care of her family. So everything hit me at once, for all I wanted to do was be at Jamie's side and be in touch with God.

But that night we went to bed early. We've been sleeping really well because you have been praying for us. I woke up at 3:30 A.M. and didn't go back to sleep until daylight. I was praying for Jamie, trying to keep my mind off what the doctor had said and just focus in on God's promises. Then God spoke.

"You know all those little notes you put up in that room in Houston? I want you to remember that My Word does not return to Me void. I have heard every prayer you prayed. I'm making a record of all the prayers the people are sending up to the throne for Jamie. I'm recording every prayer prayed on his behalf. The answer is coming. I am healing him in My time. It is finished. It is done."

I praise God that He gives us those encouraging words as we go along. I want to encourage you: Please don't stop praying. The battle is not over. It is won, but it's not over.

When Jackie finished, I stood up and told the congregation about my mother's admonition to seek the Lord at every step when the land has no trails. I told them about all the changes in our lives during the past three weeks. This is the message I gave.

My Part

There is no map for any of us to follow with the exception of this: The Bible is the only chart we have. God will direct our path. He will walk behind us, whispering in our ear, "No, not that way. This is the way, walk you in it."

I remember seeing an old chart used by Christopher Columbus when he set sail from Spain, sailing westward into an unknown area. No one had ever charted beyond two hundred miles from shore. Columbus was setting sail believing he could reach an unknown destination by a route never traveled by others. It was a journey of faith.

I looked at the map, marked by latitudes and longitudes out to a certain point. Then the lines stopped. In the white space there were great clouds drawn on the map. Then the chartmaker had written: "Beyond this there be dragons."

How do you walk an uncharted path? You walk it with God's Word in your heart and your hand in God's hand.

Yes, there are dragons out there. But they cannot harm the child of God. They have no right to destroy a blood-washed child of the King.

I have but one ambition. I have but one plea to make to God. "If You will let me walk around heaven during the week, then I will return to Your people each week and tell them what You are like and what You are saying. That is my only desire for remaining on earth. If You don't want me to do that, then just take me home."

This week I have walked with Him, and He has told me to come before you this morning and say, "Regardless of your situation, put your hand in the hand of Jesus. He alone knows the way."

When I first became a Christian, my mother taught me a little song:

My Lord knows the way through the wilderness,
    All I have to do is follow.
My Lord knows the way through the wilderness,
    All I have to do is follow.
Strength for today
    Is mine all the way,
    And all that I need for tomorrow.
My Lord knows the way through the wilderness,
    All I have to do is follow.

TWENTY-FOUR

UNEXPECTED LOVE

O
N MONDAY MORNING THERE WAS A KNOCK AT THE front door. Jackie came back in my study where I was sitting, staring at a two-foot-high pile of unanswered mail.

"Someone special has come to see you."

"Everyone is special."

"These are special specials," she grinned.

I walked into the living room. There, seated on the couch, were three old chums from Vero Beach High School — class of 1950. I rarely saw them, but our relationships had started decades earlier. John Schumann Jr. and John Jewett had been part of a close group of friends who went through grammar and high school together, then had all gone to Mercer University together — a small school in Macon, Georgia. My third visitor, Larry Catron, had not gone to the university with us but had remained a friend across the years.

As a child, John Schumann was one of my closest friends. We went to the same kindergarten, played together after school — either at his house or at mine — and did lots of crazy stuff together in high school. In college we roomed together in the freshman dormitory.

Following graduation John had returned to Vero Beach and taken over the *Vero Beach Press Journal*, which his dad owned. For ten years I had written a weekly column for the editorial page until my other writing forced me to quit. Our deep friendship had continued, however, despite the fact we saw each other less than once a year.

I looked over at John Jewett. Towering above the rest of us, he had been a star basketball player in high school. After we got to Mercer, we were on the freshman basketball team together. John, nine inches taller than I, eventually became a starter. I never made it off the scrubs. After a stint in the banking business in Vero Beach, he had gone into business with the third man in the room, Larry Catron.

Larry had been one of the "fun" friends I had in high school. As with the others, our roots had been entwined years earlier. After high school he had stayed in Vero Beach working with his uncle. He now owned and operated a prosperous beer distributing business.

We sat — the four of us — for almost two hours: talking, reminiscing, laughing at old mistakes.

John Schumann reminisced about the time we took a war surplus life raft into the saltwater mangrove swamp beyond the golf course. As night came we got lost in the hundreds of little water trails through the mangrove trees. Then the raft started to deflate, and just when we thought all was lost a fish jumped into the raft and we jumped out — only to find the water was less than six inches deep. We waded out of the swamp, following the sound of my brother John (at that time called by his nickname, Laddie) honking the horn of Daddy's pickup truck.

John Jewett brought up the incident in the freshman dorm at Mercer when I had flushed John Schumann's shirt down the commode on the third floor and flooded all three floors of the dormitory. The entire freshman class had been "campused" for that incident because the guilty party had refused to stand up and confess.

Larry reminded me of the Friday night in the seventh grade when we had attended a high school football game. Afterward we had taken our girlfriends home — riding on the handlebars of our bikes.

When all the remembering was finished, they wanted to know about me. They had heard and were concerned. The three of them listened intently, as I shared what was going on in my life. It was the first time I had the opportunity to talk to my old friends about how my relationship with Jesus had developed. They sat, nodding their heads, understanding that I was walking out what I believed.

It was time for them to go. "If the prayers of a Presbyterian elder count," John Schumann said, "then I want you to know I am praying for you daily."

John Jewett just reached out and hugged me. My head came up to his shoulders. I felt his love.

Larry Catron grinned. "Do you think God hears the prayers of a guy who drinks bourbon and beer and smokes two packs a day?"

"You sound like the kind of fellow Jesus ran around with," I said, gripping his hand.

"I'm glad to hear that because I was going to run the risk and pray for you anyway."

I walked them out to the car.

I felt loved.

In the mail was a little note from ten-year-old Nick Jagos. Just one year earlier Nick had almost died of cancer. Our church had prayed a lot for him. I remembered him sitting in the services, his hair gone from the radical chemotherapy, so weak his parents had to help him walk in and out. Yet he had survived and was healed.

> Dear Jamie: I know how you feel. But if God can heal me, He can heal you. I think you are a great guy, and I really look up to you.
>
> My favorite verse is: "My son, pay attention to what I say; listen closely to my words. Do not let them out of your sight, keep them within your heart; for they are life to those who find them and health to a whole man's body" (Prov. 4:20-22). This really meant a lot to me.
>
> Your friend in Christ,
> Nick Jagos

I felt loved.

That afternoon I answered the doorbell. Standing on the front porch was an old friend, Bishop L.E. Weaver, pastor of the Greater Faith Temple Church of God in Christ. His wizened black face was glistening with tears.

"I've been on my face all morning praying for you," he said. "I tried to stay away, but the Lord kept directing me to come out here and see you. I need you. The church in Melbourne needs you. The kingdom of God needs you. I'm not going to let the devil take your life. He'll have to get me first."

I reached out and hugged him, then led him into the house. I had preached in his church. He had preached in ours. His choir had come on several occasions and sung for us. His son had played basketball with our church team. Now here he was, dressed in his three-piece suit with a gold fob chain hanging across his vest, standing in my living room weeping — and challenging Satan on my behalf.

"Pray for me," was all I could say.

I got down on the floor, on my face. He knelt beside me and began praying. Suddenly I was back in the old camp meetings I had attended as a boy in the North Carolina mountains where preachers prayed the way Abraham Lincoln said preachers ought to pray — as if they were fighting a swarm of bees.

His voice took on a musical tone, and I knew he was no longer kneeling beside me — he was in the throne room of heaven. As he prayed I could hear my dad's voice, quoting in dialect, the preacher's prayer of the great black poet James Weldon Johnson.

> And now, O Lord, this man of God,
> Who breaks the bread of life this morning —
> Shadow him in the hollow of thy hand,
> And keep him out of the gunshot of the devil.
> Take him, Lord — this morning —
> Wash him with hyssop inside and out,
> Hang him up and drain him dry of sin,
> Pin his ear to the wisdom-post,
> And make his words sledgehammers of truth —
> Beating on the iron heart of sin.
> Lord God, this morning —
> Put his eye to the telescope of eternity,
> And let him look upon the paper walls of time.
> Lord, turpentine his imagination,
> Put perpetual motion in his arms,
> Fill him full of the dynamite of thy power,
> Anoint him all over with the oil of thy salvation,
> And set his tongue on fire....[1]

The prayer was over. The bishop had grown silent. "Now you must pray for me," he said softly. "You see, I may have cancer also." Before I could rise he had dropped to the floor, face down on the carpet. I lay face down beside him, my arm around his shoulders, and began to pray. Then we were crying: two grown men — one black, the other white; one dressed in shorts and a T-shirt, the other dressed in a three-piece, pin-stripe suit — lying side by side on the floor, weeping and praying loudly in tongues.

When the praying subsided, we both turned over on our backs, blowing our noses and wiping our eyes. Looking over at each other, we started to laugh.

I felt loved.

After the bishop left, I walked back into my study. The mail had piled so high on my desk it had fallen off onto the floor. I could barely wade through it to get to my word processor. My church staff was waiting on me to write a vision statement for the church. Vision statement. I was desperately trying to find light to walk in today. How could I write a vision statement to light the future of an entire church? There was so much to do — especially at the church — and so little time.

I thought of Jack Taylor. Jack had been preaching in Little Rock, Arkansas, when he had his heart attack. He had been hospitalized for two months — almost dying on several occasions. In the middle of that, while he was still in the hospital with the incision in his chest reopened and draining, a couple of the leaders of the church he pastored in Fort Worth had turned mutinous. Some of his pastors and elders actually flew to Little Rock so he could conduct a church business meeting from his hospital bed.

"What did you learn from all that?" I had asked Jack.

"I learned," he laughed, "that despite what you are going through, despite what happens to you, life goes on with everyone else."

"Thank You, Father, for loyal pastors and leaders in my church," I prayed. "Thank You that no one is trying to take over while I'm in this battle. Thank You that they are instead in the battle with me. Yet Jack is right. Life goes on. I can't just spend all my time concerned with myself. I need to be working and planning for the future of this church. But I just can't...."

I heard Jackie's voice at the doorway. "There's someone in the living room to see you."

"Again? Who?"

"I've never seen him before. He said God sent him to pray for you."

I almost reluctantly got up and walked through the den and kitchen into the living room. A nice-looking fellow in his late twenties stood up. "Do you remember me?"

"I'm not sure."

"It's not important," he said. "I met you once in a meeting where you were speaking. I live in Texas and heard about your situation on a Christian radio station. Day before yesterday God told me to get in my car and drive to Melbourne to pray for you."

"You mean you drove all the way to Florida just to pray for me?"

"I'll probably stop by and see my folks in Alabama on the way home, but my primary reason is to pray for you. That's all."

"Then do it," I said.

I sat down beside him on the love seat. He reached over, put his hand on my back and prayed softly for about two minutes. He prayed that I would have peace to let God direct me step-by-step. He prayed I would have strength to release all my responsibilities and rest in the Father's love. He then thanked God for my total healing and was finished.

"I've done what God told me to do," he smiled.

"I feel so helpless. I don't even know your name. Can't we give you lodging for the night or something to eat?"

"No, I'll head north, spend the night on the road, then drive on to see my folks tomorrow." He hugged me. "God bless you!"

And he was gone.

I felt loved.

In the stack of mail was a letter from Angus Sargeant, a medical doctor in High Point, North Carolina. Angus, an old friend, had gone with me twice on camping trips into the Sinai. It had been several years since I had heard from him.

He called my diagnosis a "miracle."

"From what I know of your symptoms," he wrote, "I don't know of many medical doctors who would have ordered a CT scan. I certainly wouldn't have felt your symptoms were severe enough to go to that extent."

He also enclosed a list of almost 100 names from the High Point-Greensboro area. I knew most of them. He had called them all personally and received a promise from each that they would be praying for me daily until I was healed.

I felt loved.

That night, as on every Monday, our home group met — this time next door at the Watsons'. Jackie and I walked to the meeting — through our backyard, past Sandy's cottage, down the narrow path through palmettos and pines, past my "tree house" — my little ten-by-twelve-foot isolated writing studio built on poles five feet off the ground — then on past the remnants of the old pasture fence to the Watsons' house. At the close of the meeting Jackie and I lay on our faces on the floor of the living room. The other four couples were seated on the floor with the two of us stretched out between them. I thought, This is twice today I've been stretched out on the floor, face down.

They reached out and laid their hands on us. It was a quiet time. We waited, and I could hear their whispered prayers on our behalf. We remained that way for almost thirty minutes, sometimes praying out loud, sometimes silent. Finally there was a release.

"God has a path for you," Don Lees said. "He will reveal it day by day."

I felt loved.

TWENTY-FIVE

DAMN THE TORPEDOES

TUESDAY: THE DAY THAT EVERYTHING CHANGED.

Jackie went with me to the weekly church staff meeting. We had not planned on staying long. Jackie's mother was home alone and needed help getting out of bed. She was still weak from the hip operation. Plus, Ralph and Sylvia Johnson were to arrive sometime before noon. I had looked forward to meeting with Dr. Johnson ever since he first called me from St. Petersburg and then connected me up with Dr. Swanson at the cancer center in Houston. Jackie wanted to have lunch ready.

Following communion, Mary Stone, one of the receptionists, knocked gently on the door. "We just received a phone call from Bruce Stark," she said. "He said Pat's cancer operation went well, but the tests show the doctors could not get it all. She's going to need treatment. She's not handling it well."

Bruce Stark was an artist with a national reputation. His wife, Pat, worked on the reception desk in the church office. She had undergone surgery for ovarian cancer the day before in Lakeland. At first the doctor had told her he thought he had gotten all the cancer out. Now, apparently, the report had changed. Pat would have to go through treatment as well.

All our activity stopped. The room broke into prayer. It must have been this way, I thought, that morning when they prayed for me while I was having the kidney biopsy. After a while the intensity of the prayer time eased off. I stepped out of the room and across the hall to use the phone. Moments later I was talking to Pat at the Watson Clinic in Lakeland.

"The rest of the staff is still praying, but I wanted to call. Satan is overplaying his hand, Pat. First me. Now you. He's probably going to strike others also. But we shall stick together in faith. We shall stand on God's Word together. 'No weapon forged against you will prevail, and you will refute every tongue that accuses you' " (Is. 54:17a).

I could feel something happening in the heavenlies as we talked. When she had answered the phone, her voice was weak. As we talked, I could feel God's strength coming through the phone. I prayed for her and hung up.

Sitting at the vacant desk, I felt strong also. There is a certain strength that comes only when you reach out to others, touching them in your own time of need. I stared at the empty chair across the desk. I sensed the Father sitting there — smiling and nodding His head.

The mail had come to the house early. We picked it up at our big silver mailbox as we turned into the driveway. On top was a letter from Dr. Swanson in Houston — a copy of his diagnostic report to my brother John. Another copy had been sent to Dr. McClure, the local oncologist. I waited until we got back to the house. Then I sat down on the tile steps leading from the foyer into the breakfast nook. I opened the envelope, read the report slowly — then wished I had not read it at all. It was grim.

It confirmed the diagnosis of primary renal cell carcinoma. Dr. Swanson said the tumor in my kidney was pressing up my big vein toward my heart. The cancer had definitely spread to my lymph glands, maybe farther. Then he described my prognosis:

> After discussing his X rays with the radiologist and other members of our department, it is the consensus that this is a very advanced lesion.... It is highly unlikely to be cured by surgery alone. It would be my expectation that the chances of such a patient being tumor-free at an arbitrary period of time, such as three years from now, would be well under five percent and probably more reasonably one percent or two percent....
>
> There are no protocols [treatment plans] at this institution, and probably few, if any, in other institutions that would treat him following

removal of the primary tumor. This means that it would be necessary to wait until such time as measurable disease did manifest itself....

I heartily concur that the therapies of today should be withheld until there is measurable disease because of the significant morbidity associated with all treatments....

Although Mr. Buckingham's tumor is very large and has rather extensively involved regional lymph nodes, there is no measurable distant metastatic disease, and this does makes his situation a little more unique. I think the surgery would be technically difficult, but it is certainly 'doable' with an acceptable risk if he were to so choose....

Alternatively, I think there is something attractive about seeing if his tumor is responsive to any one given protocol....

I finished reading and turned to Jackie. "Well, there it is — in black and white. The best surgeons in the world can't figure out what to do. They just recommend I wait until it gets worse."

I laid the letter on the breakfast table.

"I don't want to read it," Jackie said.

I tried to pray, but the phone rang the moment I put my head in my hands. It was Oral Roberts.

"I'm up in the prayer tower here at ORU," he said in his familiar, raspy voice. "This is my day to fast and pray for all the requests that come in during the week. But this morning I have not been able to pray for anyone but you. I finally got up, took my finger and drew an outline of your shape on the wall. Then I laid my hand on the area where your kidney is, and I began to pray in the Spirit. When I did, God revealed something to me."

He paused. "Are you about to make a decision?"

"If I don't hear anything from God before tomorrow," I told him, "I'm going to start treatment. I'm not happy about it, but I've told God I would wait until Wednesday."

"The Lord said several things to me. One of the things He said was you were to take naps in the middle of the day as 'acts of healing.' As you rest, God will heal your body.

"I don't know what the rest of this means," he said. "But as I was praying for you I felt the Lord say that the prince of demons, Beelzebub, is in your body. He is trying to kill you.

"Beelzebub is an old lion," Roberts continued. "He can only harm you if you give in to fear. Young lions never roar. They sneak up on their prey and attack without warning. The old lions have lost that ability. They put their mouths to the ground and roar. The sound goes out in all directions. The animals don't know where the sound is coming from — and they freeze. When they do, the old lion is able to attack.

"Do not panic. Do not freeze. Stay on the alert. Stay on the offensive. The Holy Spirit is battling Beelzebub in your body, refusing to let him take root. The cancer is still moving around. It is not rooted yet. There is still time."

"Time for what?" I asked.

"I don't know. That's all He said."

Thirty minutes after I hung up the phone the doorbell rang. It was Dr. Ralph Johnson and his wife, Sylvia.

After hugs and introductions (we had not met either in person), we sat down to eat. They were a handsome couple. He was my age, balding, outgoing, with muscular arms and shoulders. She was a few years younger. Her tasteful dress showed evidence of her years as a fashion buyer for some of the largest retail stores in St. Petersburg. Over lunch I told them of the phone call I had just received.

"What do you think it means?" I asked.

"I have no idea," he said, "but Sylvia and I want to pray with you as soon as we finish eating. That's the one thing God seemed to be saying to me as we drove over."

Following lunch, we went into our living room. Jackie and I sat on one love seat, the Johnsons on the other. I liked them. Both were easy to talk to, easy to listen to.

We sat quietly for a few minutes, then Dr. Johnson opened a book

"Why don't you sit back and let me read you something."

Jackie and I relaxed on the sofa, holding hands. He began:

> To view the wilderness as an end — a place of abiding, rather than a place through which one passes on his way to a land of promise — is the greatest of tragedies. Since God never intended that His children enter a wilderness and remain, each wilderness experience should be accompanied by a sense of nagging dissatisfaction, a deep longing for the Promised Land to come. Pilgrims should be careful not to try to escape the suffering God places on His children, until the object of that suffering is complete. At the same time, they should arise every morning and look upward — expecting, yea *knowing*, that one day the cloud will move.
>
> Depression, discouragement, unhappiness, feelings of unworthiness — all these are moods of the wilderness. But the promise of God is far greater and can be experienced long before one actually emerges

from the wilderness. Therefore, it is not unusual to hear, even from wilderness beds, songs in the night.

Even though the reed is bruised He will not break it off. Even though the wick is only smoldering He will not snuff it out. While each desert is a place of burning, the promise of God remains: "When you walk through the fire, you will not be burned; the flames will not set you ablaze."[1]

He closed the book and looked up. I was trying to hold back the tears, but they were pushing through my tightly closed eyelids.

"Do you know where that comes from?" he asked gently.

I could only nod my head.

"Those are the closing paragraphs on page 93 from your book *A Way Through the Wilderness*. I was reading it in the car as Sylvia drove over from St. Pete. Even though you wrote it seven years ago, it is God's word for you this afternoon. It is bread on the waters, now returning."

We prayed.

Finishing, Dr. Johnson looked me straight in the eye.

"You are to go for surgery!"

Jackie sat straight upright. "What?"

"Surgery! I feel it strongly. The sooner the better."

I looked at Jackie. Something was welling up in me, like oil rumbling from the earth after the drillers' bit had opened a huge vein of gas and oil deep beneath the surface. Suddenly an idea formed in my mind.

"Resist the devil, and he will flee from you!" I said.

"What do you mean?"

"We've been sitting back letting Satan push us around. We've not been in command. I'm tired of being on the defensive. It's time to pick up my sword and start swinging. James 4:7 says if we resist the devil, he will flee. Surgery is taking the offensive. It's fighting back. I am willing to trust everything on God's Word that if we resist him, he will flee."

Jackie was gripping my arm tightly. "Let's do it."

"Surgery fits my theology a lot better than treatment," I said. "Cancer has the nature of Lucifer. It is cells which have rebelled against God's plan for the human body — cells setting themselves up as gods over God's system for life. When Lucifer did this, God cast him out of heaven. Jesus said if we have an offending hand, we should cut it off; an offending eye, we should pluck it out. I have an offending kidney along with other offending cells. It is right to cut them out and throw them away so the rest of the body can live."

"There are medical reasons for this as well," Dr. Johnson said. "Your body is strong and will bounce back quickly from major surgery. Do it now. Do not delay."

"I'm ready."

"Where's your phone?"

"In the kitchen. Why?"

"I'm going to call Dr. Swanson in Houston."

"Now?"

But he was already on his way to the kitchen. Moments later I heard him talking to Dr. David Swanson at the M.D. Anderson Cancer Center.

"Mr. Buckingham has decided he wants surgery. When can you schedule it?"

My mind was racing. Did I decide this or did Ralph Johnson decide? Why can't we wait a few days? Then I remembered: Tomorrow was the imposed deadline. The answer had come. There was no need to wait.

Dr. Johnson put his hand over the mouthpiece. "He says there is a top urologist at the Fort Lauderdale branch of the Cleveland Clinic. That's closer to home. Your family can visit while you are recovering. He knows the doctor and will be glad to make the appointment."

"No," I said. "We're to go with Swanson."

Dr. Johnson nodded and returned to his conversation. After he hung up he said, "The earliest he can work you in is a week from Thursday."

"That's not soon enough," Jackie interjected. "I'm going to start praying right now that he will move that date up."

I got up and went into the dining room. On the table were the big brown envelopes with all the medical scans I had brought back with me from Houston. I handed them to Dr. Johnson. He opened one of the envelopes and pulled out the CT scans of the soft tissue in my abdomen. Holding the negative up to the window, he nodded.

"You can't miss it," he said. "What did the local doctors say?"

"They all said it is inoperable."

He lowered the negative and looked at me, his brow furrowed. "You hadn't told me that."

"Dr. Swanson said there was a chance," I said. "He said the operation was 'technically difficult but doable.' "

"I've never, in all my medical career, recommended surgery when other doctors said a tumor was inoperable. But if Swanson is willing...."

He just shook his head and slipped the negatives back into the envelope.

"I don't think it was you talking when you said surgery," Jackie said softly. "I think it was God talking through you."

That night, after we had told the family, called friends in the church and sent out messages to a few folks around the nation, Jackie and I lay in bed praying. A lone whippoorwill sang his mournful song in the trees in front of the house.

"How do you feel?" she asked after we had prayed for a while.

"Full of determination. I've hated the way I've been feeling — like a boxer being beaten to death on the ropes. I couldn't even get my fists up to ward off the blows. This whole thing was controlling me. Pushing me around. Now it's time to push back. I feel like Admiral Farragut at the Battle of Mobile Bay during the Civil War. 'Damn the torpedoes! Full speed ahead!' "

She squeezed my shoulder and laughed. "That's what I've been praying for. You've always been a fighter. Now you are one again — only this time dressed in the full armor of God."

TWENTY-SIX

DIVINE
SCHEDULE CHANGE

I CALLED DAVE WELDON WEDNESDAY MORNING after we finished breakfast. I came back upstairs to use the phone while Jackie finished dressing to go to the store. Sitting on the little cedar chest in our bedroom, I explained to Dr. Weldon the events from yesterday. I told him the appointment had been made for surgery. I could tell by his response that he had some questions.

"Do you mind if I call Dr. Swanson?"

"Of course not. Why?"

"You know what the doctors here have said. I just want to make certain he's not operating on you needlessly."

Twenty minutes later he called back.

"I just got off the phone with Dr. Swanson. He's going after everything. He feels there is a possibility he can get it all. If that's the case, you won't need further treatment."

My spirit soared. This was the first time anyone had said there was a chance this nightmare might end.

I hung up the phone and stood quietly in front of my dresser, looking at the little pieces of paper Jackie had pasted there. One of them was a card from John Acuff, a Tennessee attorney whose son had died the previous year.

"When you get it all said," John had written, "He loves us. Bet our life on it. Stake your future on it. Put everything you hold dear in His hand and relax and know that He means you good."

Next to it was one of those little yellow stick-ums that were posted all over the house. It was a quote from Zechariah 4:6. "Not by might nor by power, but by my Spirit, says the Lord Almighty."

"What did Dr. Weldon say?" Jackie asked.

I told her Dr. Swanson's hope of "getting it all," then said, "I've got to forget that, put it out of my mind."

"Why?"

"If I trust in that, it will be trusting in the 'arm of flesh' rather than the Word of God. I cannot allow myself to get hyped over what the doctors say about healing, any more than I can allow myself to get depressed when they say I'm going to die. I've got to stand on the Word of God. Alone."

It was about noon when the phone rang again. I heard Jackie pick up the extension in the kitchen. It was Dr. Swanson in Houston.

"For some unexplained reason one of my surgical colleagues has had a change of schedule. If you can get out here Monday, I can operate Tuesday morning — four days earlier than I had anticipated."

"My wife has been praying for that to happen."

"You may not want to know all the details, but there are some very good medical reasons for you to have the surgery as soon as possible."

"We'll be there Monday noon."

"You'll be in the Lutheran Pavilion adjoining the clinic. The lounge chair in the room opens into a comfortable single bed so your wife can stay with you after you get out of recovery."

"If all goes well, how long will I be in the hospital?"

"Eleven to twelve days. This is a big operation, and I don't know what I'll find when I get inside. I'll come in and see you the night before surgery and try to answer any questions you have then."

I hung up the phone and heard Jackie, back in the kitchen, shout, "Hallelujah!" God had answered her prayer.

There was a fax message sticking out of my machine when I walked back into my study after lunch. It was from Jim Jackson in Montreat, North Carolina. I had called him immediately after talking to Dr. Swanson. It was a copy of a

message being sent to several hundred members of his Reach Out Club —
supporters of the CBU ministry.

> Sound the alarm! The battle lines are drawn; the location and time are
> set for the enemy to be destroyed and cast down and out. The battle
> is the Lord's, and the victory is ours as we reign with Him!
>
> The alarm and battle cry are for Jamie Buckingham, who will
> undergo surgery on Tuesday morning, July 31, in Houston, Texas....
>
> So let's get busy! Start those prayers, and let's move heaven on
> Jamie's behalf. I would like you to join me on Tuesday in prayer and
> fasting beginning Monday evening. Pray specifically for:
>
> 1. The reality of God's healing hand having already performed
> miraculous surgery.
>
> 2. Skill, alertness, knowledge and discernment beyond their abili-
> ties for the surgeons and staff.
>
> 3. The brooding power and presence of the Holy Spirit over the
> operating table.
>
> 4. Peace, confidence and assurance for Jackie and their family.
>
> 5. Victory over the demonic enemy — cancer.

In the huge stack of mail on my desk was a note from Paul Dodge, the pastor
of a small full-gospel church in Melbourne. It was filled with love — and brought
a needed word of spiritual balance.

> It is good that your whole church is praying, and it is interesting that
> people all over the world are praying — but none of their prayers can
> assure healing or guarantee results. But if you are basing your healing
> on God's Word, then healing can come. However, it will come only
> as you shut the world out and shut yourselves in with God and the two
> of you [Jamie and Jackie] wrestle with the forces of hell and wrestle
> with God to overcome all the power of the enemy. It doesn't take large
> numbers of people to touch God. Only one or two. With the two of
> you, you have the added power of two in agreement.

There was one more letter that seemed to have particular significance. It was
from Stephen Berry, a prisoner in Maghaberry Prison in North Ireland. Stephen
had read several of my books and had written once before, but we had never met.

> I just wanted to say that in the situation you and Jackie and the kids
> face it is okay to express fears and longings and even tears of pain and

pity. That's the grace of the present moment given to you by God, and it is an act of faith, not faithlessness. Jesus does care about the suffering you are going through and the suffering your family is going through, and He weeps for you all — for it has never been the will of God for His sons and daughters to experience such pains.

Remember, Jamie, it is usually tomorrow we are concerned about. I've learned that from being in this awful prison. But if you think about tomorrow you miss this wonderful truth: 'This is the day the Lord hath made, let us be glad and rejoice in it.' *This* is the day, Jamie. Not tomorrow. *Today* we can rejoice and be glad, no matter what the circumstances, because we are in the Lord.

I finished reading the lengthy letter and placed it on my desk. I wondered if Stephen and I would ever meet.

That afternoon Jane Berrey called.

"Gene and I have talked," she said. "I'm going to fly out to Houston and stay with you. We are leaving Saturday night to drive to our cabin in the mountains of north Georgia. Tuesday morning Gene will drive me down to Atlanta, and I'll fly to Houston. Gene will stay in the mountains, and I'll stay with you for a week, then fly home."

Both of us were relieved. Having a nurse — especially such a close friend — to help Jackie in the room would relieve us both.

On top of this, our daughter Bonnie insisted she fly out with us and stay as long as needed. She was the only family member available to stay a lengthy period of time because her two children would be leaving the day before to spend two weeks with Marion's parents in Baton Rouge.

Once again we went to the airport and cashed in frequent-flyer bonus coupons for free tickets. Everything was falling into place.

TWENTY-SEVEN

ADVICE FROM
A SURVIVOR

MICHAEL THOMPSON CAME BY THE HOUSE FRIDAY morning. My energy level was down, and it felt good to sit at the dining room table and let him talk.

"You know I went through major surgery three years ago," he began. "Crohn's Disease is considered terminal. The surgeon said I might die on the operating table. I came through it without complications and am healthier now than I have ever been.

"This morning as I was praying for you I felt the Lord wanted me to come out and walk you through the surgery."

I sat looking at Michael. He was younger than both my sons, yet he had made a powerful impact on our church during the two years he had been with us. Despite the fact that both our schedules prevented much personal time together, my love for him had grown deep across the months.

He started by telling me what to expect when I entered the hospital, what the surgical preparation would be like and how I would feel when I came out of surgery.

"Just be prepared for the pain," he said. "You're going to hurt when you come out of surgery. But it won't last long, and you'll not remember it because you'll still be coming out from under anesthesia. Just relax and sleep. It will go away quickly."

We talked for more than an hour. Details. Things I should be prepared for. The pre-surgery enema. The tube in my nose. The PCA (patient control access) pump that gives pain medication. The necessity of coughing. How to squeeze a pillow on your stomach to soften the accompanying pain. Helpful pointers.

His final advice: "Bring something familiar from the house, something of special significance. Hang it on the wall of your hospital room so you can see it from your bed. Let it become a point of focus. Hospitals are lonely — even if your family is there. If you have something familiar from home, it will help. It will give you the focus you need most of all: memory of who you are."

After he left, Jackie looked at me. "I know what you want to take with you."

"What do you think it is?"

"Something to remind you of Israel or the Sinai."

"How did you reach that conclusion?" I laughed.

"You've always said if you needed to run away from home, I could find you camping in the Sinai Desert."

We walked together back to my study. Hanging over my word processor was an oversized photo of me, tanned, strong, wearing a desert hat and carrying my five-foot staff — standing in the rocky wilderness of the southern Sinai. In the background, towering against the azure sky, was the dark red granite mountain called Jebel Musa — the Mountain of Moses. Mount Sinai.

"That's it," I said. "Take it down and put it in your suitcase. I want it hanging at the end of my bed, reminding me I am an adventurer, an explorer, a pilgrim on my way to God's promised land."

"I have one other picture I'm going to take," she said. "Jack Taylor sent us a picture of Hook's *Laughing Jesus*. He said you needed to look at it every day and know that, like Jesus, you can laugh at the devil."

Our neighbors Denny and Susie Tharp took us to dinner that night. Denny, a retired Air Force colonel and former elder, had been a true friend during some times of church stress a few years back. It was a light, almost frivolous evening in a swanky restaurant on the harbor. Their deep love was evident. Afterward, sitting in the car in the dark driveway in front of our house, we prayed together. After they pulled out (they only lived a block away), Jackie and I stood on the walkway to our house, our arms around each other's waists.

"We are the most blessed people in the world," she said. "We have things very few people have anymore. We are surrounded by our family. We have long-term friends, many of whom have chosen to live here just to be close to us. We have a loving, caring, praying church. We have hundreds of friends all over the world. We have hundreds of thousands of people — people we'll never know this side of heaven — who are praying for us right now."

She stopped as her voice choked up. I looked up through the towering pines at the stars twinkling in the night sky. I could hear John's dogs barking. Far to the back of the property, maybe at Bruce's house, a car door slammed, and I heard children laughing. An owl hooted in the distance, reminding me of sounds from my childhood.

I thought about our friends at home, then I thought about our friends around the world. All of them were praying for us right now.

"Did you see the fax from Yechiel Eckstein?" Jackie asked. Yechiel was an orthodox rabbi from Chicago, president of a group called the International Fellowship of Christians and Jews. We had become close friends, and I served on his board of advisers. He had sent a fax that afternoon. It read: "I am praying for you each day. I shall be in Jerusalem on the day of your surgery. I will be at the Western Wall, praying for your safety and healing."

It was similar to a message that had come from Helen bar Yaacov, an Israeli tour guide who had helped me on several hiking trips. She had sent a precious letter. Not only was she praying for me, she said, but so was my tough old friend Uzi Vered, a former military commander for Israeli forces in the Sinai and now a tour director.

We walked back to the house and sat on the front step, holding hands, interceding for all these friends who were praying for us.

What was it Tennyson had said about prayer?

> For so the whole round earth is every way
> Bound by gold chains about the feet of God.[1]

TWENTY-EIGHT

MISERY WITH COMPANY

SATURDAY NIGHT CREPT IN QUIETLY. ALTHOUGH I had been trying to keep Saturday as a Sabbath, the ox was definitely in the ditch. I had spent much of the day on the phone and at the word processor, knowing I was going to be out of the saddle for an undetermined length of time. It was almost 10:30 P.M. when Jackie came into the bedroom carrying the elements of communion. I was propped up in bed, reading my Bible and trying to get some kind of handle on what God wanted me to say the next morning in the church services. As it had been for the last four weeks, Saturday night had arrived and I had no idea what I was supposed to say on Sunday. Each time I had gone into the pulpit with no notes — and virtually no idea what I was going to say. Yet the July crowds had grown larger and larger until the building was packed with almost a thousand in each service. A summer miracle.

Gradually something dawned on me. For years I had been reading the Bible looking for things to preach to the people. I would try to find a scripture that met a known need — then preach on it. But I had not done that for the last four weeks. Instead of preparing sermons, I had been preparing myself. I had spent my weekdays talking with God, then showed up on Sunday and talked to the people.

"You are no longer a preacher," Gene Berrey had joked. "Now you're a prophet."

I remembered something one of my seminary professors had said thirty-five years ago. "A preacher speaks on Sunday because he has to say something — a prophet speaks because he has something to say."

I had discovered that when you spend time with God, you always have something to say.

Jackie sat down beside me on the bed. She was carrying the silver chalice I had bought in Israel along with a small piece of pita bread.

I scooted over beside her and heard the kitchen door open downstairs.

"Come on up," I called out.

Tim walked in, dressed in his softball uniform. He had been playing with the church team and had just gotten home. His elbow was bloodied from sliding into base.

"Why not join us for communion?"

He stood looking down at us. "Do you remember when I had all that faith to believe you had been healed, then your biopsy showed the cancer?" Tim asked.

"I remember," I smiled.

He sat down on the cedar chest at the end of the bed. "Well, that wasn't faith — it was wishing. Now Kathy and I and the boys are reading the Bible together. Faith, it seems, is believing what God has said. I believe it. That's why I know you're healed."

Jackie broke the bread. Tim dropped to his knees beside the bed. Together we received the body of Christ. Then we drank from the common cup.

"Dad, there's one more thing," Tim said. "I've talked with Bruce. We're glad Bonnie is going with you to Houston. But we're coming out next weekend. I know you've said we didn't need to. I know you've said you need us around here. I don't know where we're going to get the money. But even if we have to start walking tomorrow, we're coming to Houston next weekend to be with you."

I felt pride welling up in my chest — pride in my sons that they felt that strongly. "I understand," I replied. "Saundra called this afternoon. She said people had already given money to the church designated to take care of all your expenses so the two of you can fly out and back. They are also taking care of Bonnie's expenses. We want you to come."

The phone rang. Tim handed it to me. It was Jane Berrey, calling from Savannah, Georgia. Her voice was tense.

"We stopped here to spend the night on our way up to the mountains. Gene's in the hospital. He may have had a heart attack."

I hung up and tried to say something to Jackie, but no words came out. She knew, from overhearing, that something was seriously wrong. I finally told her what Jane had said.

"He started having pains earlier in the evening. Jane insisted he go to a hospital. He didn't like the first hospital. They looked in the yellow pages and found a second hospital in Savannah — St. Joseph's. They admitted him, and he's there now. He wanted to go back to the hotel, but Jane insisted he stay in the hospital. They have him on medication."

"We need to call the home group and get people praying," Jackie said. She took the phone and began to dial.

Tim got up to leave. "Stay for a minute," I said. "As soon as Mom finishes these calls, we need to pray. I'd like for you to be here with us."

My mind flashed back to all the fun things we had done with the Berreys. The four of us had spent a week sightseeing in Nova Scotia one summer. A couple of years later we vacationed for two weeks in Alaska, most of it spent in a trapper's cabin on a lake inaccessible except to the float plane that had flown us in — then returned eight days later to see if we were still alive. Gene had gone with me on one of my trips to the Sinai and just a few months before had been part of the small group from our church I had taken on a hiking trip in Israel.

"You guys have been friends for a long time," Tim said, referring to Gene.

"We've done a lot of things together," I answered.

I thought back several years before. I had been invited by the Indonesia director of Wycliffe Bible Translators, Dick Hugoniot, to come to Irian Jaya — Indonesia's eastern province on the big island of Papua New Guinea — to speak to all the missionaries at the remote jungle base of Dona Biera. Gene volunteered to go with me to "carry your suitcase."

In Irian Jaya there had been a great revival among the Dani Indians. Tens of thousands were converted. They were now sending out missionaries from their tribes to other tribes in the jungles. On the last day of our visit Gene and I met a group of them.

"There are about fifteen native Dani evangelists down at the sawmill," Dick Hugoniot had said. "They heard there were two apostles who had come from America. They want you to come pray for them to receive the Holy Spirit."

I looked at Gene. He grinned. "You're the apostle. I'm the bellboy."

Half an hour later we met with the scantily-clad Dani evangelists. Their leader spoke to us in the Dani dialect. Dick interpreted.

"He says they have been praying that God would send them an apostle from Jerusalem to lay hands on them and impart the Holy Spirit. I told him you were from America but had been to Jerusalem many times. He thought Jerusalem and

America were the same place but said it made no difference. God had sent you, and they were ready to be baptized in the Holy Spirit."

When he finished, the Dani men all knelt in the sawdust on the floor of the old sawmill. Gene, Dick and I went from one to another, laying hands on their heads and praying softly, asking God to send His Holy Spirit. Everyone we prayed for began to pray out loud. I could not tell what language they were using because I did not understand their dialect. But it was a spontaneous outburst of joy.

When I finished, the leader came forward, embraced me and then shouted at the others. They walked off down the trail — singing lustily. Gene and I stood for a long time, our arms around each other's shoulders, feeling privileged above all other men.

Now Gene was in a strange hospital in a strange city — close to death. Jackie had alerted the home group and the prayer teams. Tim, Jackie and I prayed.

That prayer continued throughout the night. I woke often and found myself praying. Sometimes I was praying for Gene, sometimes for myself. At times I got us mixed up in my mind and did not know whom I was praying for.

There were times during the night when I could actually feel a battle going on in my gut. I could feel movement, much as I suppose a pregnant mother must feel movement. Something was happening inside me. There was no pain. Just a sensation of some kind of battle going on in my abdomen. I would come out of sleep and find myself praying for Gene, then myself, then praying for the good cells in my body that they would be strong and fortified in their war with the evil cells.

I was up before dawn, knowing I had to preach at both morning services — still having no idea what I was going to say. But this seemed evident to me. The devil had overplayed his hand. If he had just left this alone and been satisfied to attack me, I would have remained confused. But this attack on one of my best friends, on Jane who was to have met us in Houston to help in the hospital room, on one of our chief elders in the church, suddenly dropped things into perspective.

Oddly, there was almost a feeling of comfort, the same kind of feeling I had when I thought Len LeSourd had suffered a stroke — that more than one of us were under attack. Now I was even more certain who the enemy was. Now I knew how to fight.

TWENTY-NINE

SUNDAY V

T HE SPIRITUAL WARFARE OF THE NIGHT HAD LEFT me weak. Confused. I woke up praying every forty-five minutes, it seemed. What was going on? I remembered a line from Marc Connley's play, *Green Pastures*. Gabriel was looking over the parapets of heaven at the great flood which floated Noah's ark. The "Lawd" had asked him how things were going down there. "Everything dat's nailed down comin' loose, Lawd," Gabriel said. I had that distinct feeling that the water was rising — only I didn't know if it was God's water or the devil's.

I lay in bed quietly, hoping God might whisper to me. But there was only silence and the soft sound of the outside world beginning to awaken.

I got up and felt my way through the dark bedroom toward the bathroom. I stopped at my dresser and groped to find the little six-ring binder from the Community of Jesus. Closing the door of the bathroom to keep the light from waking Jackie, I sat on the edge of the bathtub. I opened the book and read all the messages I had received from my friends on Cape Cod. I finally reached the page where I had written in my own messages from God.

"Why aren't You still speaking?" I asked aloud.

Instantly I sensed that silent voice, now so familiar.

"I have given you My Word, My son. Study it!"

I knew what He meant. John began his Gospel by writing, "In the beginning was the Word...and the Word was God" (John 1:1). God is His Word. The Word of God is the extension of God's being. What He said, He still says through the Bible. I did not need more subjective words from God, more whispers at dawn. Those messages, necessary during my times of crisis, were simply an act of grace. It was God's way of letting me know He was there, caring and acting. Now He wanted me to walk in faith, not knowledge. He wanted me to rely, not on the subjective word, but on His proven word — the Bible.

I sat, nodding my understanding.

"I will do what You ask," I said softly.

Then I added: "All I ask is You keep my mind alert and my body comfortable enough — regardless of the treatment I might need — so I can fulfill Your call on my life. I don't dread change, even physical suffering, but I ask that it not be so severe that I spend all my time concerned with my survival rather than serving You, hearing Your word and proclaiming that word to Your people. That is my plea."

My sermon at both services was simple. I told the people the events of the week, including our decision to go for surgery. I told them of Gene's heart condition, pausing in the middle of my message to lead the church in a prayer for him. I then read James 4:7, calling the people to humble themselves before God but to resist the devil. I closed with 1 Peter 5:5-9 which says essentially the same thing but closes with, "Resist him (Satan), standing firm in the faith, because you know that your brothers throughout the world are undergoing the same kind of sufferings."

My brief sermons, however, were not the significant events of the morning. The first event took place at 9:30 between the two services. Announcements had been made for the last two weeks about this special moment — an exercise in spiritual warfare. As we had planned, the families gathered in the big parking lot in the center of the property.

I stood in the middle of the parking lot under a big oak tree. I had brought my *shofar*, a long, crooked ram's horn I had purchased in Israel many years before. In the Old Testament the Levis blew the ram's horn to assemble the people and to announce the beginning of special occasions in the temple.

The blowing of the horns was to be the signal for the families of the church to march out and stand along the far perimeters of the church property. Then, when the horns were sounded again, the people were to shout, rebuking Satan away from the church property and away from all who were members of the church. Turning in to face the church property, we were also to ask God's blessing and healing on all who made up the body of the Tabernacle Church.

I caught my breath and blew a mighty blast on the old ram's horn. The huge crowd of almost two thousand people began to fan outward — singing and praying out loud as they went. Jackie and I walked out to the main entrance. I raised the shofar again and blew a long note. Then, as Joshua's army did at Jericho, the people began to shout. I had thought they might shout just once or twice then sneak back into the building. Instead, the crescendo grew louder and louder until it was almost deafening. Circling the property, people were standing, hands raised, rebuking Satan — resisting him.

Then, without any outside signal, they turned and faced into the four-acre circle. This time the sound was softer, musical, as the people pled with God to protect the church, to protect the leaders, to protect me.

The entire scenario lasted about twenty minutes, then gradually the people began to drift back toward their cars or into the buildings. However, I noticed many remained — especially at the various entrances into the property — on their knees, praying. It was a moment of great spiritual power — unlike anything we had ever done as a church.

The second significant action of the day came during the second service. Our children, sixth grade and younger, usually remained in the church services until after the worship period. Then they withdrew to another building for "childrens' church."

That morning, before the children left, Michael Thompson left his position at the piano and stepped to the pulpit.

"One of the things we have learned at the Tabernacle," he said, "is the prayers of little children are always answered. Children do not have the hang-ups of doubt and sophistication which plague adults. When they pray they enter directly into the throne room of God. They don't even knock to see if God is busy — they just come into His presence because they believed Him when He told them the door was always open for kids.

"For the last thirty days, the children of this church have been praying for Jamie. Jamie's grandchildren have been praying for him. My children pray for him several times a day. Every time the children of this church come together, they pray for our leader. Jamie is going into surgery on Tuesday morning. I want Jamie and Jackie to come forward. The children of this church are going to come to the platform, lay hands on them, and pray for them before they leave."

Jackie and I knelt in the middle of the stage. The children, more than 250 of them — some toddling in diapers, others almost ready to bud into adolescence —

streamed forward from all over the building. They filled the platform and stood around the altar. I saw my own grandchildren among them. As many as possible crawled up to where we were so they could touch us. The rest either touched another child or stood with their hands raised.

Michael gave the microphone to Nick Jagos, the sixth-grade boy who had almost died of cancer the year before — the one who had sent me that precious note telling me his favorite scripture from Proverbs. Nick began to pray, but then his voice was drowned out by the voices of hundreds of little children who began to pray out loud also.

Buried under that pile of children, with Jackie squeezing my hand, I began to cry. It was the same kind of convulsive crying I had done during those early morning men's prayer meetings when I had laid on the platform, just inches from where I was kneeling. I could not hold back the tears. I sensed Jackie's tears also. I had never felt the "presence of God" with such power as I did at that moment when the children prayed.

Finally it was over. I looked up. Standing, with her arms around my neck, was Robin and Jon's little freckle-faced five-year-old Heather. "I love you, PaPa," she grinned. "Jesus healed you."

At the close of the service, Don Lees came to the pulpit with an official pronouncement.

"The staff and elders believe this is a time for prayer and fasting. We are calling the body into a fast which shall begin Monday at 9:00 a.m. and will end Tuesday at 6:00 p.m.

"A fast is your offering unto God. It is a privilege to fast unto the Lord. It is not a tool to bribe God to answer our prayers in behalf of our leader; rather it is an offering of praise on our part.

"Prayer, on the other hand, has various parts and components. One of these is to do battle. Another is to call forth the protecting angels. Another is to intercede on behalf of our brother and his family, to intercede on our own behalf, and to intercede on behalf of this church.

"During this time of prayer and fasting — tomorrow and Tuesday — you are to meditate on Isaiah 58. Read it prayerfully several times.

"God wants us to stand as pure vessels before Him. This is not only a time to stand against the evil one, but a time to praise God for all He has done. Therefore, pray for pure hearts, then acknowledge God for who He is, what He has done, and what He is going to do this coming week."

As soon as we got home from the church service, we put in a call to Jane Berrey at St. Joseph's Hospital in Savannah.

"Gene's in surgery right now," she said. "He had a massive heart attack during the night. The doctor said if he had not been in the hospital and receiving medication, he would have died."

"Is he OK?"

"The doctor is confident he can save him, but he is having to do a quadruple bypass. The only heart doctor available is a seventy-year-old Chinese cardiac surgeon. He has been with him constantly since early morning. Now listen to this: he is one of the most famous cardiac surgeons in the world — and he just happened to be here and just happened to be on call today. Does that sound like God or not?"

She was chuckling.

"Brooks Watson and Don Lees are on their way up right now," I said. "They left immediately after church in Brooks's plane. They will rent a car and come straight to the hospital. Saundra is driving up this week with Gena [the Berreys' youngest daughter]. I just wish we could be there ourselves."

I waited a moment, then continued. "Jane, I've seen the enemy in this. He is all fright and no power. We leave early in the morning for Houston. God is going to protect us all."

THIRTY

KNEELING IN THE STARTING BLOCKS

CURRY VAUGHAN CAME TO THE HOUSE EARLY Monday morning to drive us to the airport. Each of the children — with the exception of Bonnie, whom we would pick up on our way to Orlando — had already come by to hug and pray before they went to work. Sandy and Jerry had moved in so they could take care of Jackie's mother and watch the house. As Curry came in the back door I saw he was holding a silver communion chalice, a small silver plate and a bottle of vintage wine.

"I know you guys don't drink," Curry grinned. "And you know that Nancy and I are lifelong teetotalers. But years ago someone gave us this bottle of wine. I've saved it, knowing there would come a special occasion when I would use it for holy communion. This morning is that occasion."

I glanced over at Jackie. She was nodding.

"Only because it's you, Curry," she said, "and only because it's for this occasion!"

We sat at the breakfast table. Our bags, packed the night before, were on the floor. The back door, which opened onto a large screen porch, had been left open. The house was quiet, but the chirping of the birds as they flitted back and forth to the backyard feeder and the chattering of the squirrels chasing each other up and down the pine trees provided background music for the communion celebration more beautiful than could have come from any church orchestra.

Curry served us, using those ancient, familiar words: "This is my body, which is broken for you.... This cup is the new testament in my blood..." (1 Cor. 11:24-25, KJV). He concluded by quoting from Isaiah 53:5 (KJV): "With his stripes we are healed."

The doorbell rang. It was Janna Hogan, one of our Tab people who had called many times with prophetic encouragement. She was standing on the front steps barefooted and without makeup. "You know how much I love you if I come to your house without makeup," she laughed, "but I have received a special word from God as you leave for Texas."

She handed me an envelope, then reached up and kissed me on the cheek. "Godspeed, beloved! You will walk in His safety, surrounded by His angels."

She was gone. I opened the envelope. Inside was a handwritten message. "When you go under the anesthesia Tuesday morning, and the whole world is praying for you, forget them. Fix your eyes on the face of Jesus and relax in His presence."

I thought of John Sherrill's earlier word to me about surgery. He had told me to allow the Holy Spirit to prepare my subconscious as well as my conscious mind.

Both Michael Williams and Curry Juneau met us at the Houston airport. They had never met, so it was a joy to introduce them. Curry was our official ride into town, but Michael said he wanted to meet us at the airport just to pray with us. After loading our bags in the Juneau car we all stood in the airport parking building, holding hands in a circle. Cars were passing by, but we were oblivious as Michael prayed. I found myself smiling: prayed for when we left Melbourne, prayed for when we arrived in Houston. It can't get any better than this.

I helped Jackie and Bonnie check into the now-familiar Marriott Hotel. Bonnie would stay there, joined by Bruce and Tim when they came out for the weekend, until she had to go home. Jackie would spend the first night with her and then stay with me in the hospital room the rest of the time. Curry then drove us around to the medical center and said he would be back early the next morning before I went into surgery.

The rest of the afternoon was spent going through preliminary exams and paper work. Finally, about 4:00, an orderly showed up with a wheelchair to take me from the clinic to my room in the adjoining hospital.

"Do I have to ride in that? I'm not sick," I balked.

"Hospital regulations," the orderly laughed.

"You're going to have to get used to taking orders rather than giving them, Dad," Bonnie giggled.

"This is going to be good for him," I heard Jackie say behind my back as I settled into the wheelchair.

Minutes later, after going through a labyrinth of halls and elevators, I was pushed through the spacious nursing station on the sixth floor of the Lutheran Pavilion and left in room 6026 — which was to be my home for the next seventeen days.

Jackie reached in the little shoulder bag she had been carrying and pulled out a brand-new pair of blue pajamas. "I refuse to let you wear to bed what you do at home," she said. "So I went out and bought these."

"I don't want to lie in bed yet," I said. "I need to hang on to health just as long as I can. Let's explore first, then we'll come back here before you have to leave for the evening."

An hour later we were back in the room just in time for Jack Taylor to arrive.

"What are you doing here?" I asked, surprised.

"I'm here to pray for you and to sit with Jackie and Bonnie while you're in surgery," he said.

"Remember this," Jack added after he prayed for me. "It ain't no big deal. And you're hearing that from someone who walked right up to the pearly gates before getting sent back."

"Thanks, friend," I grinned. "If it's no big deal, why don't we just swap places right now?"

"Because you don't want to go where I've been," Jack laughed.

Dr. Swanson and Dr. Giannakis came in about 8:30 P.M. I had finally agreed to put on my new pajamas and, after learning how to control the bed, was propped up talking to Jackie and Bonnie. Dr. Swanson carefully outlined the procedures for the next morning.

"The orderly will come for you at 6:30 A.M. You'll be in operating room 1…the surgery will take between three and five hours…you'll be in the surgical intensive care unit about twenty-four hours, then they will bring you back to this room."

He then explained what might happen in surgery if things did not go right. They did not know what they would find when they entered my abdomen. His primary objective was to remove the tumors in my vena cava, remove as many of the tumorous lymph nodes as possible and remove the kidney. However, I might need as many as ten pints of blood to replace what was lost, and there was a possibility the cancer could have spread to many other areas. He then asked me to sign a permission slip, not only to operate, but to remove a number of other organs — including my colon — if, once he got inside, he discovered they needed to come out.

"We have come this far by faith," I said. "Tomorrow is no different. Take out whatever is bad — just be aggressive."

"You need to realize," Jackie said to Dr. Swanson as I was signing the sheet, "that tomorrow morning you and my husband will be the most prayed-for men in the world."

He smiled. "That's nice to know." Both he and Dr. Giannakis shook my hand — and were gone.

Jackie and Bonnie remained for another thirty minutes. The room was quiet. The door, which opened onto a large open area where the nurses' station was located, was closed. Jackie sat on the edge of the bed. Bonnie stood at the foot gently rubbing my feet. It was a small room with just enough room for my bed, the recliner chair which opened up into a single bed, a small night stand and a tiny closet. The nurse had brought in a second chair which was placed under the TV. There were a total of twenty rooms in this particular pod. All were occupied by urology patients — although some had accompanying problems such as cancer of the liver or pancreas. We prayed, then they left to walk back over to the hotel.

Tomorrow would arrive much earlier than usual.

Shortly after they left, a stocky black nurse came in. "Time to clean you out," she laughed. What followed was more of an adventure than an indignity.

"All the Bible requires is clean hands and a pure heart," I joked as she squeezed the 100 cc enema bag to make sure I was filled up before rushing into the bathroom to empty. "But you've added something else — clean guts."

"Sparklin' clean," she laughed. Then she asked, "You a preacher?"

"Sort of."

"The Bible says God loves a cheerful giver. So when you go in the bathroom and sit on that toilet, do a lot of laughing, 'cause you gettin' ready to give everythin' you got."

I needed that. I needed her.

Later another nurse came in and inserted an IV in my arm. I didn't know it then, but I would live with those needles and tubes — day and night — for the next two weeks.

After she left I lay quietly on my back on the hospital bed. There was a dim light burning on the wall behind my head. I reached over and picked up my Bible.

Since the members of the flock back in Melbourne were all meditating on Isaiah 58, I should join them. There was just enough light to read by. I began slowly, reading out loud. Every verse seemed to bring new meaning to life. Don Lees had wanted us to read, I thought, so we could concentrate on the meaning of fasting. But suddenly I reached verses 8 and 9, and it was as if a laser light came through the window and illuminated those two verses:

> Then your light will break forth like the dawn,
>   and your healing will quickly appear;
> then your righteousness will go before you....
>
> Isaiah 58:8a

I shifted my gaze. There was a tiny footnote symbol beside the word "righteousness." I glanced at the bottom of the page where the clarified meaning was given — "your righteous One."

I felt what seemed to be an electric current running through my body. I had touched something powerful and was suddenly being energized. I went back and read the verse over again.

> Then your light will break forth like the dawn,
>   and your healing will quickly appear;
> then [your righteous One] will go before you,
>   and the glory of the Lord will be your rear guard.
> Then you will call, and the Lord will answer;
>   you will cry for help, and he will say:
> Here am I.
>
> Isaiah 58:8-9

I picked up my pen and wrote in the margin: July 30, 1990. M.D. Anderson Cancer Center, Houston, TX!

"Thank You, Father. Thank You for this assurance from Your Word that tomorrow morning when I am wheeled into surgery, the 'righteous One' will be at one end of the gurney and the 'glory of the Lord' at the other. What a wonderful place to be."

THIRTY-ONE

ANGELS ON ASSIGNMENT

I SLEPT WELL THE NIGHT BEFORE SURGERY, BORNE aloft by the prayers of countless saints and loved ones. I felt as if I were floating high above a battlefield, safe from all harm. In fact, there was not only a sense of peace but a sense of joy — almost a giddiness. For a month I had shed more tears than I dreamed imaginable; now I woke up chuckling. Strange — but wonderful.

At 5:30 A.M. the door opened, allowing light from the nurses' station to form a tiny yellow path across my bed. Jackie and Bonnie eased in. They quickly shut the door behind them and then came over and kissed me. How fresh and alive they looked! Their eyes were sparkling with excitement.

"This is the finest day of your life," Jackie said. "We prayed in the room before we left, and God said the victory was ours."

All Bonnie could say was, "I love you, Daddy."

Bonnie: my tenderhearted daughter. She was the one who had inherited my mercy gift. I remembered returning from a mission and research trip to Thailand several years before. I had shown the family some slides I had taken in a refugee camp. Bonnie had looked at three or four then burst into tears. One summer when the children were small we had driven to our cabin in Western North Carolina. Going through the little town of Blackshear, Georgia, we had passed the ancient, brick, two-story jail, which sat on Main Street. Several inmates on the second floor were standing at the windows, their arms and hands extended through the bars. Bonnie had begun to cry and continued crying all the way to Augusta — two hours away. How tender was her heart.

Now she had graduated from Oral Roberts University, had worked as art director for the Oral Roberts Evangelistic Association, had married Marion, who was now the vice president of a bank, had given birth to two beautiful children — and all she could trust herself to say was, "I love you, Daddy."

She made my heart feel warm.

Moments later Curry and Bev Juneau arrived. Then Jack Taylor. They stood around my bed praying. I heard Jack, in an authoritative voice, assigning angels to come and take their place in the hospital — to guard the operating room in particular.

A nurse came in and did something to the IV in my arm. Then she handed me a shower cap.

"Am I going to take a bath?" I joked.

"Just put it on so all those Florida germs won't jump out of your hair into your incision," she grinned.

Another nurse came in and gave me a hospital gown that was open in the back. "No need to tie it in the back. They're going to take it off as soon as you get in the operating room."

"Well, the pajamas didn't last very long, did they?" I said to Jackie. "Everyone, turn your backs. This obviously won't take long to get into."

An orderly arrived. Things were getting busy. Jackie and the others squeezed into the corner of the room so he could wheel the gurney into the room.

Then there was a knock at the door. It was my sister, Audrey.

"I knew you weren't expecting me," she said. "But I couldn't stay away. My pastor called yesterday and gave me money for the plane ticket. Darroll's sister lives here, and she met me at the plane last night. I'll stay with her — but I'm here to represent Mother B., John and Clay. And I'm here because I love you."

I got out of bed, aware that my gown was flopping open in the back and barely covering other areas I was hesitant to expose before such a large crowd. The orderly hung the dripping IV container on a pole at the end of the gurney. I climbed up on the narrow stretcher and lay down.

The group followed the gurney, like a New Orleans Mardi Gras parade, as the orderly pushed it down the hall to the elevator. Everyone crowded in, and moments later we were at the surgical floor. The orderly pointed to a waiting area. "The family and friends can wait here. The doctor will send someone to let you know how things are going. When the surgery is over, he will come out and give you a report."

Jackie, Bonnie and Audrey kissed me, careful not to mess up my shower cap. Then I was in motion again, down the hall through two sets of double doors and finally parked outside what I assumed was operating room 1. The clock on the wall said 6:45 A.M. I was alone.

An orderly came out of the operating room and checked to make sure I had my shower cap. "When will I be shaved?" I asked. I remembered Michael Thompson telling me they would shave the entire center portion of my body.

"After you're asleep," he laughed. "And you don't want to know what else they're going to do, so don't ask."

A young doctor appeared. He introduced himself. It was an Irish name like Donovan. Something was happening. I wasn't remembering things as well. I assumed they had put something in my IV to slow me down.

"I'm your anesthesiologist," he said.

"You're not the same one I talked to yesterday."

"No, but he gave me all the information I need."

He then asked me again about allergies and family history of various things. He was very upbeat. Encouraging. I was beginning to feel high, as if I were floating.

The doctor disappeared, and a pretty, young, redheaded nurse came through the door from the operating room. "I'm your anesthetist nurse. I'll be right by your side all the time you're in surgery."

She squeezed my arm. I realized that somehow she knew who I was. She told me she was a believer and was going to be praying for me. I grinned. God was already putting His angels around me.

She disappeared, and I remained on my back on the gurney, alone. I felt surrounded by grace, uplifted by peace.

Another orderly appeared. "Are you Jamie Buckingham?"

"Yes."

"There's someone down the hall who wants to see you."

I was confused. What was going on?

"Who is it?"

"One of the hospital chaplains."

Oh, no, I moaned inwardly. I'm doing too well. I hope it's not a liberal nonbeliever.

It was obvious I had no choice. The orderly pushed my gurney through the double doors and down the hall toward the waiting room. Before we got there he stopped.

I looked around for the clergyman. The only person I saw was a chubby, young black woman with an angelic face. "I'm Chaplain Blondela James," she smiled.

"You're a hospital chaplain?" I asked, astonished. Maybe, I thought, the drugs were already taking effect.

She laughed. "I'm a minister with the Church of God in Christ, and I'm on staff here."

"You're a Pentecostal!" I almost shouted.

Her eyes were sparkling. "Shhh! Not so loud. They might throw us both out. I've read so much you've written. I heard you were here and wanted to come pray with you before you went into surgery."

I laughed and closed my eyes. A sister. Maybe an angel.

Moments later the orderly returned. "They're ready for you."

He pushed me into the operating room. I was struck by how cold it was. I could tell it was a huge room with a high ceiling and many different lights on various tracks. There were several people in the room, all in surgical masks. I could recognize Dr. Swanson.

I looked at the Irish anesthesiologist. I was shivering from the cold. "When King David was old and cold, they put young virgins in bed with him to keep him warm," I said.

Everyone in the room laughed. I thought, Why in the world did I say something stupid like that? I should be praying. Instead I'm cracking corny, almost obscene jokes. Have I lost my mind?

Someone replied, "We've been looking for girls like that but can't find any on the staff."

They all laughed again. What kind of surgery was this going to be? The patient is cracking jokes, and the doctors and nurses are all laughing. Two men lifted me off the gurney and onto the operating table. I was feeling good. What a marvelous adventure.

I lay peacefully while they adjusted tubes. Someone had taken my gown off. I was totally naked — like Jesus on the cross.

I remembered a line from *Peter Pan*. Peter was sitting on a rock in the middle of the lagoon, and the tide was coming in. "To die," he said. "To die would be an awfully big adventure."

What if I died on this table? But God had said I would not die. Not here. I would live and declare His Word and His works.

Someone asked me to place my left arm a little closer to my side. The anesthetist nurse, the redheaded one, squeezed my shoulder again.

I could see Dr. Swanson peering over his mask. "Good morning. Are you ready?"

"God is in control!"

Another squeeze from the redheaded angel.

"OK. We're ready. I'm going to increase your anesthesia, and you'll go straight to sleep."

I remembered Janna Hogan's words about focusing on Jesus. What does Jesus look like? Maybe He looks like Chaplain Blondela James. She was the last unmasked face I had seen.

Then it happened. Instantly. It wasn't until twelve days later that I remembered what I saw in that moment, just as I went into deep unconsciousness. When I did remember, I was lying in my hospital room talking to Jackie and Bonnie. It was almost two weeks after surgery. My mind was just beginning to clear from the effects of the long, deep anesthesia when suddenly it all returned.

Lying on the operating table, I had raised my head slightly. Why, I do not know. I raised it just high enough to look around the room one more time before going to sleep. Standing in the corners of the room and all around the walls — not up close, but surrounding me on all sides — were giant heavenly beings.

No one else seemed to see them, but they were there. They were standing shoulder to shoulder. They seemed to be masculine. They were between nine and ten feet tall. They were dressed in off-white tunics of some kind. Their faces were oyster-shell in color. They did not seem to be holding weapons of any kind. They were motionless, just standing with their backs to the wall as if at parade rest — looking straight ahead. On the side of the room to my right there were at least twenty. I was aware of equal numbers standing around the other three walls. Huge celestial beings. Waiting. Watching. Guarding. On assignment.

Then I was gone.

I cannot write this, almost a year later, without my eyes filling, without my throat clogging with emotion. So powerful was the moment. So powerful is the recall.

Later, as I was telling Jackie about it, I said, "They weren't doing anything. Just standing there."

She replied: "Oh, they were doing something. That's why you're here."

Jamie in front of Mount Sinai in Israel

THIRTY-TWO

"YOU GOT YOUR MIRACLE!"

I WOKE IN A GREAT FOG. I WAS LYING ON MY BACK in a strange room. There was no pain, but something was stuck in my throat — something so huge I could not talk.

Dr. Swanson was leaning over me. "You're fine. I was able to remove the tumor and lymph nodes. You're going to be OK."

Then Jackie was speaking from the other side of the bed. I couldn't see her, but I could hear her voice. "Honey, you got your miracle! The cancer is gone."

Dr. Swanson had left. I tried to talk but couldn't. Whatever it was in my mouth and down my throat kept me from talking. Why hadn't Michael warned me about this?

I tried to ask Jackie if I was going to need additional treatment. But all that came out were strange sounds. She kept misunderstanding me. I heard her begin to cry. "Something's wrong with him," she told Bonnie.

I was trying to say, "Tell me more. Give me details." But the sounds were garbled.

Jackie was gone. I learned later she had fled into the hall, nauseated and unable to handle the wild noises as I, frustrated, tried to get her to say more than "You got your miracle."

Bonnie was still there. She held my hand. She knew what I wanted. She began to talk, slowly, deliberately.

"Your surgery took six and a half hours. You lost all your blood, and they gave you ten pints to replace it. Dr. Swanson said you were very strong throughout the surgery. He had to call in a thoracic surgeon while he was operating on your vena cava because the tumor was close to your chest. He said he got all the tumors and took out all the swollen lymph glands. He had trouble with your kidney, though. They couldn't get it out. Four hours into the surgery the other doctors wanted to stop, wanted to close you up. The kidney was rooted in place. But they couldn't get the bleeding to stop. Dr. Swanson said the only way to stop the bleeding was to remove the kidney. He got very aggressive. He said he took all your small intestines, put them in a plastic bag and laid them on your chest. Then he attacked the kidney. He had to pry it loose with both hands. He said he got all the cancer he could see. No further treatment is necessary."

Bless her heart — she had told me what I wanted to know. I squeezed her hand and drifted back to sleep.

The next twenty-four hours passed in a blur. The only pain was when they lifted me to weigh me. They put me in some kind of sling and cranked me up off the bed. I felt as if I were being torn in two, but it only lasted a moment. The tube in my throat bothered me more than anything. Every so often they would "irrigate" it — suck the mucus from it. When they did, I thought I was going to drown. I learned after the third time that if I was swallowing while they were doing it, I could keep the gagging down to one convulsion.

My lips were dry. I motioned for the nurse, who hovered nearby in the recovery room. I made a "writing" signal, and she handed me a pad and paper.

I wrote "water."

"No, you can't have any."

I wrote "lips."

"Oh, sure," and she took a small sponge and moistened my lips. It was like finding a spring in the desert.

I was aware of other tubes. One was up my nose. It hurt. Dr. Swanson had told me they hoped to put a drainage tube in my side so the nasal gastric tube would not be necessary. I found out later that the surgery was so extensive they could not drain my stomach that way, meaning I had to live with that nasal tube for two weeks. It was the most difficult part of the healing ordeal — except for the time when I threw up after they took it out. Another tube, for oxygen, was in the other nostril. I found out later there was also a catheter going up into my bladder, but checking what was going on between my legs was the last thing on

226

my mind at that time.

There was a clock on the wall, but I couldn't tell if it was 6:00 P.M. or 6:00 A.M. I kept dozing off. Then the nurse pulled the respirator tube out of my throat. Suddenly I could talk. Only a whisper, but my voice was back and I could swallow. Wonderful.

Someone was listening to my lungs with a stethoscope. "There are no breathing sounds," he said, alarmed.

Another man, a fellow named Steve, grabbed the stethoscope and put it against my chest. "No, he's breathing. He just has a large chest capacity. His lungs are so clear you can't hear the air moving through them."

Praise God I don't smoke, I thought.

I dozed on and off, waiting for the pain. It never did come, except when they violated my body. I knew if they would just leave me alone, I'd be OK.

Over and over Jackie's word "miracle" kept ringing in my mind. I found myself smiling all the time. I could remember Dr. Swanson's grinning face. I had not only survived; I no longer had cancer.

Time went slowly. I thought I had been in the recovery room for three days. Actually it was only about four hours.

I looked up. John Osteen was looking down at me, grinning.

"Do you know who I am?"

I nodded.

"Tell me who I am."

"Johnny," I heard myself whisper. "Bless you for coming."

Noon the next day, less than twenty-four hours after coming out of surgery, two orderlies gently eased me onto a rolling gurney and took me back to my room. Jackie, Bonnie and Audrey were waiting. They had decorated the room to welcome me back. Healing promises of the Bible, in large printing on legal-sized sheets of yellow paper, were all over the walls. Flowers had arrived from home — and from friends. And on the wall, right at the end of my bed, hung two pictures: one of Jesus, His head thrown back in a hearty laugh; the other of me in the Sinai Desert with my five-foot hickory staff and the Mountain of God in the background.

The days passed in a blur. Jackie moved into the room and was there until I was dismissed, fifteen days later. The following day the doctor removed the catheter. That afternoon a powerfully built black male nurse, who had learned his medical techniques working with a MASH unit in Vietnam, got me to my feet to take my first steps.

"Listen to your nurse," he counseled me gruffly. "All doctors do is cut and stitch. Nurses heal."

I was too weak to argue with him. Besides, I sensed he was right.

That night Jan Kiley arrived.

Jan and Phil Kiley had belonged to the Tabernacle before they moved out of state two years earlier. Jan's arrival was a total surprise.

"Phil and I prayed, and we felt I should fly over from California to be here and help out any way I could."

Now I had four women in the room taking care of me. They quickly decided they could rotate so no one would be worn out. Only Jackie insisted on staying all the time — with only time out to go down to the cafeteria to get something to eat. I was being fed through a tube in my arm and would not eat anything by mouth for almost two weeks.

The following day my head was clear enough to pray again. I had missed praying out loud with Jackie. It was good that my voice was returning.

Tim and Bruce arrived on Saturday morning. That afternoon I was able, for the first time, to walk down to the elevator, ride it to the ground floor and walk outside the building. I was pushing a wheeled contraption that had the IV bag and tubes as well as a bag for the nasal gastric tube from my nose that was collecting the bile from my stomach. Bruce and Tim went with me, walking slowly down the sidewalk beside me in the hot Texas afternoon. I tired quickly, but it was a delightful feeling to get outside and walk on my own.

The following day Audrey and Jan Kiley returned to their homes. Bruce and Tim left that evening. Other friends arrived. Charles and Frances Hunter, who had called almost daily, came to the room. They were dressed in matching pink outfits. Frances laughed. "You had nothing to worry about. If the surgeons had not gotten all the cancer, we would have killed the rest of it in Jesus' name."

John and Dodie Osteen came by. John was dressed in red cowboy boots and a Western jacket and tie.

Michael and Donna Williams came by and prayed. John and Diana Hagee called regularly from San Antonio. It was good to hear his booming optimism over the phone. Folks from home called daily.

Chaplain Blondela James arranged for me to come downstairs and speak to the hospital chaplains. I went to the meeting dressed in my bathrobe and with the nasal gastric tube hanging out of my nose. Even in the middle of recovery I was back in service. It felt good.

Cards, letters, flowers and tapes came from all over the nation. People received prophecies for me and read them onto tapes. A retired professor from Clemson University wrote a song and sang it on a tape for me.

Those were precious times, lying on my hospital bed, listening as Jackie read the letters and cards, praying for everyone who contacted us, listening to the tapes — something I had never had time to do before.

Bill Bright sent two Scripture song tapes produced by Campus Crusade. We played them until they were almost worn out. The room was filled with music and praise. Sometimes the nurses would come and just stand inside the door, reading all the Scripture verses on the walls and listening to the music.

"I don't know who's going to follow you in this room," one little Hispanic nurse said, "but whoever it is will sure be blessed, because God is here."

Perhaps the most precious tape came from my old friend Ben Hoekendijk in Holland. It arrived airmail, and a courier brought it up to the room just at dusk. We put it in the tape player and relaxed, listening.

Just before leaving for the hospital I had sent a letter to Ben's wife, Wiesje, telling them of our decision to go for surgery. Ben and Wiesje were about our age. I had met them through Corrie ten Boom almost twenty years before on my first trip to Holland. Ben, an evangelist, was often called the Billy Graham of the Netherlands. A brilliant writer, he had published his own magazine as well as a number of books. Jackie and I had stayed in their home, and they had visited with us on several occasions.

Then, in early spring, he had lost everything. His board of directors, angered over his success and unable to tolerate his free spirit, had taken over his ministry and forced him out. I had wept for Ben and Wiesje as they went through the heartbreak of losing everything they had poured their lives into: their television ministry, the publishing business, as well as the annual *Vierhouten* convention for young people that drew more than twenty thousand kids from all over Holland. They had lost their salary from the ministry as well as their retirement fund. They were back to where they had begun, many years before, living by faith.

Trying to find himself and hear God, Ben had sailed his little one-masted sailboat around Scotland and Ireland, south to the Bay of Biscay and on to Spain. He was on his way back when Wiesje got my message. He had pulled into a harbor along the French coast to spend the night and call home. She told him the news. The next day, sailing alone south of England, he had taken his little tape recorder and gone up on the tiny forward deck. There he poured out his heart to me. He did not know at that time whether I was going to live or die. He was just expressing his deep love for his American friend.

He closed out his soliloquy with a searching prayer for my healing. Then I heard him sob. The tape continued to play. I could hear the gentle sound of the sails flapping in the wind, the lapping of the water against the hull, the pinging of the lines against the mast — and in the background Ben's soft sobs as he grieved for me.

The tape finally ran out. Jackie and I waited in the darkened room listening to God, who was so near.

"We are blessed people," she finally said.

I could only nod in the semidarkness. I didn't trust myself to speak.

August 7 — one week after the operation — Dr. Swanson and Dr. Giannakis came into the room as they had every afternoon. This visit was different, however. They had not come to see how I was doing but to report on a miracle.

Minutes before I had sneezed. That was the one thing Jack Taylor had warned me against. "It's better to fall down a flight of stairs than to sneeze after surgery," he had said. I had felt it coming and grabbed the pillow and held it tightly against my tummy. It buffered the pain across the incision, but after it passed, the second worse thing that can happen to a surgical patient occurred. I began to hiccup.

These were not just polite little hiccups. They were gargantuan. The kind that pick you up off the bed and then slam you back onto the mattress. Strangely, there was no pain. Just these tremendous hiccups.

I began timing them, as a pregnant woman times labor pains. They were ten seconds apart, and I was afraid they were going to get worse.

"Do something," I told Bonnie.

She rushed out of the room to the nurses' station. Moments later she reappeared with a brown paper sack — a small grocery sack. "The nurse said to hold this up against your face and breathe in it."

"That's an old wives' tale," I howled. "Here I am in the most sophisticated hospital in the nation, surrounded by the most technical machines the human mind can devise, and the nurse hands me something out of the Dark Ages?"

I started to ask if they were still using leeches to draw blood, but a huge hiccup stopped me. I grabbed the paper bag and breathed into it.

Looking over the edge of the bag, I could see Bonnie and Jackie at the end of the bed, their faces in their hands. At first I thought they were crying. After all, they were responsible for this and surely were concerned that I could rip out all my stitches. Then I realized they were not crying. They were convulsed in laughter. They were laughing at me because I had the hiccups.

It was at that instant the doctors came in the room.

Dr. Swanson looked around. Here was a room filled with Scripture verses taped all over the wall next to a picture of his patient standing like Moses on Mount Sinai, two women laughing so hard they had tears running down their cheeks and his patient lying in bed breathing into a paper sack.

Embarrassed, I lowered the sack.

"I have the hiccups," I mumbled.

"Well, I have good news," he said, grinning.

Walking over to the side of the bed, he grabbed my hand and shook it. "Congratulations!"

"What for?"

"I told you I had removed as many of the swollen lymph glands as possible, and I sent these off to pathology. I gave them a lot of tissue to examine. The pathologist looked at it all very carefully and has finally reported that your lymph glands were not tumorous."

"You mean there was no cancer in the lymph glands?"

"Yes! That's *exactly* what I mean. I got all the cancer I could see. It had not spread to the lymph glands, and we would not recommend further treatment at this time. Get well and go home."

It took a while to get well. My stomach didn't like the nasal gastric tube and reacted — meaning I had to stay a little longer. But after a total of seventeen days, one of Curry Juneau's elders drove us to the airport, and Tim picked us up in Orlando. Sandy and the grandchildren had decorated the house with big banners: "Welcome home to the place you love!"

How right they were.

THIRTY-THREE

NO LIFETIME
WARRANTY

I RECEIVED A COPY OF DR. SWANSON'S DISCHARGE summary for Dr. Weldon in Melbourne. The only paragraph that interested me was the one titled "Prognosis."

> The patient's final pathology revealed all nodes to be negative. The tumor thrombus and tumor were removed entirely with negative margins, making the patient a stage III renal cell carcinoma and with no obvious remaining disease. The patient should do well if no metastatic disease develops.

He gave me everything I could have asked for except one: a guarantee the cancer would never return.

THIRTY-FOUR

ONE DAY TO LIVE

THE DAY BEFORE I LEFT THE HOSPITAL, CURRY Juneau had come into the room. He was agitated.

"I was just listening to a local Christian radio station," he said. "They announced that you had but one day to live. I called them and set the record straight."

I laughed. "Thanks. Someone must have misunderstood what I meant when I said that from this time on I was going to live one day at a time."

Curry chuckled. "I guess there's not a lot of difference, is there: one day to live and living one day at a time?"

I remembered Gene Berrey's question at that first home group meeting after I knew of the cancer. "If God were to say, 'Jamie, I'm going to give you a choice. You can come on home to Me now and enjoy all the wonderful blessings of heaven; or you can stay on earth, but you may suffer much pain and even heartbreak.' Which would you choose?"

I had told Gene, "I can't make a choice. I would have to tell God: 'Lord, whatever You want me to do — go or stay — I will do.' "

I guess that's what living one day at a time means.

But re-entry into the world was tough. I recalled Jack Taylor's warning: "Life goes on." And it did. Everyone was gracious. Michele was working overtime keeping the magazine on deadline. Sandy came in daily to answer my mail and return phone calls. The pastors and church staff did their best to keep the church machinery oiled — but I was a different man. Not only had my desires changed, so had my motivations. I was not only slower physically, but I had no desire to stay on the treadmill. The idea of strolling through life, talking to God, had great appeal to me — far more than the mill-race of notoriety and travel. All I wanted was to be with my family, friends and God.

Our first out-of-town trip was in early October. Jackie and I returned to Houston for two days of testing. As we were getting ready to leave, we sat down with Dr. Swanson.

"It's embarrassing to have a patient who is healthier than his doctor," he said. "Just get regular checkups for the next two years."

The nightmare was over. I knew, in the back of my mind, that there was always a possibility the cancer would return. But now was not the time to think of that. Now was the time to rejoice. That other thought would be there always, reminding me that God was leading us into a new life-style: a life lived by faith alone.

We flew from Houston to Phoenix, where our good friends John and Barry French met us and drove us up into the high desert to a retreat center at Community of Living Water near Cornville. Every year for the past dozen years, ever since John and Barry had built the center, Jackie and I had gone there to teach. This year I was returning to teach with David Manuel in a writers' conference. David and I had been friends since we worked as editors for Logos Publishers in the early 1970s. He continued to write from his home on Cape Cod as a member of the Community of Jesus.

On Friday we returned to Phoenix as house guests of the Frenches. That night we joined their family for dinner at an elegant restaurant (the only one in Arizona where you really do need a coat and tie). David, sensing my melancholic struggle with "re-entry," later wrote me a haunting observation on the evening.

There we were with the French clan at Voltaire's. The setting was elegant, the conversation convivial. I glanced over at you, and it was like looking at a nineteenth-century polar explorer who had been trapped in the ice for a year. Safe home in London now, he was the guest of honor at a dinner of the poobahs of the Royal Geographic Society. He was dressed as they were, smiling and nodding...but from his eyes, he was still back on the ice-sheathed deck of his ship, gazing into the silent night at the endless, jutting icepacks under the full moon.

Don't be too quick to re-enter London society. The understanding that you have gained is worth more than anything you were doing before. And don't be concerned about not fitting in. God has separated you unto Himself for a season. Pray for patience — and for the grace to be meticulously obedient. In due course He will reveal His plan; meanwhile, don't let well-meaning friends pressure you this way or that, no matter how worthy or urgent their request. As you said, you're not called to be a pastor, or an editor, or a communicator. You're called to walk with Him.

I knew that. I just didn't know what it might entail.

THIRTY-FIVE

THE BEST
GUARANTEE OF ALL

IN LATE OCTOBER JACKIE AND I SPENT A WEEK IN our little cabin in Western North Carolina. One rainy morning we got up to drive across the mountains to meet the Berreys, who were driving over from their cabin in north Georgia. We were going to meet them halfway for lunch. Gene had fully recovered from his bypass surgery and, like me, had developed an entirely new outlook on life.

Coasting down our steep driveway, I heard an inner voice. "This could be your last trip. You could be killed on that slick, mountain highway."

The tone of the voice wasn't really threatening — it was more like a gentle reminder. I recognized it from two weeks before. I was at home in Florida, pulling on my sweatpants to play basketball on the half-court behind our garage — my first time back on the court.

"You could drop dead on the basketball court tonight," the voice had said.

There had been a momentary flash of fear. I had just faced death. I wanted to think life — not death. Yet I remembered that earlier in the year Pete Maravich, former professional basketball star, had died suddenly while playing basketball with James Dobson. Later Dr. Dobson also had a heart attack while playing basketball. (Praise God, he recovered.) Death, the voice reminded me, is always a breath away.

I argued. "Surely You wouldn't allow that after just healing me."

His answer was gentle — but firm. "You now live on borrowed time — time loaned by Me. *When* I call you home is My business. Your business is to walk humbly with Me and live in a ready position."

I remembered Jesus' words. "Therefore do not worry about tomorrow, for tomorrow will worry about itself" (Matt. 6:34). James was more pointed: "Why, you do not even know what will happen tomorrow. What is your life? You are a mist that appears for a little while and then vanishes. Instead, you ought to say, 'If it is the Lord's will, we will live and do this or that' " (James 4:14-15).

That morning on the rain-swept mountain highway I realized the purpose of my summer of miracles. The cancer had appeared not just to give me the chance to repent and be cleansed of my selfish approach to life, but to prepare me for a new kind of life-style. From this time on I was to live as though I had but one day to live.

I remembered visiting with my daddy in Vero Beach three days before he died. Even at eighty-eight his mind was still sharp, alert. But his body had just worn out. After sitting on the side of his bed and talking for a few minutes, I got up and walked back in his little study. For years he had done all his family and business bookkeeping in a big, black ledger book with green pages. It invariably lay open at the page where he was working so when mother rolled him into the study in his wheelchair, it was easily accessible. That afternoon when I walked into the little study, the book was closed. His fine-tipped ink pens had been wiped off with a paper towel and were laid side by side next to the old inkwell. He had balanced — and closed — his books. He would never need to open them again.

Somehow, I suspected, that was what God wanted of me. I should live so that at the end of every day I could close my spiritual ledger and know the books were balanced.

Following the summer miracle, I had felt invincible. Almost immortal. Now there was a growing feeling that God was not going to allow me the luxury of knowing the future. Rather what He wanted was for me to walk intimately with Him, as Adam did in the cool of the garden. No guarantees. Just God.

One night, walking out the soreness of the operation, I talked to Jackie about it. There was just a touch of fall in the air, as much as we ever get in Florida, and Jackie was wearing a light sweater.

"I love you," I said softly. "I love touching you. Why can't I be as close to God as I am to you?"

"Maybe you are and just don't know it."

"But what does He want from me?"

She reminded me of the biblical drama which played itself out early one morning on the beach of the Sea of Galilee. After a fish breakfast, Jesus had pulled Peter aside. "There are no guarantees for long life or earthly success if you follow Me, Peter," He had said.

I remembered the scenario. Jesus had said that Peter was going to be crucified. Peter had reacted. Pointing to John, he had said, "What about him?"

"I alone control the length of a man's days," Jesus told Peter. "How long John lives is none of your business. You must follow Me" (see John 21:18-22).

That night after we got in bed I picked up my Bible and turned to the books Peter had written. It must have been a frightening moment, hearing Jesus prophesy that his life would be taken from him violently. Yet years later, looking back, he was able to write about being "shielded by God's power" (1 Pet. 1:5).

"Cast all your anxiety on him," he said with the confidence that comes only by walking through anxiety, "because he cares for you" (1 Pet. 5:7).

I read on as he closed out his letter. "And the God of all grace, who called you to his eternal glory in Christ, after you have suffered a little while, will himself restore you and make you strong, firm and steadfast" (1 Pet. 5:10).

There it was. God does not reveal the future. He reveals Himself. That, it seemed, was the best guarantee I could ever have.

THIRTY-SIX

FIGHTING
TO LOSE

THE PAIN BEGAN AROUND CHRISTMAS. LOWER
back. Then down into my hip and thigh. Finally below the knee. Dr. Weldon,
suspicious that the cancer might try to return, ordered X rays, a bone scan, then
a CT scan. All were clear. Yet the pain persisted.

I tried a chiropractor. It got worse. He put me in a back brace. It didn't help.
Finally, on Good Friday, Dr. Weldon ordered a magnetic resonance imaging scan.
He was looking for a pinched nerve or a herniated disc in my spine. Instead he
found a small tumor fastened around two vertebrae in my lower spine. Another
cancer had invaded my body. The attack was on again.

Jackie and I met with our home group just an hour after Dr. Weldon called
the house with the news. It was the Monday after Easter. The tumor was located
along the lower region of my left spine and was putting pressure on the nerves —
causing the pain. It had already eaten into a couple of vertebrae. He felt certain
it was from a microscopic cell which had been left in the body following surgery.
Untreated, it would quickly cripple — then kill.

We were late getting to the home group, feeling we needed to make the announcement to the family first.

I was encouraged by Tim's faith. "Last summer you were attacked by a big demon," he laughed. "This is just a little one. All we need to do is flick it off in the name of Jesus, just as you would a mosquito off your arm."

"Not only that," Sandy said with determination, "we know how to pray now."

And they did, starting then.

Our home group met that night at the home of Don and Helen Crossland, who had recently become part of our group. We arrived just as they finished eating. As they had last summer, the home group stopped everything else and focused on our problem.

"How do you feel about it?" Don Lees asked.

"Embarrassed! I hate to put the church back through another crisis."

"God is not only working on you," Don said, nodding his head, "He's working on this church as well. Last summer we got all excited and acted spiritual. Now we're back in our old routines. God loves us enough — He loves you enough — to shake us until we all walk by faith."

"I'm confused, though," I said. "We've walked close to God. We've radically changed our life-styles. Jackie has me on an anti-cancer diet, drinking fresh carrot juice, eating grains, beans and fruit. I've stopped drinking coffee and eat very little meat. We've tried to do everything right — now this."

"Is it possible you'll have to live the rest of your life this way?" Gene Berrey asked.

"What do you mean?"

"I never know when I might have another heart attack. Every little pain is a reminder to pray. Maybe that's what God is saying to all of us."

I had suspected Satan would counterattack. Just that week I had read in Luke 4 of Jesus' bout with Satan on the Mount of Temptation. After Satan was defeated, Luke wrote, "He left Him [Jesus] until an opportune time" (Luke 4:13). If the attacks had continued against Jesus, why should I be exempt?

"Despite the fact I feel armed and ready," I told the group, "I'm still shaken. Here I am, ready to get on with life, and now I have to turn aside for another battle."

"Which one of us has a promise for more than today?" Laura asked. "God is just showing us, through you, how the rest of us are to live."

"Well, I wish He'd start showing you through someone else," I said with a half-laugh.

"Do you really?" It was Linda Lees. "When you say that, it means you want Him to take His hand off your life and leave you alone."

"Satan is stupid!" Jackie said. "He's hit us at our strongest point. We are standing where we stood: healed by the stripes of Jesus. Jamie had just started to work on the book about last summer's miracles. Now this. It's the devil's attempt to stop the book. He wants to kill Jamie too. But Jesus has already paid the price for our healing. We'll just have to prove it again."

Strange, but in the midst of what could have been devastation, we felt peace. God was still in control.

The next morning in the church staff meeting, Art Bourgeois read from Psalm 95:8-9: "Do not harden your hearts as you did at Meribah, as you did that day at Massah in the desert, where your fathers tested and tried me *though they had seen what I did*" (italics added).

As he read I was suddenly back in the Sinai, hiking across the sand near the Gulf of Suez. Our small group of campers had come to the Oasis of Marah. More than three thousand years before, the children of Israel had stopped here. Just three days earlier they had faced an impossible situation. Standing on the other side of the sea, with the armies of Egypt in hot pursuit, they were trapped. Nowhere to turn. Moses, standing on the shore, had held out his staff. The sea parted, and they walked through on dry ground. Then the sea closed on their enemies, and they were home free.

Until they reached Marah, three days later.

Parched, out of water, they saw the oasis and raced across the sand. But the water was bitter, laced with minerals. That is why the place was called Marah, the Hebrew word for bitter. The people couldn't drink it. They panicked and turned on Moses.

In desperation Moses asked God what to do. God told him to throw a certain bush into the water, which caused the water to turn sweet. They drank and were saved.

But the question remains: Didn't God know the waters of Marah were bitter? The answer is yes. God was giving the Israelites a test — a test they failed because of *meribah*, their quarreling (Ex. 15:22-27).

The minerals in the bitter water were calcium and magnesium — a powerful laxative. The water would not have killed them; it would have cleaned them out. God wanted to change their life-style by not only getting them out of Egypt — but by getting Egypt out of them.

But they were so overcome by the circumstances they failed to remember what God had done just three days before. They forgot the big miracle at the sea because they had a second encounter with difficulty — the bitter water at the oasis.

Because of their lack of faith, God said He would not let them enter the Promised Land. They were, He said, "a people whose hearts go astray," who did not know His ways.

245

Art continued to speak. "God's way is to allow certain obstacles into our lives so we will change, grow and become like Jesus. Once we make that decision, He quickly removes the obstacles and lets us move on to Elim, a place of rest and abundant provision."

I made a decision that morning in the staff meeting. I would not be one whose heart went astray. Like Jackie, I would stand where I stood last summer — on the finished work of Christ. However, if in order to become the kind of man God wanted me to be I had to drink a bitter cup to be cleansed and strengthened for the journey — then I would do it with joy.

That afternoon I called Dr. Johnson.

"I want to talk to David Swanson," he said. "I'll call you back later this evening."

Not only did he call Dr. Swanson, but he called Dr. Weldon in Melbourne. They all agreed I should receive radiation. The treatments would last only a minute at a time with minimum side effects. However, they had to be administered daily — Monday through Friday for five weeks. Dr. Johnson insisted Jackie and I come to St. Petersburg and stay with them during the week while taking the treatments at his Bayfront Cancer Center. Then we could drive home on the weekend so I could be with the family and preach at the Tab.

"My role," he said, "will be to oversee the treatment. Then, while you're lying on the table in that big lead-lined room under the radiation camera, Jackie and I will be just outside the door praying in the Spirit."

Once again I cancelled activities and trips. We would drive over to St. Petersburg every Monday and return home Friday morning — for five weeks. The weekdays would become a time of spiritual retreat, seeking God for the future.

Words of prophecy started coming. Some from the church, others from friends around the nation. All had to do with "dying to self" and "resting in the Lord."

John French called from Arizona. His wife, Barry, had a word of prophecy for me. "Count yourself a dead man."

I remembered the story by one of the modern Greek playwrights who wrote of a novice monk who went to stay on an island with a wizened old priest. One afternoon the young cleric, eager to learn, walked with the venerable man along the craggy shore. As their robes swirled in the wind, he finally asked his big question.

"Father, do you still wrestle with the devil?"

"No, my son," the elderly man answered, stroking his white beard. "I have grown old, and the devil has grown old with me. He does not bother me as before. Now I wrestle with God."

"Wrestle with God? Do you hope to win?"

The wrinkled old man looked his young consort in the eye. "Oh, no! I hope to lose."

Now I found myself in that same position. During the summer I had wrestled with Satan. Now I was back in the wrestling match. Only this time Satan was not my adversary. He was a defeated enemy. I was battling with God, who was trying to change me into the image of His Son. And I was resisting.

As the radiation treatment gradually shrank the tumor, I had time, lots of time, to spend on the wrestling mat. One quiet afternoon, sitting in Dr. Johnson's home in St. Petersburg, I found myself struggling with Jesus' words from Luke 9:24. "Whoever wants to save his life will lose it, but whoever loses his life for me will save it."

Did this mean I should not take measures to save my life from the cancer? Surely not, for God had told me to resist evil. No, it meant I was not to save my life for my sake — but so I could be at God's disposal, delighting to do His will.

Reading on in the book I found: "Anyone who does not carry his cross and follow me cannot be my disciple" (Luke 14:27).

For years I had equated the cross-life with laying down things that were wrong. Back in July I had gotten serious about taking a moral inventory, purging myself of things wrong.

This time, however, God wanted more. He was asking me to relinquish the things that were right.

That afternoon, like Jacob at Peniel, I wrestled with God. To give up that which was wrong in the face of death had been easy. But to surrender just when you saw hope for living — ?

"Do You mean I must nail *everything* to the cross?"

"You are to count yourself as a dead man," I felt Him reply.

One by one the list of things "most precious" scrolled across my mind — much longer than last summer's list of sins. It included not only the things I liked to do but the things He Himself had promised. Dreams. Ambitions. Ministry. Family. Health. Long life.

Little things were highlighted: playing basketball, climbing mountains in Israel and walking the beach with my wife. All were to be nailed to the cross — with no promise of return.

"What about my writing, Father? Don't You want me to write the story of last summer's miracle?"

"That too must be nailed to the cross."

Christians, I discovered, don't die easily.

247

That night I sat in a chair in the bedroom while Jackie pulled down the covers. My back was hurting — and I was confused. I knew the Bible promised healing. We had stood on that promise the summer before, and God had faithfully fulfilled His Word. Every afternoon at 3:12 P.M. the past week I had lain on my back on that narrow table in the lead-lined room. As the radiation machine buzzed, I had cursed the cancer cells as Jesus had cursed the fig tree. Outside the door Ralph and Jackie had held hands, praying in the Spirit. Now God was telling me to be willing to lay my life down. What did it all mean?

I had been reading about the life of J. Hudson Taylor, the pioneer missionary to China. He had lost two wives, had buried three children in China, had been paralyzed for two years, had seen his precious new converts beheaded because of their faith — yet had grown stronger through it all. There was no way I could ever match his spiritual devotion.

Hudson Taylor said in times of despair he had been strengthened by 2 Timothy 2:13. I picked up my Bible and found the passage. "If we are faithless, he will remain faithful."

"Don't be so uptight," I felt God whisper. "Let Me sort it all out. Just live one day at a time."

That helped.

I eased myself into bed, groaning from the intense pain in my hip and lower back. I finally got comfortable. Jackie rubbed me for a while, then reached over and took my hand. We prayed.

"God may be my adversary, but He is not my enemy. I'm like a child wrestling with his dad. I know that when He eventually pins me to the mat, He'll reach down and kiss me."

The next morning the pain had eased some. Sitting on the side of the bed listening to the mockingbirds singing in the Johnsons' backyard, I felt God say it was OK to start back to work on the book — this book. He also said I could stake my life on His promises of the Bible — regardless of the pain.

Within two weeks from the time I began treatment, the pain was almost gone. It was a good sign. The tumor was shrinking.

Then, just as I was completing the treatment, a new set of pains in my back and leg appeared.

Dr. Johnson reminded me this could be "good pain." The nerves which had been damaged by the tumor could be regenerating. This was confirmed by another CT scan taken days before I finished treatment.

"But," he pointed out, "it can return at any time. The only guarantee you have from this time on is God."

That night, sitting in the semidarkness of the Johnson family room while Ralph played Scripture choruses softly on his synthesizer, I prayed.

"Father, I'm in trouble. I need Your help."

He answered gently. "Would you call on Me for help if you were not hurting?"

He knew, from past experience, how prone I was to become self-sufficient the moment I began to feel better.

Then He added: "I like it when you ask Me to help you."

The afternoon following the CT scan, Ralph Johnson came upstairs where we were staying in their beautiful home. He was laughing, clapping his hands. The tumor was shrinking, he said, responding to the treatment.

"By the way," he added, "I let the radiologist look at your original CT scan — the ones made in Melbourne last summer. He couldn't believe me when I told him you were alive and healthy."

I was sitting at my word processor, working on this manuscript. Jackie was in a recliner chair on the other side of the room, reading. After Dr. Johnson gave us the news, he walked out, pulling the door shut behind him. He knew we needed to be alone during that moment. We would celebrate with Ralph and Sylvia later.

Jackie came over to where I was sitting. There were papers all over the floor. Bibles and books were piled high on Ralph's desk, which I was using. My little Zenith laptop was in the middle, its bright screen filled with words telling the story of God's incredible goodness. Writing the story had reminded me: We, all of us, are mere actors on His stage. Happiness and success are ours only when we let Him direct our movements — and write our lines.

Jackie knelt in front of me and put her head in my lap. She was crying softly, praising God for His mercy.

I stroked her silky, blonde hair. Her ordeal had been far tougher than mine, for she had carried the burden for us both.

"I am grateful beyond words for God's mercy," I told her softly.

"Today I praise You because the news is good," I prayed softly. "Help me reach the place where I can rejoice — not in the news — but in You. Only."

Jackie reached out from her kneeling position and put both arms around my waist. The room grew quiet.

We were not alone.

A few days before this book went to press, Jackie and I drove back across the state to St. Petersburg. It had been two months since I finished radiation treatment — and almost one year to the day from my first medical exam. Dr. Johnson wanted another CT scan.

We spent the night in the now familiar upstairs bedroom in the Johnsons' home.

Early the next morning I woke to the sound of rain splattering against the glass window next to the bed.

"It's raining," Jackie's sleepy voice came from the pillow beside my head.

"Rain is a biblical sign of blessing," I said.

I felt good. I swung my legs off the bed and sat up, realizing there had been no pain in the movement. Nor had I had to do what I had been doing since surgery — hook my heel on the edge of the mattress to provide leverage to sit up.

I sat, listening, as Jackie read Psalm 25 slowly. We paused and prayed after each verse. "Guard my life and rescue me; let me not be put to shame, for I take refuge in you" (v. 20).

"Your body is the temple of the Holy Spirit," a silent voice said.

I felt alive. Confident.

An hour later we were in the corridors at Bayfront Cancer Center. Dr. Johnson had taken off most of the morning to walk me through the exams — chest X ray, blood work and, finally, another CT scan. He and Jackie were standing in the hall when I came out of the scanning room. They were talking with a middle-aged man.

"This is the patient I was telling you about last night," Dr. Johnson said excitedly. "His cancer is in remission, but best of all he's just accepted Jesus as his Savior. I've given him a copy of your book *Power for Living*. He wants you to autograph it."

Just as he handed me the little blue book with white letters on the cover, a nurse's aide walked by.

"Oh!" she said excitedly. "That's the book that changed my life. I accepted the Lord after reading it. Then I gave it to a lost friend."

I laughed. "Well, Dr. Johnson has several extra books in his office."

She was gone, bubbling with excitement and witnessing to the others getting on the elevator.

"Regardless of what the exams show," Ralph Johnson said, wiping tears from his eyes, "that makes life worthwhile."

Driving back to the Johnsons' house to await the results of the tests, I remembered a line from Thornton Wilder's *Our Town*. The character Emily had asked, "Do any human beings ever realize life while they live it?"

Wilder's answer was no. But I agreed with Dr. Johnson. When you are in Christ, you not only realize life, you realize it abundantly.

Early afternoon Dr. Johnson arrived at the house. We were packed, ready to drive back to Orlando and catch a plane to Tulsa. The next day I was to speak at the annual ministers' conference of the Charismatic Bible Ministries on the ORU campus. Oral Roberts had called. He wanted me to give a "stirring" testimony of last summer's miracle. I knew, however, that I had more to talk about than that. Miracles, yes, for I would not be here had God not intervened. But there was so much more.

"Good news!" Dr. Johnson said as he came into the kitchen. "The tumor in your back looks like it is shrinking. Your vertebrae seem to be rebuilding. Best of all — there is no new cancer. Your lungs and liver — where we were looking for trouble — are clear."

"Is the cancer gone?" Jackie asked.

"We don't know. We just know it's not growing. I guess you can say it's in remission."

That evening, on the plane to Tulsa, Jackie and I held hands and prayed.

"Are you disappointed?" I asked her.

She smiled and shook her head. "God has you right where He wants you — where He wants us. Totally dependent on Him."

I squeezed her hand and remembered what the inmate in an Irish prison had written me. "This (today, only) is the day the Lord hath made; let us be glad and rejoice in it."

And tomorrow, and tomorrow, and tomorrow, we'll rejoice.

Jamie and Jackie

DEDICATION

WHEN IT WAS ALL OVER I GOT A SIX-WORD LETTER from my friend John Howe, bishop of the Episcopal Diocese of Central Florida. He wrote: "See what happens when Episcopalians pray?"

To that I add:

And when Pentecostals pray,

and Baptists (Southern, American, Independent, Fundamentalists, Primitive and others),

and Methodists,

and Catholics,

and Presbyterians,

and charismatics,

and Seventh-Day Adventists,

and Lutherans,

and Nazarenes,

and Quakers,

and Mennonites,

and Jews,

and at least one bourbon-drinking beer distributor.

To them all I say, "Thank you! May we always pray for and love one another."

Jamie Buckingham
Palm Bay, Florida

253

NOTES

Preface

1. Jamie Buckingham, *Miracle Power* (Ann Arbor, Mich.: Servant Publications, 1990), pp. 3-4.

Chapter 7

1. Quoted in James D. Morrison, ed., *Masterpieces of Religious Verse* (New York: Harper & Brothers, 1948), p. 410.

Chapter 10

1. The book was called *Mission: An American Congressman's Adventure in Space* published by Harcourt, Brace and Jovanovich. It was written by Jamie for U.S. Congressman Bill Nelson — a member of the Tabernacle Church who was at that time the leading Democratic candidate for governor of the state of Florida. Nelson trained as an astronaut and flew aboard the spaceship Columbia just ten days before the explosion of the Challenger.

Chapter 11

1. Quoted in Morrison, p. 602.
2. Quoted in Morrison, pp. 69-70.

Chapter 12

1. Jamie Buckingham, *Tramp for the Lord*. (Old Tappan, N.J.: Fleming H. Revell Company, 1974), pp. 86-87.

Chapter 24

1. James Weldon Johnson, *God's Trombones* (New York: The Viking Press, 1927), p. 14.

Chapter 25

1. Jamie Buckingham, *A Way Through the Wilderness* (Old Tappan, N.J.: Fleming H. Revell Company, 1983), p. 93.

Chapter 27

1. Quoted in Morrison, p. 410.

"**I** believe that every Christian has a ministry—a Holy Spirit-inspired dream to fulfill. As editor-in-chief of *Ministries Today*, I am fulfilling a dream God gave me to help raise up, encourage and minister to leaders and potential leaders in His church. I want *Ministries Today* to inform you, assist you—and inspire you to pursue your own unique ministry in the body of Christ."

Jamie Buckingham
Jamie Buckingham
Editor-in-Chief